BERNARD SPENCER

COMPLETE POETRY

BERNARD SPENCER

COMPLETE POETRY
TRANSLATIONS & SELECTED PROSE

EDITED BY PETER ROBINSON

BLOODAXE BOOKS

ISBN: 978 1 85224 891 8

First published 2011 by
Bloodaxe Books Ltd,
Highgreen,
Tarset,
Northumberland NE48 1RP.

www.bloodaxebooks.com
For further information about Bloodaxe titles
please visit our website or write to
the above address for a catalogue.

Supported by
**ARTS COUNCIL
ENGLAND**

Cover design: Neil Astley & Pamela Robertson-Pearce.

Printed in Great Britain by
Bell & Bain Limited, Glasgow, Scotland.

CONTENTS

12 PREFACE

15 INTRODUCTION

Complete Poetry

AEGEAN ISLANDS AND OTHER POEMS (1946)

Poems before 1940

47 Allotments: April

49 A Hand

50 Plains as Large as Europe

51 There was no Instruction Given

52 Houses are Uniformed

54 Evasions

55 Portrait of a Woman and Others

56 A Cold Night

57 Part of Plenty

58 Cage

59 Ill

60 A Thousand Killed

61 Suburb Factories

62 Waiting

63 How Must we Live?

64 My Sister

Poems 1940 to 1942

67 Aegean Islands 1940-41

68 Greek Excavations

69 Salonika June 1940

70 Delos

71 Base Town

73 Death of an Airman

74 Letters

75 Libyan Front

76 Egyptian Delta

77 Acre

78 Frontier

79   Cairo Restaurant
80   The Ship
81   Behaviour of Money
83   Yachts on the Nile
84   Olive Trees
85   The Building of the House
86   Peasant Festival
87   Egyptian Dancer at Shubra
88   Passed On
89   In an Auction Room
90   Sarcophagi

WITH LUCK LASTING (1963)

93   The Beginning
94   Delicate Grasses
95   Notes by a Foreigner
97   From my Window
98   Mediterranean Suburbs
99   Fluted Armour
100 Out of Sleep
101 A Spring Wind
103 On a Carved Axle-Piece from a Sicilian Cart
104 The Boats
105 At Courmayeur
106 In a Foreign Hospital
107 Regent's Park Terrace
108 Letter Home
109 Morning in Madrid
110 The Café with the Blue Shrine
111 Castanets
112 In Athens
113 The Rendezvous
114 The Lottery Sellers
115 Train to Work
116 At 'The Angler'
117 The Administrator
118 Night-time: Starting to Write
119 Sud-Express

120   Boat Poem
122   Table Tennis
123   The Leopards
124   A Sunday
125   Cripples
126   Watchers
127   The Wedding Pictures
128   By a Breakwater
129   Lop-sided
130   Donkey
131   Full Moon
132   The Agents
133   Chestnuts
134   Blue Arm
135   Near Aranjuez
136   On the Road

COLLECTED POEMS (1965)

Poems from Vienna

139   The Empire Clock
140   On the 'Sievering' Tram
141   The Invaders
142   A Number
143   Properties of Snow
144   Clemente
145   You
146   Dr Karl Lueger
147   To Piers Spencer, five months old
148   Traffic in April

UNCOLLECTED AND UNPUBLISHED POEMS

Early Poems 1929 to 1932

151   'The lights with big elegant fingers'
152   Schedules
153   Collection
154   Festa

156 'Above, the fingers of the tree'
157 Departure
158 'Those near and dead who think there is another'
159 After Love
161 Poem ('After the wheels and wings of this intense day')
162 Clouded, Still, Evening
163 Poem ('White factories lancing sky')
164 Two Poems ('My pulling on my shoes')
164 ('Her hands waking on her lap')
166 Poem ('Who sees the rain fall into the Spring land')
167 'For seeing whole I had been too near my friends'
168 'Such height of corn, so many miles'

Uncollected Poems 1935 to 1946

170 'Most things having a market price'
171 'I, Jack, walking on the hill's shoulder'
172 The Runner
173 Winter Landscape
174 The House
175 Going to the Country
176 Picked Clean from the World
177 They Tell a Lie
178 In Memoriam
180 The Top-Storey Room

Uncollected Poems 1947 to 1963

182 Pino
183 The Clock
184 For Signorina Brunella Mori
185 A Ward
186 Black Cat
187 Castille
188 This Day
189 Witness
190 Written on a Cigarette Packet
191 From the Military Academy
192 The Train Window

Occasional and Unfinished Poems

195 *from* Conducted Tour after Edward Lear
196 'From Cairo this: scorn upon verse from Alex'

197   'For madmen, darkness whip and chain'

198   'I met you, George, upon a refuse dump'

199   Casa di P——

201   'The girl in the black mantilla with the ink splash eyes'

202   'Look at my suit'

203   'Rocks like a Dürer landscape, torn and hacked'

204   'The story is of battles and of conquest all the way'

Translations

George Seferis: THE KING OF ASINE AND OTHER POEMS (1948)
(with Nanos Valaoritis and Lawrence Durrell)

Part I: Myth of our History

207   1. 'The messenger'

207   2. 'Still another well within a cave'

208   3. Remember the Baths by Which You Were Slain

208   4. Argonauts

210   5. 'We never knew them'

210   6. M.R.

211   7. South Wind

212   8. 'What do they seek our souls as they travel'

213   9. 'The harbour is old, I cannot await any longer'

213   10. 'Our native place is enclosed, all mountains'

214   11. 'Your blood sometimes froze like the moon'

214   12. A Bottle in The Sea

215   13. Hydra

216   14. 'Three red pigeons in the sun'

216   15. *Quid πλατανων Opacissimus?*

217   16. And the Name is Orestes

217   17. Astyanax

218   18. 'I am sad because I let a broad river flow between my fingers'

218   19. 'And if the wind blows it does not cool us'

219   20. 'In my breast the wound opens again'

219   21. 'We that set out on this pilgrimage'

219   22. 'Now when so much has passed before our eyes'

220   23. 'A little further'

220   24. 'Here terminate the works of the sea, the works of love'

Part II: Ancient Dances

221   1. Santorin
222   2. Mycenae

Part III: Poems from 'A Book of Exercises'

224   1. Five Japanese Poems
225   2. Epitaph
225   3. Epiphany, 1937
226   4. In the Manner of G.S.

Part IV: Poems from 'Log Book 1 and 2'

229   1. Mathias Pascalis among the Roses
230   2. Our Sun
231   3. Morning
231   4. The Return of the Exile
233   5. The King of Asine
235   6. Stratis the Mariner among the Agapanthus Flowers
236   7. Calligraphy
237   8. Old Man on the River Bank
238   9. Stratis the Mariner on the Dead Sea

Odysseus Elytis: THE MAD POMEGRANATE TREE
(with Nanos Valaoritis)

241   The Mad Pomegranate Tree

Eugenio Montale: FOUR POEMS

243   The Lemon Trees
245   'Don't ask us for the word which cuts and shapes'
246   'Bring me the sunflower so that I can transplant it'
247   'To shelter, pale and preoccupied'

George Seferis: TWO POEMS

248   The Mourning Girl
249   Denial

Selected Prose

253   The Exhibition of Dutch Art at Burlington House
255   Note on Auden
256   Ideas about Poems
257   Keith Douglas: An Obituary Note
258   The Wind-Blown Island of Mykonos
261   Dialogue on Poetry
265   Madrid Journal
271   New Poetry
275   I Will Abroad
279   Ankara Notebook
282   Anatolia Notebook
284   Poems by Bernard Spencer
286   Lawrence Durrell
289   Context
291   University of Madrid Lecture
298   Interview with Peter Orr
304   Bernard Spencer Writes…

307   NOTES
342   BIBLIOGRAPHY
347   INDEX

PREFACE

When Bernard Spencer died in September 1963 he left behind a published *oeuvre* of three books: *Aegean Islands and Other Poems* (1946), the translations (with Nanos Valaoritis and Lawrence Durrell) from George Seferis, *The King of Asine and Other Poems* (1948), and *With Luck Lasting* (1963). He had sent 10 recent poems to Alan Ross at *The London Magazine*, poems published there just before and after his death. Ross initiated the history of gathering Spencer's work with *Collected Poems*, published by his own Alan Ross Ltd in 1965. This volume contained the 1946 and 1963 collections and, in 'Poems from Vienna', the last poems. It included none of the poet's translations, and did not search out any uncollected or unpublished poems. Though the texts are mostly reliable, there are a few cases of variant readings from the first editions, which may have resulted from oversights or editorial revision.

Roger Bowen, a British academic at the University of Arizona, set out in 1978 to discover as much as he could about Spencer, with the idea of writing a critical biography. A chance meeting with Jacqueline Simms, then poetry editor at Oxford University Press, led to the publication of his edition of the *Collected Poems* in 1981. Bowen followed Ross in reversing the order of the two sections in *Aegean Islands* (where the poems before 1940 appear after those written between 1940 and 1942), and of adding after *With Luck Lasting* the 'Poems from Vienna'. To these he adjoined a section of 'Poems Previously Uncollected and Unpublished (1935–1963)' containing 22 poems and 4 unpublished translations from Eugenio Montale. He selected from Spencer's early poems for a first appendix, and printed two statements about poetry in a second.

In 2008, I received a small project grant from the British Academy to catalogue the Bernard Spencer Archive at Reading, enlarged the previous year with bequests from his widow, Anne Humphreys, and Roger Bowen. With this grant I was able to fund a research assistant, Verity Hunt, and together we compiled and published a catalogue of the papers to coincide with a Bernard Spencer Centenary Conference, at Special Collections in Reading, organised for the end of October 2009. This new edition of Spencer's writings grew out of that work, and my notes here are indebted to Verity Hunt's collaboration. Bowen listed 5 excluded poems in a bibliographical note and 8 Oxford poems that he had selected out. He noted the existence of 2 translations from Odysseus Elytis (1 published twice, in fact), lost Rafael Alberti translations, and a lost 'Madrid Journal'. He referred to 4 uncollected prose pieces. His edition, with notes on manuscript remains and first publications, contained almost entirely reliable texts. I have, for example, changed a typo in 'Night-time: Starting to Write', a misreading from the manuscript of 'This Day', a slip over one word in 'Castille', and I follow the typescript text of 'Casa di P——'. Details of all such changes are given in my notes, notes much indebted to Bowen's pioneering edition.

The time is now ripe, I believe, for a collection of Spencer's poetry that is as complete as possible. I have added the translations, the early Oxford poems, the few occasional poems, and the even fewer uncompleted poems in the Reading archive. I have found one additional fragmentary poem beyond those listed by Bowen, two occasional pieces, and two translations of lyrics by Seferis that were broadcast on the BBC but never published. From the complete poetry I have excluded a few fragmentary lines and a stray couplet. From the translations I have excluded 'Fair is the garden where my love doth haunt', a rough pencil draft with variants in archaic idiom, whose original I have not been able to identify. From the prose I have excluded an early review of John Lehmann and two untraced printed items: 'Talking of Barry', which appeared in Cairo in 1944, and a half-humorous piece about his lung operation reported published in a magazine called *Envoy* in, most probably, 1949, and mentioned in correspondence between Bowen and G.S. Fraser.

Aside from these, I have brought together Spencer's occasional published prose, from a 1929 review of an exhibition of Dutch art to a Poetry Book Society Statement from the year of his death. I have included an interview and an article on Lawrence Durrell from the Spanish newspaper *Insula*, both of which, only existing in Spanish, I have translated for publication here. The 'Madrid Journal', thought to have been lost in 1981, turned up in the possession of a family friend, and was returned to Anne Humphreys. It is published here, along with two journal fragments from the poet's period in Turkey. There remain in the Reading archive numerous lectures that Spencer used in his teaching for the British Council. From these, I have published the 1962 talk on his poetry. I have not include any of Spencer's letters, which, if added to from other archives and sources, might one day make an informative and moving volume.

I would like warmly to thank Anne Humphreys for her kindness and permission to publish Spencer's works, and to Piers Spencer for his enthusiasm and support. My greatest debt is to Roger Bowen who has been as attentively supportive as possible. Jonathan Barker, Roderick Beaton, and Nanos Valaoritis have advised on the resolution of secondary rights issues. Roderick Beaton, Adam Piette and Isabel Vila Vera have helped with Greek, French and Spanish. My thanks go to Verity Hunt, to Richard Price and Duncan Heyes at the British Library, and to Guy Baxter, Jen Glanville, Fiona Melhuish, and Nathan Williams at Special Collections, University of Reading. As ever, I am indebted to Ornella Trevisan, both for her knowledge of Spanish and for every other sustenance.

PETER ROBINSON

INTRODUCTION

Bernard Spencer does not come across as a confident poet. John Betjeman remembered him as 'delightful humorous company and diffident about his own work... I should think a rejection slip would have set him back for years.'[1] The first publications of his poems in magazines support such a view. Spencer tended to send his work only to editors where he could expect a sympathetic hearing. From 1935 to 1939, Geoffrey Grigson published him in *New Verse*, where Spencer also helped as an assistant.[2] Between 1942 and 1945 they appeared in *Personal Landscape*, the Cairo magazine for which he was one of the founding editors. In the immediate post-war years he was published in Tambimuttu's *Poetry (London)*, and his first collection, *Aegean Islands and Other Poems*, appeared from its imprint in 1946. John Lehmann was among Spencer's most loyal supporters, publishing his collaborative translations from George Seferis in 1948, including him in volumes of *Penguin New Writing* and, from 1954, in *The London Magazine*, a place that remained a home for his verse after Alan Ross took over its editorship. Ross was also to publish his first *Collected Poems* in 1965.[3] Spencer's creative diffidence shows too when talking to Peter Orr, on the 27 August 1962, about conceiving and composing poems:

> But definitely it is a feeling as if some sort of signal has gone on and the fact that inside you, from that moment, is a so-far-unexplored area of feeling and emotion, which is almost disagreeable to hold on to. And the poet, for all reasons, must then work on this or let it hang about, preferably for some time before he starts working on it, and this will turn into a poem, with luck.[4]

He adopted the phrase 'with luck lasting' from 'Boat Poem' for the title of his second collection of poems, the last published during his lifetime.[5] When Lawrence Durrell came to write a memoir of his recently dead friend he recalled Spencer seeming to try his luck by hoping it had changed: 'We sat round a kitchen table for an all too brief hour and exchanged all the gossip of the day. He had recently married a beautiful young Scots girl and she had changed his luck for it. At least he had managed to find a publisher for his poems'.[6] *With Luck Lasting*, published by Hodder and Stoughton, was a Poetry Book Society Recommendation for the summer quarter of 1963. That title would, in the short term, prove woefully unapt, its appearance being followed so quickly by his never entirely explained accidental death in the early hours of 11 September 1963.

Charles Bernard Spencer was born into a collateral branch of the Spencer-Churchill family in Madras, India, the second son of Sir Charles Gordon Spencer, a high court judge, on 9 November 1909.[7] He was sent to England in 1911, to be brought up by relatives and guardians with his elder brother John and sister Cynthia, at first in Southampton, then in Crowell, Oxfordshire. From 1918 the latter part of his childhood was spent at Rowner, near Gosport, one of the reasons why yachts, boats, and ships figure so prominently in his poetry, as, for example, in the third verse of 'Yachts on the Nile'. In his fragmentary 'Autobiographical Notes', Spencer describes his early years following his return from India:

> I have no memories at all of that country, because after being ill several times – I suppose India in those days was a rougher place for babies than it is now – I was brought back to England and farmed out with guardians, Rectors & Vicars and their families, from the age of eighteen months till I was seventeen. So belonging to a country clergyman's household, my brother, my sister and myself were regarded as socially too good for the company of village children and by the local gentry as not good enough by and large for the company of theirs. Consequently we made our own amusements, often separately, and this, along with any books I managed to get hold of, was probably a helpful stimulus to the imagination. I read pretty fluently by the time I was three, and I remember when I was less than five being extremely satisfied on Sunday evenings with a large family Bible which had illustrations by Doré.[8]

After a period at a dame school in Eastbourne 'where I had a reputation for telling long adventure-stories', Spencer attended prep school at which 'I developed a passion for acting, was good at English, Latin & Greek and no other form subject, made violent friendships, drew pictures of battles, was myself bellicose, learned poetry easily by heart, and wrote my first poems, which were humorous accounts of the exploits of my group.' Spencer elsewhere recalls his early love of language being manifested by reciting from *The Lays of Ancient Rome*, ingesting a newspaper entire, and outdoing Tolstoy with a story that lasted two whole years.[9]

In 1923 he followed his brother to the traditional family school of Marlborough, where he was a contemporary of Anthony Blunt, and met the more senior John Betjeman and Louis MacNeice. There he seems to have been more involved with the art club than the literary society, though he did, in his own words, make 'a fuller discovery of the Romantic poets, especially Keats, William Morris, Rossetti, Flecker and early Yeats. Towards the end I read the Sitwells. I remember, as important contrast, causing surprise by buying a copy of George Herbert, who is still one of my favourite poets.' In the Michaelmas term of 1928, he went up to Corpus Christi, Oxford, as a Gentleman Commoner, where 'as important as my books were my friendships with such contemporaries as Isaiah Berlin, Stephen Spender, Humphrey House & Arthur Calder-Marshall, and also the world of ideas & books I met through Maurice Bowra.' He was now, as he adds, 'publishing and editing verse'. In 1930 he co-edited *Oxford Poetry* with Stephen Spender and the following year with Richard Goodman.

In the summer of 1932 Spencer graduated with a second-class degree in Greats. Once out of university, he has not proved easy to follow during the rest of the 1930s, though a number of significant occasions are recorded. Some letters and a poem, for example, sent to Rosamond Lehmann (to whom he had been introduced by Spender) have survived in her archive at King's College, Cambridge. Selina Hastings, in her biography of the novelist, dismissively reports the young poet's brief infatuation with his hostess.[10] In November 1934 he was with the family when his father died at the family home of Tarwood House, South Leigh, Oxfordshire. Between 1935 and 1938 he helped Geoffrey Grigson edit *New Verse*, and it was there that most of his mature early work appeared. On 1 August 1936 he married Nora Kathleen Gibbs at the Hampstead Register Office. The poet Bernard Gutteridge gives a glimpse of these years in his 2 October 1963 condolence letter sent to the poet's second wife, Anne:

> Bernard, Dylan [Thomas] and Louis MacNeice were the first poets I ever knew; and of them Bernard was always the closest – especially in those two last gloomy years before the war when he was always one of the gay reliefs. I first met him in Geoffrey Grigson's house in Hampstead for dinner, just the three of us and Norah. It must have been twenty seven years ago this autumn. He wore green corduroys, a red and white checked cotton shirt and a bow tie and a gay jacket and was, as he remained, one of the best-looking people I had ever met.

I was entranced by them both and was with them once or twice every week from then on, I believe. Supper in Soho at Durands (a bombed hole opposite the York Minster); drinks on the red plush and the marble tables at the Café Royal with Ernest Copplestone; parties at a flat off the Bayswater road which had dark reddish-purple cocoanut matting all over the floors; dancing in a pub on Haverstock Hill; and then the war...[11]

Spencer's 'Autobiographical Notes' describe his post-Oxford period as 'a year at film making, then a living scratched up out of schoolmastering and advertising.'[12] He worked as a Classics teacher at Chipping Norton Secondary School, Hillside School, Reigate, Harrow View House, Ealing, and Westminster School. He was for a time a copywriter in Royds' Advertising Agency, the Strand, and, in addition, co-wrote the biography of a Victorian politician, Sir Henry Cunninghame, which appeared in 1938.

These years of uncertain direction were given shape and a more clearly documented track on 16 February 1940 when Spencer – born with a congenital heart condition that rendered him unfit for military service, and permanently in precarious states of health – joined the newly formed British Council and travelled with his wife by train via Belgrade and Athens to Salonika in Greece. There he became a Teacher at the Institute of English Studies, where he also acted as the Librarian. Grigson records a reported anecdote, that in 'Salonika policemen on traffic duty would notice Norah with delight. Then they would see Bernard, and turn away from her, and stare at him.'[13] She returned to London for a holiday before the Fall of France and appears to have been refused permission to return to Greece.[14] Through the war years Nora worked at the Ministry of Supply in London in a secretarial post. During July and August of 1940 Spencer was on Mykonos and Delos with Lawrence Durrell and Nanos Valaoritis, his future co-translators of George Seferis' poetry.[15] On the 28 October the Italians invaded Greece and in that month air raids on Salonika began. The Hotel Luxembourg was hit and Spencer's room demolished. The British Institute was damaged in several bombardments and closed. By Christmas, Spencer was in Athens awaiting a transfer to Fuad I University in Cairo. His British Council record says he was posted to Egypt in December, to take up the lecturing position in March. It seems, however, that he left Greece by ship in January, evacuated with Robert Liddell.

As well as lecturing at the university, Spencer gave talks on painting and literary subjects at the Institutes of Cairo and Alexandria. They were joined by the great exile from Greece in May. During the late summer, in the gardens of the Anglo-Egyptian Union, Durrell, Robin Fedden and Spencer came up with their idea for the magazine that would become *Personal Landscape* (1942-1945). This is the second journal of the three with which his poetry was to be principally associated, a milieu and publication about which the also exiled Seferis recalled that 'the goodwill and humour of *Personal Landscape* were among the few things that gave me comfort'.[16] In a 1966 memoir, Fedden provides a portrait of Spencer at this point in his life:

> Though I had met Bernard Spencer once or twice in England, his memory for me will always be associated with Greece. Both the man, with his fine clearly-drawn features, and his verse shared something of the country's spare taut quality. He was not easy to know, for a friendly manner concealed a reticence hard to pierce and a formidable irony. When he later arrived in Egypt [...] he came to stay with me in Zamalek. Subsequently for a time we were fellow lecturers at Cairo University. I think Spencer never much liked Egypt, and never felt the attraction either of the old Cairo across the Nile – the great mediaeval city that time has spared – or of the ancient Egypt on the fringes of the desert. Wherever we went, he created his own self-sufficient world. In this world he made room for a group, usually a small group, of devoted friends. It was a world in which his poems, all too few, slowly and obscurely matured, to emerge clear, moving, and incisive.[17]

Among Spencer's acquaintance at this time was Keith Douglas, encountered in Cairo during May and June of 1942 when, according to Desmond Graham, he 'spends time with David Hicks, editor of *Citadel*, and meets Bernard Spencer'.[18] In his biography of Douglas, Graham offers two versions of the younger poet's relations with Spencer. His apparent denigration of his elder is given in a footnote. Spencer is 'a minor poet who once edited things with Spender – but to do him justice, has forgotten it'.[19] This is more dismissive of the prominent Spender than the lesser known Spencer, sounding like a report of gossip about the co-editor of *Personal Landscape*, or, more likely, a piece of self-denigration. Spencer had not published a collection at that date, while Douglas, eleven years his junior, was about to appear in a shared *Selected Poems* with J.C. Hall and Norman Nicholson. Spencer appeared already to have outlived his moment. Graham, though, continues: 'Hicks, like others in Cairo at this time, recalls, however, that Spencer and Douglas became good occasional friends'.[20] Douglas's '*Vergiss-meinnicht*' (May-June 1943), first appearing in *Personal Landscape* in 1944, shows knowledge of Spencer's 'Death of an Airman', 'Letters' and possibly 'Libyan Front', the first two published in Cairo a couple of years before his poem was written. As Adam Piette suggests, Douglas's creative 'choices took energy from' among other poets 'the detached intensities of Bernard Spencer'.[21] Spencer's 'Keith Douglas: An Obituary Note', in the last *Personal Landscape*, shows a clear-sighted admiration for the soldier's poetry.[22]

In June 1942, the period of the 'Flap' when the fleet withdrew and papers were burned because Rommel had reached El Alamein, Spencer spent time in Palestine. When Durrell's wife Nancy left him in July, he moved in with Spencer, 'who had a first-floor flat at 27 Sharia Malika Farida, opposite the Mohammed Ali Club, where editorial meetings for *Personal Landscape* now took place, and where the magazine had its mailing address,' Gordon Bowker notes in his biography of Durrell, adding that he 'like Spencer, seems to have turned to other women for comfort. The flat became known as the Orgy Flat – the scene of many a wild party'. On 11 November, a gathering to celebrate the new issue of *Personal Landscape*, Robin Fedden's marriage to Renée Catzeflis, and Durrell's departure for Alexandria took place at this same flat.[23] It was in Cairo that Spencer first met his lifelong friend and supporter Ruth Speirs, whose translations of Rilke first appeared in the magazine, and to whom several of his poems are addressed. Though the dates on the post-1930s section of Spencer's *Aegean Islands and Other Poems* (1946) suggest he wrote no poetry in the latter years of war, he certainly wrote his occasional sonnet for the 'flyting' with the Alexandrians, and there are indications that he began collaborating with Durrell and Valaoritis on translating Seferis during the early months of 1944. In the November of that year Olivia Manning's 'Poets of Exile' in *Horizon* asserted that Spencer

> has long deserved a wider public. His poems are in the direct tra-
> dition of English poetry, and are marked by sincerity, exact obser-
> vation, and a deep feeling for nature. They are patient, honest,
> individual, and always come out of the life he is living. Unlike
> Durrell's work, they never pretend to be more than they are; unlike
> [Terence] Tiller's, they never give the impression of straining after
> something not quite realised. Spencer's tone is unmistakably his
> own. His values, likes and appetites are recognised by the average

man as normal and universal. (In this he resembles MacNeice, but he has none of MacNeice's dazzle.) He abhors flashiness and is very careful not to let slickness run away with him. He relies on level statement for much of his strength, but on the rare occasion when he is saying something that demands slickness, his command of technique is obvious.[24]

Manning then illustrates this command of technique, resistance to facile success, unique tone, and value by quoting the first four verses of the Cairo poem 'Behaviour of Money'. Durrell had the right to use the diplomatic bag to convey material back to London, and it was he who sent Spencer's poetry to T.S. Eliot at Faber & Faber. From London, Eliot's advice was that he should wait until there was a complete book of post-Thirties poems. The Faber editor's secretary, Anne Ridler, then passed the manuscript to Tambimuttu, who recalls that Spencer was in touch with him about the manuscript while still in Egypt.[25] Thus it came about that his first collection was published by Editions Poetry London in the year after war ended.

Spencer's wife Nora joined him in Cairo in early 1945, where she appears to have done some broadcasting. The confidential British Council report by a Mr Furness in January notes:

> In such contacts as I have had with him, I have found him satis-factory to deal with, though except among his intimates he has a rather unforthcoming manner. He used often to strike me as some-what melancholy, but I have the impression that he has been more contented of late, especially since his wife joined him a few weeks ago.[26]

In August the couple returned to England 'on account of ill-health' according to another British Council document.[27] Tambimuttu wrote to Durrell on Patmos at about this time reporting a reunion of the Cairo exiles – Ruth Speirs, Bernard Spencer and Gwyn Williams – in London.[28] By the autumn, Spencer was writing educational notes at the Council's Film Department in the capital, waiting for a permanent position in the overseas service of the Council. Nanos Valaoritis had also now arrived in London, and the two began again making translations from Seferis' poems. Working with Valaoritis will have helped prompt 'A Spring Wind', first published that year. Spencer mentions the poem in a 1 June 1946 letter to Seferis, in which he also requests permission to publish their translations, because John Lehmann has got some paper, 'a rare thing in England' at the time, as he notes.[29]

On 1 July, Spencer was posted to a lectureship at the British Institute in Palermo, Sicily, leaving England on the 28 August to take up the post on 1 September. Spencer had begun writing again, as his poem 'On a Carved Axle-Piece from a Sicilian Cart' also indicates. 'On the Road', written during the following year, may perhaps be recalling their journey through harvest France to take up the post in southern Italy. During that winter Nora became ill with TB, dying of heart failure caused by the disease in Rome (where the couple had gone in the spring to find treatment) on 13 June 1947. She is buried in the Protestant Cemetery, just behind Antonio Gramsci's grave. In a letter to Ruth Speirs written soon after, Spencer says 'that for weeks and months – really for years – there had been a wretched, exhausting struggle against death. Not that I realised how close it was till the end'. He admits he has begun to recover from 'feeling tired and dazed' by 'going into company as much as possible'.[30] In the immediate aftermath of his wife's death he would lecture at a three-week summer school for Italian teachers east of Rome, and then holiday in the north of Italy, near Switzerland with a newly-married David Hicks. The poem 'At Courmayeur' was probably occasioned during this August of 1947.[31]

On 1 September, Spencer was posted to Turin, as Lecturer at the British Institute. Durrell is reported by his biographer to have met the recently widowed Spencer in Lisbon during November 1947, where the poet is said to have been working for the British Council. While there is no evidence for such a posting to Portugal it is at least possible that Spencer made a journey to visit his friend who was on route for Argentina. Spencer returned to London on 17 May 1948 himself suffering from tuberculosis, and on 1 September went to Leysin, Switzerland, for treatment involving surgery on the lungs performed under local anaesthetic. By December he was back in London, doing light duties at the Council's Davis Street offices. *The King of Asine and Other Poems* by Seferis appeared from John Lehmann in 1948. Valaoritis recalls that it was well received, with fourteen reviews and congratulations from T.S. Eliot,[32] while Roderick Beaton, Seferis's biographer, wrote in 2003 that this 'is very much a poets' translation, and deserves to be read'.[33] Lehmann would publish Spencer's poetry in *The London Magazine* after he had re-founded the journal in February 1954. 1948 also saw the appearance in the USA of the Doubleday edition of *Aegean Islands*, and the beginning of an influence on some American poets of which Spencer may have remained almost entirely unaware.[34] The poet's experiences from the death of Nora to the end of the decade suggest a serious loss of orientation, underlined perhaps by the fragment collected here for the first time in which he sees 'Spain coming in through the window / *what do I owe all this to? /* what was I before?' [35]

Spencer's post-war life did indeed take on a more steadied shape when in September 1949 he was posted to Madrid as a lecturer at the British Institute. He began again to find poetry in his surroundings, as 'Notes by a Foreigner', 'From my Window', and 'Mediterranean Suburbs' exemplify, while 'Madrid Journal' gives a glimpse into his life during these years. It is also from this point that complete manuscript records of Spencer's compositional processes begin to survive. On 1 September 1955 he was posted to Athens, an interlude that came to an end the following year, though not before it had produced two of his finest later poems, 'In Athens' and 'The Rendezvous'. Introducing the latter poem for a Third Programme radio broadcast, recorded on 30 July 1959, Spencer's comment is politic in not specifying too much: 'in a town which you know and love there is an outbreak of political feeling; mobs march through the streets rioting; soldiers are called in. Civilised values are forgotten in the excited satisfactions of the masses.' [36] The deportation of Archbishop Makarios on 9 March 1956 from British Cyprus resulted in rioting both on the island and in Athens, where the British European Airways offices had their windows smashed. Sir Anthony Eden, the then prime minister, would have been one of those 'Ministers in tight morning coats' who 'miles from here have done their work' [37] in lines deleted from the draft and replaced by the more neutrally discreet 'now governments have done their work', a phrase referring both to the British, originally picked out for sole blame, and the Greeks who had deployed troops to restore calm, and were making representations at the United Nations for sovereignty over the island. The cries of crowds and the slammed doors in 'The Rendezvous' are anti-British, including the poet, a cultural representative of his country overseas.

The poem also registers, more strongly in the draft, a much-travelled Englishman's informed detachment from the world vision of his then government. He begins his poem with the 'twist-about' street, an adjective that sets the pitch for a work concerned about ways that individual feelings are both contrasted with and distorted by political interests and conflicts. Bowen has suggested that Spencer's poem reveals 'despairing incredulity', [38] but that might mean he didn't understand what was causing the people to riot. Yet he clearly does, as his revision of the 'governments' line indicates. There is too much detachment (as in that sardonic 'etc', or his characterising the graffiti writers as 'the fanatic or the duped, / even children') for 'despairing' to be the dominant note. Yet just as Spencer's 8 and 10 April 1956 notes to Ian Fletcher concerning an ICA reading of the poem[39] reveal a by no means innocent poet, his manuscripts show the skills of selection and pointing with which he shaped a disarming simplicity from an awareness of the most complex and intractable of situations.

Nor should we forget that 'The Rendezvous' attunes a disharmony of loves, the patriotic and the romantic, through a tryst in the conflicted circumstances of the Greek capital. Spencer's poem more than hints that such encounters, as in Hardy's 'In Time of the "Breaking of Nations"', will survive both mass violence and international conflict. Asked by Orr about his influences, Spencer replied: 'I think Thomas Hardy, very, very especially'.[40] He was allusively to recall Hardy's poem in 'Properties of Snow', written in Vienna after the bitter winter of 1962-63. Rather than the 'maid and her wight',[41] though, it is 'the marching of a company of infantry' which, over the snow, seems 'the killed from a battle whispering by'. Writing to Fletcher with advice about travelling in Spain from the Old Felbridge Hotel, East Grinstead, on 12 September 1956, Spencer added along the right side of the second sheet: 'It looks as though the Greeks are throwing me out of Athens. Shall probably be in England when you get back.' [42] He was based at the Council's London headquarters until January 1958 when he took up a temporary appointment as a lecturer at the University of Ankara, Turkey, which ended in July of the same year. This sojourn produced 'Delicate Grasses', 'Lottery Sellers' and probably 'Donkey', as well as fragmentary travel notes set in Ankara and Anatolia, published here for the first time.

By September of the same year he was back in Madrid, once again a lecturer at the Institute, and it was in the Spanish capital that he would meet his second wife, Anne Marjoribanks. On 31 December 1960, *The Twist in the Plotting*, a limited edition of twenty-five poems, was published by the Fine Art Department at the University of Reading. This volume was commissioned and overseen by Ian Fletcher. On 6 April 1961 a party was held at the British Institute, Madrid, to celebrate publication. In July, Spencer and Anne were in Ibiza, where archival material shows he wrote 'Boat Poem', the holiday being followed by a visit to London to have a check-up with his doctor. On 29 September the poet was back in Madrid where the marriage to Anne took place. In July of the following year, the couple left the Spanish capital and in October 1962 Spencer was transferred to Vienna, as a lecturer at the university, employed by the British Council. Spencer concludes his fragmentary 'Autobiographical Notes' with a snapshot from this moment in his life: 'I have recently married, for the second time. My wife and I now living in Vienna. Her interests are clothes, balls, houses, most animals, children, the drama, pictures. My interests, apart from books, are people, places, and most of the Arts. I relax by doing nothing at all, by sleeping around the clock, or by getting into company & talking.'[43]

On 7 February 1963 the poet's son Piers Bernard Spencer was born, prompting the composition of what may be his last completed poem, 'To Piers Spencer, five months old', whose title suggests it was written in July. That year the family summered in Italy on the Adriatic, with a visit to Venice. However, the holiday was interrupted because of a breakdown in Spencer's health. Already deliriously ill and with a high fever, he was inexplicably allowed to leave the Viennese clinic where his condition was being investigated. His body was discovered at 5 a.m. on 11 September beside suburban railways lines, the state of his shoes suggesting he had walked a considerable distance, and with head injuries that made it likely he had been hit by a local train. His widow wished to have questions asked about why he was allowed to leave the clinic, but the Council did not want to strain relations with Austria. Various suggestions have been made for the poet's fever and sudden decay of mental powers ranging from an undiagnosed brain tumour to an enlarged prostate causing ureic acid to infect the brain. After an autopsy, which among other things confirmed the presence of no alcohol, Spencer was cremated in Vienna. His ashes were returned to England and buried with his parents in Wheatfield, Oxfordshire.

Diffident poets, such as Bernard Spencer appears, may contain behind their defensive manner a serious doubt. Sometimes, too, they may have reserves of confidence on which they can draw to produce, if they're lucky, profoundly uncertain poems. Spencer was gifted in this way. Within his small *oeuvre*, poem after poem sounds true. That sound sense of reliable poetry was achieved under the shadow of an urge to doubt the entire business. Yet within this shadow the conditions for his success are found in outline.

'Night-time: Starting to Write', another poem set in Madrid, discovers the poet at his desk engaged in the dubious activity described in the interview with Peter Orr when he identifies 'a so-far-unexplored area of feeling and emotion, which is almost disagreeable to hold on to' and which the poet 'for all reasons, must then work on':[44]

> Sounds and night-sounds, no more; but then I catch
> my lamp burn fiercer like a thing bewitched,
>
> Table and chairs expectant like a play:
> and – if that Unknown, Demon, what you will
> stalks on the scene – must live with sounds and echoes,
> be damned the call to sleep, the needs of day,
>
> Love a dark city; then for some bare bones
> of motive, strange perhaps to beast or traveller,
> with all I am and all that I have been
> sweat the night into words, as who cracks stones.

If these 'bare bones / of motive' are like those of a skeleton at a feast, they are also fundamental to structure and articulation. The autobiographical foundation for Spencer's art is professed in 'all I am and all that I have been'. In his introduction, Bowen indicated two virtues of autobiographical poetry. He quotes Spencer's admission that 'For me, poetry always begins at home, wherever home may be', and also his writing to Alan Ross that his poems are 'always factual'.[45] Dubious and self-doubting features are present in 'Night-time: Starting to Write', where the poet's need to take himself seriously so as to compose such poetry struggles with a sense that to do both might be play-acting. Self-doubting autobiographers want the shaping form that poems may discover, can be sceptical of the patterning they find, but would not be without it. The poem has a manuscript variant for ' – must live with sounds and echoes' which reads ' – must play a loved-loathed role', a phrase sustaining the theatricality of the occasion, but which takes the already perilous self-dramatisation towards a melodramatic self-regard. Spencer was right to supplant that with a half-line drawing the poem back towards the business of the composing poet, alive to 'sounds and echoes'. 'Night-time: Starting to Write' is nonetheless engaging with the ambivalent impulses in that 'loved-loathed role'.

When it is carefully noting the sounds of night in its opening six lines, the poem evokes an impression of the random circumstances that may

sponsor composition, presenting them with a casualness underplaying the
sense that these random instances are thus already composed:

> Over the mountains a plane bumbles in;
> down in the city a watchman's iron-topped stick
> bounces and rings on the pavement. Late returners
> must be waiting now, by me unseen
>
> To enter shadowed doorways. A dog's pitched
> barking flakes and flakes away at the sky.

Here the poet skilfully pitches the dog's barking around a line-end, then
has the noise echo down the next line, like the street, with its 'barking
flakes and flakes'. At this point, though, self-consciousness about his poetic
role interrupts this muted activity with that troubled theatricality already
noted. It is as though the thought of being a poet (cursed or blessed by
the urge to arrange words) misleads the true attentiveness of the poet in
the direction of a pose, a remnant of romantic self-definition. The problem
with that expression 'loved-loathed role' is that while it characterises the
doubleness in contemporary poets' lives as writers – what they do, and
how they may have to appear – the expression is more from the repertoire
of the artiste, than from the artist's pen. Yet this too acknowledges the
risks involved in Spencer's carefully underplayed art.

His aesthetic preferences for poetry that begins at home were first out-
lined in the mid-1930s with work he published in *New Verse*. What Durrell
was to evoke in the following decade in 'Alexandria', when he referred to
'B. with his respect for the Object',[46] was a quality Grigson asserted in his
preface to an anthology of the magazine's poets published in 1939, writing
that to be 'an imaginative poet, of the best kind, you need to see objects as
themselves and as symbols, all at once' and 'to impart ideas through objects'.[47]
Spencer had praised Auden in the November 1937 double number devoted
to him for 'brutalising his thought and language to the level from which
important poetry proceeds' – curiously equivocal praise prompted by the
thought that to 'go soft and sermonise' or appeal to pity (it being 'an emo-
tion you can't live with for long at a stretch') were faults to be avoided.[48]
When he came to contribute an 'Ideas about Poems' to *Personal Landscape* in
1942, this sense of poetry as 'brutal' was not only attributed to J.M. Synge,
and offered as a requisite for skirting a host of contemporary dangers, but
also tacitly overcome in an act of 'joining'. As he writes, 'pity and disgust

might provide the necessary impulse to begin writing', but true poetry 'is a dance in which you take part and enjoy yourself'. The brutalising of the self, if that's exactly what it is, was then only a means for avoiding conventional responses from 'a more urban and controlled society' that would frustrate the poet with 'a tenderer heart and a weaker stomach'.[49] Once detached from these, the poet could write, not merely with detachment but a 'joining' involvement – and 'joining' does, after all, presuppose a prior distance. 'In what sense am I joining in / Such a hallooing, rousing April day' he asks in his first collected poem, 'Allotments: April', and Spencer's work frequently answers that question by exploring trajectories from separation to enjoyment.

This 'respect for the Object' is, then, shorthand for a combined detached-attachment that allows the object to be seen for what it is, respected in being so, and then as a focus for connection:

> she puts a sheaf of tulips in a jug
> And pours in water and presses to one side
> The upright stems and leaves that you hear creak,
> Or loosens them, or holds them up to show me,
> So that I see the tangle of their necks and cups
> With the curls of her hair, and the body they are held
> Against, and the stalk of the small waist rising
> And flowering in the shape of breasts

Nearly forty years after this was written, Grigson anthologised it in a collection of love poetry,[50] and a love poem 'Part of Plenty' certainly is: yet in order for the poet to present this valuable experience he must first detach himself from any assumed emotion, so as not to bribe readers with it, even as he comes round at the poem's close to affirm how 'What she does is ages old, and she is not simply, / No, but lovely in that way.' Even here, it is 'that' and not *this* 'way' and the poet's wife remains as a third-person 'she'. In *The Private Art*, Grigson writes that 'I see again, as I read, Norah's youth, her hands, her gestures, her arms and elbows and long neck and small waist. I don't know another poem in which the shape and nature of a particular woman is so fixed, so preserved, so in action.'[51] That the anthologist sees a combination of the 'fixed' and 'in action' here, is thanks to a reduction of the poet's presence to an object pronoun ('to show me') and then as subject for the simplest of verbs ('I see'), and, by that means, to a respect not only for the objects of sight – what Grigson calls 'Norah Spencer and tulips together, as if they were each other' – but for the reader, who is not required to take on trust any emotion in life that the two people may and must have shared.

'Part of Plenty' was placed next to 'A Cold Night' in Spencer's ordering of *Aegean Islands*, and there we read of 'the soldiery who lie / Round wounded Madrid' and how, also cold in winter, 'I turn back to my fire. Which I must', because 'one needs time too to sit in peace / Opposite one's girl, with food, fire, light'. Some critics, faced with such moments in Spencer's poetry of the 1930s have been tempted to call such gestures quietist,[52] but the honesty of this moment comes not only from the acceptance of individual limits, but also from a simultaneous acknowledgement of their cost. If the value of personal experience is that it needs protecting, then praise for 'time too to sit in peace' is not vitiated by the acknowledgement of suffering elsewhere but guaranteed in its precariousness as deserving defence. This doesn't make Spencer's poetry unable to take sides in the Spanish Civil War, but, on the contrary, shows it naturally committed via its beliefs about private life to the Republican side. Franco's forces are called 'soldiery who lie', recalling Yeats' 'drunken soldiery'[53] in 'Nineteen Hundred and Nineteen' and promoting the pun on 'lie' by exposing the word at its line end, while Republican Madrid is described as 'wounded'. Spencer's political intelligence and sense of perspective have brought him to such insights as Auden would reach two years later in 'Musée des Beaux Arts' with its views on 'suffering' and 'just walking dully along'.[54]

The good poet's attention to technique contains recognition of such involuntary conditions of things and, within the space of art, reconfigures them as voluntary relations. We can see this in those two senses of 'must' in 'A Cold Night': the modal expressing both compulsion and choice. This partial freeing of the will not only serves to help achieve acceptance of the inevitable, as in elegy, it also encourages and advocates a more humanly fulfilling life 'in' the world, but not merely 'of' its constrictions – such as those senses of humiliation and incapacity that the demands and powers of money can exert. Spencer's 'Behaviour of Money' is imaginatively embroiled in such involuntary constraints, and in their conversion into a more positive emotion. First published in *Personal Landscape* in 1943, the poem concerns the rampant inflation that gripped the Egyptian capital's monetary system during the vicissitudes of the Desert campaigns. As a civilian employee at Cairo University, Spencer would have been paid in the local currency, while military personnel, such as Keith Douglas, were paid in sterling. The poem's form, invented for the occasion, mimics the spiralling instability of the local currency. From the suggestion of a personification in the second stanza ('But money changed. Money came jerking roughly alive') Spencer evolves the monstrous figure of the fifth to seventh stanzas. Finally, we are brought to contemplate 'the sprawled body of Money, dead, stinking, alone!' The second part of the poem is largely composed of questions. Those in stanza five to seven are spoken as the panic of 'the people in bed' who want to know 'what's to become of us?' Yet the final five questions are outside the speech marks, identified with the voice of the poet speaking. They thus inhabit the panicking cries of the people in bed, but turn that tone to one of curious perplexity:

> Will X contrive to lose the weasel look in his eyes?
> Will the metal go out of the voice of Y? Shall we all turn back
> to men, like Circe's beasts?
> Or die? Or dance in the street the day that the world goes crack?

The poem comes to no conclusions, but is suspended between these proliferating possibilities: one resembling the hopes for human improvement outside corrupted and corrupting monetary systems; another predicting mere anarchy and suffering at the failure of any such structures; and a third, like a revolutionary impulse, dancing at the collapse of an exploitative order. These options economically summarise many of the hopes and fears from the crisis years of the previous decade.

Perhaps 'Behaviour of Money' might appear to fail to decide between these options out of weakness. Rather, it affirms the possibility of the different outcomes, but to different degrees, and does this by means of the poem's stanza form, exemplifying what Olivia Manning meant when she affirmed in her 1944 essay that 'his command of technique is obvious':[55]

> Money was once well known, like a townhall or the sky
> or a river East and West, and you lived one side or the other;
> Love and Death dealt shocks,
> but for all the money that passed, the wise man knew his brother.
>
> But money changed. Money came jerking roughly alive;
> went battering round the town with a boozy, zigzag tread.
> A clear case for arrest;
> and the crowds milled and killed for the pound notes that he shed.

The stanza is constructed of three alexandrines (lines 1, 2 and 4), the first pair separated from the final one by a trimeter (making up line 3). The series of short third lines work to upset the order of the first pair, by introducing a surprise, or a contrary force: 'Love and Death dealt shocks' and 'A clear case for arrest'. The natural forces of love and death upset the pattern of life we've grown used to, or, as money starts to run out of control in alexandrines that become 'roughly alive' with a 'zigzag tread', something must be done, and the poet attempts to regulate the circulation with his reigned-in line 3. Yet each quatrain's final line reinforces the state of affairs sketched by the first pair of alexandrines. Thus, despite line 3 of stanza 1, 'the wise man knew his brother' and, despite the need to arrest money's course, 'the crowds milled and killed for the pound notes that he shed'. This pattern is not maintained pedantically throughout, which would be technically inept. Rather, it remains as a shadowy series of expectations behind the proliferating disturbances, the hectic circulation, and sudden bouts of panic that occur in stanzas 4 to 7. How does this pattern influence the stanza's conclusion? The stanza form suggest that lines 1, 2 and 4 will accord with each other, while the third lines will differently resist them. 'Shall we turn back / to men, like Circe's beasts?' thus singles itself out as a particularly desired hope, but one that is surrounded by unlikelihood. The 'metal' and the 'weasel look' may equally worsen. When the world goes 'crack' (a weak-sounding verb) we may well not dance for joy. In the final stanza, the poet's form endorses the hope of line 3, but hedges it around to attenuate its tenuousness. Here too, at variance with earlier stanzas, there is a slant-rhyme patterning from the 'eyes' in line 1 to the 'Y' in line 2, coming to rest on the 'die' in the poem's final line. If the expectations of line-lengths invite us to hope that we will 'turn back / to men', the concealed rhyming warns us to expect the worst. If the world's banking system collapsed and died, so too might we.

Spencer was on the lookout for rhymes. In the interview with Orr, he noted that 'reading by yourself a poem that is unfamiliar to you, you are in fact, through experience, already looking at the shape of it, and in the first few lines you are observing whether there is a rhyme going on or not'.[56] He offers thus an illustration of how readers come into a promissory relationship with form when reading a poem, a process which begins with the reader granting its speaker a certain tacit authority, to be ratified, or not, by the subsequent experience of the work. Again this concerns the issue of what a poet's and a reader's listening to poetry can mean. Good rhymes involve both luck and judgment: luck that the word exists, and judgment that, once found, they are aptly kept or dropped. And it is in the matrix of verbal luck and judgment that relationship can be shifted from one of involuntary, economic necessity, to more preferable states of desired wellbeing. In 'Behaviour of Money' there are no answers to the panicky and quizzical interrogatives – no answers, that is, except the rhymes. When you rhyme on 'the world goes crack', your congruence of sounds is attempting to make repairs. Such repairs can't change the painful facts of careering money, and Spencer's rhymes might seem no more than the interior decoration in Eliot's criticism of I.A. Richards' remark that poetry 'is capable of saving us' when he adds: 'it is like saying that the wall-paper will save us when the walls have crumbled'.[57] In bad times, though, we can always be grateful for small mercies.

Thus random and chaotic circumstances can sponsor composition, though they cannot be that composition. Spencer's poetry is formed against the pressures of an underlying sense of things being broken up, unconnected, unrelated; and to be accurate to such an awareness his poems must accommodate the pressure of a merely accidental proximity of things, even as they work to transform accidental proximity into meaningful structure. 'In a Foreign Hospital', from the period after his first wife's death from TB, when he was undergoing treatment for the same disease in Switzerland, must remain faithful to the accidents of life and death, to things that befall; but it cannot rest assured with so blank an aspect. Thus it enlists occurrences, immediate circumstances, seeking through them the reassurances of congruence, of answering form:

> the man in the next room with the low voice,
> the brown-skinned boy, the child among its toys
> and I and others. Against my bedside light
> a small green insect flings itself with a noise
> tiny and regular, a 'tink; tink, tink'.

Then 'looking at the shape of it' and 'observing whether there is a rhyme going on or not', as Spencer describes the activity in his interview with Orr, a reader tacitly notes that 'In a Foreign Hospital' both has a rhyme going on and doesn't, for, of the first 6 lines, 2 pairs rhyme and 2 eschew rhyme. But it is only when the final line of the poem is reached that the rhyme with 'tink' (the final line of the first of two stanzas) is discovered:

I am free to keep my watch with images,
a bare white room, the World, an insect's rage,
and if I am lucky, find some link, some link.

Like 'Allotments: April', 'The Administrator', and 'The Empire Clock', this poem ends with the repetition of its clinching phrase; the device mimes a sense of recognitions sinking in, helping them to sink in as it does. So the shapes of both stanzas have a precarious, stabilising regularity that establishes itself only as opportunities appear to present themselves, the stanzas seeking form even as they would not, cannot, and must not insist upon it. Yet the concluding rhyme that draws together the ends of each stanza presents a moment of faithful hope which resounds beyond the tentative if-clause that heralds it: finding in the rhyme the link that it only hopes to discover. The effect is a secularised form of the appeal for intercession in the final stanza of George Herbert's 'Denial', which, contrasting with the unrhymed suspensions of the final lines to previous stanzas, metaphorically answers the prayer it articulates by means of its own mended rhyme:

O cheer and tune my heartless breast,
        Defer no time;
That so thy favours granting my request,
        They and my mind my chime
        And mend my rhyme.[58]

Spencer had also recalled that 'when I got a school prize at about seventeen, I was much laughed at for having chosen George Herbert as the book and everyone thought that extremely stuffy of me' when talking to Orr, while he also praises Herbert for his 'sense of a tight pattern' in his 1962 University of Madrid lecture.[59] When related to the desire to find a form for his experience, luck for Spencer resembles a form of doubting faith. When luck runs out in his life, it seem to be a relative of Hardy's fatalism, but, again, filled with doubt: 'Why was this something we had not foreseen?' Much of his poetry addresses the conditions of life and time that prompt this unanswerable question from 'The Building of the House'.

His repeated adoption of the word 'twist' implies a retrospective sense of links between things more articulated than their accidental proximity, only caught in a disturbed relation not desired or expected, and one which often gravitates towards death. 'For Signorina Brunella Mori' turns a compliment with the device in its four lines:

33

> Tell me, you Romans, who but the dark Brunella,
> > giovane, bella,
> could ever give such a startling twist to the hoary
> > 'memento mori'?

In 'Base Town' it is 'The twist of reason' that moves the poem towards 'the knowledge that to die, / Some stony miles north of our wintering / Was a more ordinary thing'. 'Train to Work' contemplates the 'endearing stranger' on the seat opposite: 'condemned to sure death, he sits / (with his mackintosh belt twisted), / poetry roaring from him like a furnace'. However, it is 'In Athens', occasioned by the accident of a woman passing the poet in the street, which provides the definitive example, and in doing so gave Spencer the title for his 1960 interim collection, *The Twist in the Plotting*. Holdings at the Spencer archive at Reading makes it possible to follow the poet's discovery of this key phrase, chosen by Ian Fletcher from a list of possible titles suggested by the poet.[60] Earlier drafts do not contain these words, which emerge only in revision:[61]

> It is so much like
> the twist in the plotting of things she should pass here
> so near where they talked well on love
> two civilisations ago, and found
> splendid and jeering images

Adam Piette has evoked the work this poem achieves: 'It is as though the poet, in learning to compose the poem, were addressing a love poem to or within himself, trying to marry his compositional voice as closely as he can to the voice of the body as it addresses the mind with the secret poem about the woman encountered two civilisations ago.'[62] Spencer's erratically sure-footed free verse twists around the line-ends in search of such a relation, discovering as it does unlikely images, and linking them with internal chimes: 'here' is found to be 'so near' as we round the line (though still distanced by the enjambment), while what is found in the next line turns out to recall the here and near by 'jeering'.

In other poems his lines similarly 'descend with us the ill-lighted stair / stone by stone with all their doubts and turnings' in 'Casa de P——'. They have the switchback precipitous movement of mountain roads in 'At Courmayeur', in memory of Nora: 'Guesses went wide; but zigzag past that ridge / the road climbs from the Roman town; there stand / the glittering peaks, and one, the God, immensely / tossing the clouds around his shoulders'. In such poetry each line-end seems endangering like a potentially fatal illness, the senses thankfully reprieved if the syntax continues, postponing for a little longer the larger death of the poem's end. In a passage from Lawrence Durrell's memoir a resemblance to Edward Thomas's poetry is proposed: 'and his best poems will certainly live as long as the best of Thomas'.[63] If this is so, it may be because Spencer's poems are true to the unforeseen but ever-present possibility of fatal accident, rather than the searching stare at his almost certain death that Thomas's poetry embraces.

Yeats's apocalyptic 'Things fall apart' draws energy from the contemplation of chaos; but a Hardyesque poet for whom 'if way to the Better there be, it exacts a full look at the Worst' must enact the snapping of links, even though preferring to find they can hold.[64] When Spencer was arranging his work for *With Luck Lasting* he placed 'Regent's Park Terrace' immediately after 'In a Foreign Hospital', juxtaposing poems that contrastingly diverge. The second of the pair shapes 'The noises round my house' into a broken music of such sounds as the trains: 'which speed with the declining / sadness of crying along the distant routes / knitting together weathers and dialects'. There is a deft knitting and unthreading in that third line, where the internal rhyme binds remote weathers, but the lacking end-rhyme acknowledges that though the dialects are connected by travel, they are not so bound together, and asserts, as they must, the different in languages. As an employee of the British Council, Spencer passed the greater part of his working life abroad; a significant number of his poems encompass the separations and distances of being away from home, and of being a stranger in someone else's town. 'Regent's Park Terrace' concludes with a recognition that such noises of travel 'unpick / the bricks of a London terrace, make the ear / their road'. The poem's form comprehends the gaps between things that such unpicking shows (it is there again in the line-endings) and crosses those distances like rail-gaps.

His poems comprehend being 'Bored and humbled by every disintegrating day' ('Fluted Armour'), and discover across the gaps between things a shape which understands that 'we are also born for a message to begin, / a narrow room, a tomb, / a portent and a danger that may give / a grace and meaning' ('Cairo Restaurant'). Furthermore, in doing these two precariously well, Spencer achieves a third thing. His poem 'On a Carved Axle-

Piece from a Sicilian Cart' praises the artistry of the painter who, 'harking back out of Christendom, imagined / a chariot of glory / and Aphrodite riding wooden waves', answered thus:

> those metaphysical gaps and fears
> which drain the blood of the age or drive it mad;
> the 'why are we guilty?' and the 'who must punish?'

Though Spencer's love poetry is evidently drawn to the pagan 'Queen of Love' in this poem, his own experiences of separation through war and then total loss at the hands of love and death suggest that for him such harking back could be only a partial answer. In 'Delicate Grasses' the lure of natural phenomena 'miles from any peopled spot' tempts the poet:

> I drift their way; I need what their world lends;
> then, chilled by one thought further still than those,
> I swerve towards life and friends
> before the trap-fangs close.

In his Madrid lecture Spencer comments that 'I was half-attracted to it and half afraid...What is the trap? What was I afraid of? Later, at his request, I read the poem out to John Betjeman, and he cried out "Oh! Eternity!" That is as good an answer as any.' [65] The conflict of emotion is embodied in the contrasting senses of the statement and its formal arrangement. Spencer listens for occasional, chanced upon rhyme in his poems, but he is at least half-afraid of the certain closure performed here. If the more provisional patterns of Spencer's poems seem at first to merely wallpaper over the metaphysical gaps, they do so with some knowledge that the cracks are still to be found underneath. This is how his poetry, to recall Eliot's criticism of Richards, can help save us by not claiming to be capable of doing any such thing. Noticing this is also simply to alter the emphasis in what Martin Dodsworth noticed was the 'acute sense in him of an underlying unity and an all too obvious division'.[66] Nevertheless, paradoxically, the very consciousness of gaps underlying a precarious unity allows his poems access to as much reassurance as human perspectives could hope to give.

In this the influence of Eugenio Montale may have also been formative. It was Bowen collected for the first time in 1981, along with twenty-two stray poems and nine undergraduate pieces, four translations from the Italian poet's first collection *Ossi di Seppia* (1925). Montale's influence can be heard in a line from 'The Agents' (1957), written about a decade after his two week stay at the Albergo Nazionale in Pino Torinese where those versions were most probably made: 'your fierce script like glass jags that top a wall' appearing to recall 'una muraglia / che ha in cima cocci aguzzi di bottiglia' from 'Meriggiare pallido e assorto',[67] rendered by Spencer as 'a wall / crowned with sharp splinters of bottle'. His version of 'I limoni', 'The Lemon Trees', takes him to another image of linkage and breaking, through which we are carried by the plot-twists of enjambed syntax:

> sometimes the feeling comes
> of discovering a flaw in Nature,
> the dead point of the world, the link that does not hold
> the thread to unravel which finally lands us
> in the centre of a truth.

Reviewing Montale's second collection, *Le occasioni*, in 1940 Vittorio Sereni found that the elder poet did not 'sacrifice speech to a pretence of immediate song', and though this might be called a 'minor poet's initial attitude' without 'ambitions to eternal poetry', on the contrary, he adds, 'the configuration of his images, the echo of his words leave in us a memory of the absolute'.[68] From Spencer's poetry a similar echo, like an echo of Herbert's patterns, may be left in us. It is a spiritual relation with absence like his sense of a town at dusk in the conclusion to 'Notes by a Foreigner':

> The echo-light no town
> (of this at least you are sure), can parallel;
> when things mean more yet fade, like places
> you half remember, a now-not-beating bell.

What might have appeared to Spencer's contemporaries as a marginality of subject and focus in his poems can now be seen as a European poetry in English, and with its own distinctly English sensibility. His poems may seem to proclaim themselves, in their scale, their infrequency, and their waiting on occasions, as minor work. Nevertheless, lyric poets in our times who find themselves unbolstered by convictions or unshakable beliefs, or insufficiently by the non-literary capacities for endurance we share to different degrees, or by the boundless confidence and technical mastery of the prolific, may be more open to the threateningly meaningless in life, to the deep blankness of things, and more able to test the resources of the art in those unpropitious circumstances. Bernard Spencer's remaining faithful to the scale of his inspiration and the twists in the plotting of its situations allow his poems to face some of the hard quandaries that poetry in our age has hoped to confront and overcome. How lucky the English language appears to have his poetry in it.

PETER ROBINSON

NOTES

Some passages in this Introduction have been revised from my earlier writing on Spencer, whose sources are given in the Bibliography.

1. John Betjeman, 'Louis MacNeice and Bernard Spencer', *The London Magazine* vol. 3 no. 9 (Dec 1963), p. 64.

2. For a retrospective evaluation of Spencer that does not keep faith with those decisions to publish, see Geoffrey Grigson, *The Private Art: A Poetry Note-Book* (London: Allison & Busby, 1982), pp. 62-3.

3. See Peter Robinson, 'Bernard Spencer in *The London Magazine*', *The London Magazine* (Dec 2008-Feb 2009), pp. 68-72.

4. Peter Orr (ed.), *The Poet Speaks: Interviews with Contemporary Poets* (London: Routledge & Kegan Paul, 1966), p. 237 and, as 'Interview with Peter Orr', see below, pp. 302-3.

5. For a full account of the composition of this poem and its significance in the poet's work, see Peter Robinson, 'Bernard Spencer's "Boat Poem"', *English* vol. 58 no. 223 (Winter 2009), pp. 318-39.

6. Lawrence Durrell, 'Bernard Spencer', *The London Magazine* vol. 3 no. 10 (Jan 1964), p. 46.

7. For the outline of Spencer's life and career, as for many of the details that appear in what follows, I am indebted to the researches of Roger Bowen, his writings on the poet, and especially the Introduction to his edition of the *Collected Poems* (Oxford: Oxford University Press, 1981), pp. xiii-xxxiii.

8. This, and the following three citations, are from 'Autobiographical Notes', Special Collections, University of Reading: BSP 2/14/2 [MS5369].

9. 'University of Madrid Lecture', see below pp. 291-2 and p. 340.

10. See Selima Hastings, *Rosamond Lehmann* (London: Chatto & Windus, 2002), pp. 147-48. 'Stephen Spender was a regular visitor, bringing over from Oxford another poet, Bernard Spencer. Spencer became infatuated with his beautiful hostess, which was gratifying in a way, but tiresome in another: "he's hopeless – so dreary & boring, so depressed and convinced of his own hopelessness," she complained to Spender.' The correspondence in her archive at King's College, Cambridge, shows some of what might have been gratifying.

11. Bernard Gutteridge to Anne Marjoribanks Spencer [now Humphreys], 2 October 1963, held at Special Collections, University of Reading: BSP 4/3/16 [MS2413].

12. 'Autobiographical Notes', Special Collections, University of Reading: BSP 2/14/2 [MS5369].

13. Grigson, 'Bernard Spencer', *The Private Art*, p. 63.

14. See Olivia Manning, 'Poets in Exile', *Horizon* no. 10 (October 1944), p. 272.

15. For his memories of this moment, see Bernard Spencer, 'The Wind-

blown Island of Myconos', *The Spectator*, vol. 36 (5 September 1946), pp. 307-8, reprinted below, pp. 258-60.

16. Cited in Roderick Beaton, *George Seferis: Waiting for the Angel, a Biography* (New Haven and London: Yale University Press, 2003), p. 228.

17. Robin Fedden, *Personal Landscape* (London: Turret Books, 1966), n.p. [9-10].

18. Keith Douglas, *The Complete Poems*, ed. Desmond Graham (Oxford: Oxford University Press, 1978; third edition, 1998), p. xxxv.

19. Desmond Graham, *Keith Douglas 1920-1944: A Biography* (London: Oxford University Press, 1974), p. 148*n*.

20. Ibid. Graham mistakenly gives the year of Spencer's death as 1957.

21. Adam Piette, 'Keith Douglas and the Poetry of the Second World War', *The Cambridge Companion to Twentieth-Century English Poetry*, ed. Neil Corcoran (Cambridge: Cambridge University Press, 2007), p. 123.

22. See 'Keith Douglas: An Obituary Note' p. 257 below.

23. Gordon Bowker, *Through the Dark Labyrinth: A Biography of Lawrence Durrell* (London: Sinclair-Stevenson, 1996), pp. 148-50.

24. Manning, 'Poets of Exile', p. 277. In their biography, *Olivia Manning: A Life* (London: Chatto & Windus, 2004), Neville and June Braybrooke repeat the assumption that the poet Castlebar, in *The Levant Trilogy* (1977–1980), is 'partly based on Bernard Spencer' (p. 123). Gerry Harrison, currently writing a biography of Manning's husband, Reggie Smith, rejects this *clef à la roman*.

25. Tambimuttu to Bowen, 18 March 1980, Special Collections, University of Reading: BSP 4/3/110 [MS 5370].

26. Photocopy of Spencer's application for membership of the Permanent Overseas Service, citing 'Reports on Work', Special Collections, University of Reading: BSP 5/2/3 [MS 5370], p. 2.

27. British Council document dated 30. 8. 1945, Special Collections, University of Reading: BSP 5/2/2 [MS5370].

28. Bowker, *Through the Dark Labyrinth*, p. 172.

29. The letter is preserved in the Seferis collection at the Gennadius library, Athens.

30. Photocopy provided by Bowen of a 1 July 1947 letter from Ruth Speirs to Lawrence Durrell, mostly containing direct quotation from Spencer's letter to her. His reply to Durrell's letter of condolence is preserved at the University of Southern Illinois, Carbondale.

31. G. S. Fraser, 'The Absence of the Dead', *The Traveller Regrets* (London: Editions Poetry, 1948), pp. 2-3, was also prompted by Nora's death. Fraser had met her in Spencer's company in London during 1946.

32. Nanos Valaoritis, 'Memories of Bernard Spencer', unpublished document in my possession.

33. Beaton, *George Seferis: Waiting for the Angel*, p. 494.

34. See William Kittredge, 'Dialogue with Richard Hugo', *Dialogues with*

Northwest Writers, Northwest Review vol. 20 no. 2 & 3 (1982), p. 131, and Richard Hugo, 'Some Kind of Perfection', *The Real West Marginal Way: A Poet's Autobiography*, ed. Ripley S. Hugo et al. (New York: Norton, 1986), pp. 154-8.

35. BSP 1/78/1 [MS 5369], Special Collections, University of Reading, see below, p. 202.

36. 'Poems by Bernard Spencer', BBC Third Programme, 1959, see below, p. 285.

37. See Special Collections, University of Reading: BSP 1/28/1 [MS 2413].

38. Bowen, 'Introduction' to Spencer, *Collected Poems*, p. xxiv.

39. See Special Collections, University of Reading: BSP 4/1/18 and 19 [MS 2413].

40. See 'Interview with Peter Orr' below, p. 298.

41. Thomas Hardy, *The Complete Poetical Works of Thomas Hardy*, ed. Samuel Hynes, 5 vols. (Oxford: Oxford University Press, 1982-1995), ii, p. 296.

42. See correspondence in Peter Robinson, 'Twists in the Plotting: Bernard Spencer's Second Book of Poems', *Publishing History* no. 62 (2007), pp. 81-102.

43. 'Autobiographical Notes', Special Collections, University of Reading: BSP 2/14/2 [MS5369].

44. See 'Interview with Peter Orr' below, p. 303.

45. Bowen, 'Introduction' to Spencer, *Collected Poems*, p. xv.

46. Lawrence Durrell, *Collected Poems 1931-1974*, ed. James A. Brigham (London: Faber & Faber, 1980), p. 134.

47. Geoffrey Grigson (ed.), *New Verse: An Anthology* (London: Faber & Faber, 1939), p. 20. Spencer's contribution of seven poems ('Allotments: April', 'Poem' [later 'My Sister'], 'Evasions', 'A Cold Night', 'Part of Plenty', 'A Thousand Killed' and 'Waiting', pp. 35-46) was the third largest after Auden's ten and MacNeice's eight poems.

48. See 'Note on Auden' below, p. 255.

49. 'Ideas about Poems', *Personal Landscape* vol. 1 no. 4 (1942), p. 2, and see below, p. 256.

50. Geoffrey Grigson (ed.), *The Faber Book of Love Poems* (London: Faber & Faber, 1973), p. 227.

51. Grigson, 'Bernard Spencer', *The Personal Art*, p. 63.

52. See, for instance, Adrian Caesar, *Dividing Lines: Poetry, Class and Ideology in the 1930s* (Manchester: Manchester University Press, 1991), pp. 126-7.

53. W.B. Yeats, *The Collected Poems*, 2nd edn., ed. Richard J. Finneran (Basingstoke: Macmillan, 1991), p. 207.

54. W.H. Auden, *The English Auden: Poems, Essays, and Dramatic Writings 1927-1939*, ed. Edward Mendelson (London: Faber & Faber, 1977), p. 237.

55. Manning, 'Poets in Exile', p. 277.

56. See 'Interview with Peter Orr' below, p. 300.

57. T.S. Eliot, 'Literature, Science and Dogma', *The Dial* no. 82 (March 1927), p. 243. He is reviewing I.A. Richards, *Science and Poetry* (London: Kegan Paul, 1926).

58. George Herbert, *The Complete English Poems,* ed. John Tobin (London: Penguin Books, 1991), p. 74.

59. See 'University of Madrid Lecture' and 'Interview with Peter Orr', below pp. 292 and 298.

60. See Robinson, 'Twists in the Plotting', *Publishing History*, pp. 81-102.

61. See Peter Robinson, '*The Twist in the Plotting*: Special Collections Featured Item for November 2009', which contains some relevant facsimile reproductions and transcriptions of these holdings: http://www.reading.ac.uk/special-collections/featured-items/sc-featured-items.aspx

62. Adam Piette, 'Pronouns and Place in Bernard Spencer's "In Athens"', *The Reader* no. 13 (Autumn 2003), pp. 50-1.

63. Durrell, 'Bernard Spencer', p. 43.

64. Yeats, 'The Second Coming', *Collected Poems*, ed. Finneran, p. 187; Hardy, 'In Tenebris (II)', *Complete Poetical Works*, ed. Hynes, i, p. 208.

65. 'University of Madrid Lecture', see below, p. 295.

66. Martin Dodsworth, 'Bernard Spencer: The Poet of Addition', *The Review* no. 11-12 (1964), p. 79.

67. Eugenio Montale, *L'opera in versi*, ed. Rosanna Bettarini and Granfranco Contini (Turin: Einaudi, 1981), p. 28.

68. Vittorio Sereni, 'In margine alle Occasioni' (1940), *Letture preliminari* (Padua: Liviana Editrice, 1973), p. 10. The translation is mine.

COMPLETE POETRY

AEGEAN ISLANDS AND OTHER POEMS

(1946)

POEMS BEFORE 1940

Allotments: April

Cobbled with rough stone which rings my tread
The path twists through the squared allotments.
Blinking to glimpse the lark in the warming sun,
In what sense am I joining in
Such a hallooing, rousing April day,
Now that the hedges are so gracious and
Stick out at me moist buds, small hands, their opening scrolls and fans?

Lost to some of us the festival joy
At the bursting of the tomb, the seasonal mystery,
God walking again who lay all winter
As if in those long barrows built in the fields
To keep the root-crops warm. On squires' lawns
The booted dancers twirl. But what I hear
Is spade slice in pebbled earth, swinging the nigger-coloured loam.

And the love-songs, the mediæval grace,
The fluting lyrics, 'The only pretty ring-time',
These have stopped singing. For love detonates like sap
Up into the limbs of men and bears all the seasons
And the starving and the cutting and hunts terribly through lives
To find its peace. But April comes as
Beast-smell flung from the fields, the hammers, the loud-speaking weir.

The rough voices of boys playing by the hedge
As manly as possible, their laughter, the big veins
Sprawled over the beet-leaf, light-red fires
Of flower pots heaped by the huts; they make a pause in
The wireless voice repeating pacts, persecutions,
And imprisonments and deaths and heaped violent deaths,
Impersonal now as figures in the city news.

Behind me, the town curves. Its parapeted edge,
With its burnt look, guards towards the river.
The worry about money, the eyeless work
Of those who do not believe, real poverty,
The sour doorways of the poor; April which
Delights the trees and fills the roads to the South,
Does not deny or conceal. Rather it adds

What more I am; excites the deep glands
And warms my animal bones as I go walking
Past the allotments and the singing water-meadows
Where hooves of cattle have plodded and cratered, and
Watch today go up like a single breath
Holding in its applause at masts of height
Two elms and their balanced attitude like dancers, their arms like dancers.

A Hand

The human hand lying on my hand
(The wrist had a gilt bangle on)
Wore its print of personal lines
Took breath as lungs and leaves and
Tasted in the skin our sun.

The living palm and the near-to-bone:
Fine animal hairs where the light shone.

The handed mole to its earth, the stoat to the dark
And this flesh to its nature nervously planned;
To dig love's heart till everything is shown,
To hunt, to hold its mark
– This loved hand.

Plains as Large as Europe

Plains as large as Europe is
Where each of us walks and is alone
In my giving a cigarette to a passer
As anyone might have done
Were clearly known and shown.

But there was real and final friending
Going beyond the mere gentleness
Of little need and little favour.
For us who would soon part
In the sea-wind whirled street

For me who had come three hundred miles;
A certainty of vaster love, and a hunger
Burlier to bind us simply as men
Than any home river
Or the grass of graves there.

There was no Instruction Given

There was no instruction given
But closed faces of elders seen at school
Were voices blabbing out some clue:
We were children and learned amo,
But the years passed and the bells stopped;
In the morning, 'What do you mean to do
Now all things are crumbling new?'

Another age hammers out amo
With love and the very hills breaking and new:
And it's, Learn – if you can – upon the quick
How the stubborn break inside like bones.
How once the wheel spun true
And there were our hearts, there were Reigate and London:
Now ghosts; or all trampled new.

Houses are Uniformed

Houses are uniformed in black
Here wage-work lies heavier;
I think their colour, and I walk
Asking my way to the memory
Of your flesh and loved behaviour.

In a room after dinner
Manoeuvering Italy or France
And the bookie-governments backing a winner,
Voices rise. Near-despair
Grits on tired nonchalance.

I imagine your voice, but I hear
Voices at some different time;
'I work, I take pay, but there
Is no more good in the work. Our life
Has moved, has another name.'

Lives flat, neither sweet nor sour
Ascetic faces in the street.
A nervous haunting left from the war
Confessed at midnight over drinks;
It is our passion these hit.

If we could leave the brain
Or some deputy in place
To bear the voices, measure the stain
– But the same scene is love's scene
Its Alexandria or Greece.

A contrast passing the spoken
Gives thought of you
A journey visa-ed and broken,
Not quick as a telephone
Or the hand that stings the bone through.

Touch of skin, touch of hair
What domes wheel above and grate?
Into what marsh air
Spring love's smoothed-underground
Flowers, its unthumbed shape?

Evasions

How many times have you smiled a reckoning smile
Either when there was some question of money
Or to humour one of the dead who live around?
– Oh, but that's been going on since the world began.

How many times face to face with your lover
Have you housed apart contracted with fear and cunning
Hidden from the body and that violent weather?
– Oh but that's been going on since the fall of man.

How many times smelling the smell of poverty
Have you tired and turned for good to your cornfield and garden
(And cornfield and garden grew foul pods and rotted)?
– Oh but that's been going on since the world began.

Portrait of a Woman and Others

Let me out of my life
Said the line skewing
From eye up brow, renewing
Always, but most in sleep.
How long must I keep
Hard skull and knees,
She said, and serve these
Like a loathing wife?
Free me from my body's sloughing
With its tireless tide-measure,
From the rest and the whip of pleasure.
Let me out of my life.

She never breathed this out.

I wonder, now it is Spring,
Throwing like beams each thing
The tiger and the daffodil
And hunting on that hill;
Though rock holds its great head
Opposed, you would think, and dead true
Does all nerve and all grace
Turn also back on its face?

It can be we are not alone,
Contradicted by the X-ray bone.
It can be that each thing keeps
As we do, deep among deeps
A will not for winter and such sleeps
But for what really reaps.

A Cold Night

Thick wool is muslin tonight, and the wire
Wind scorches stone-cold colder. Boys
Tremble at counters of shops. The world
Gets lopped at the radius of my fire.

Only for a moment I think of those
Whom the weather leans on under the sky;
Newsmen with placards by the river's skirt,
Stamping, or with their crouching pose,

The whores; the soldiery who lie
Round wounded Madrid; those of less hurt
Who cross that bridge I crossed today
Where the waves snap white as broken plates

And the criss-cross girders hammer a grill
Through which, instead of flames, wind hates.

I turn back to my fire. Which I must.
I am not God or a crazed woman.
And one needs time too to sit in peace
Opposite one's girl, with food, fire, light,

And do the work one's own blood heats,
Or talk, and forget about the winter
– This season, this century – and not be always
Opening one's doors on the pitiful streets

Of Europe, not always think of winter, winter, like a hammering rhyme
For then everything is drowned by the rising wind, everything is done
           against Time.

Part of Plenty

When she carries food to the table and stoops down
– Doing this out of love – and lays soup with its good
Tickling smell, or fry winking from the fire
And I look up, perhaps from a book I am reading
Or other work: there is an importance of beauty
Which can't be accounted for by there and then,
And attacks me, but not separately from the welcome
Of the food, or the grace of her arms.

When she puts a sheaf of tulips in a jug
And pours in water and presses to one side
The upright stems and leaves that you hear creak,
Or loosens them, or holds them up to show me,
So that I see the tangle of their necks and cups
With the curls of her hair, and the body they are held
Against, and the stalk of the small waist rising
And flowering in the shape of breasts;

Whether in the bringing of the flowers or the food
She offers plenty, and is part of plenty,
And whether I see her stooping, or leaning with the flowers,
What she does is ages old, and she is not simply,
No, but lovely in that way.

Cage

That canary measures out its prison.
To perch as quick as camera–shutter, perch
Is left for the little hoop where it can swing.
The next thing is the wiry wall, and cling
With tail and twiggy feet. Then back to perch.
Then it fluffs out its throat and sings, content,
As I can judge, born barred.
There follows its tour of the globe, watch till you tire;
Perch, hoop, and wire,
Perch, wire, and hoop.
A minute shows its life, but I watch hard,
Fascinated, who have to write
An account of myself in five hundred words
For a sociological group.
Neat fists of wire clench around caged birds;
Human cages narrow or retreat.
The dead laws of a stiffening State
Shoot up forests of oppressive iron;
The shouting of each military saviour
Bolt bars of iron;
Money, houses, shudder into iron.
Within that fence I am whatever I am.
And I carry my inherited wish to be free,
And my inherited wish to be tied for ever,
As natural to me as my body.
Unlike the bird in the cage, feather to wire,
I lean out some hours,
I lunge to left, I lunge out to right
And hit no bars that way, only mist's pretence;
I cannot estimate my powers.
But, measuring man and bird,
In this respect the likeness stays:
Much of my life will go to exploring my fence.

Ill

Expectant at the country gate the lantern. On the night
Its silks of light strained. Lighted upper window.
'Is it you who sent for me?' The two go in
To where the woman lies ill, upstairs, out of sight.

I hear sky softly smother to earth in rain,
As I sit by the controls and the car's burning dials.
And always the main-road traffic searching, searching the horizons.
Then those sounds knifed by the woman's Ah! of pain.

Who dreamed this; the dark folding murderer's hands round the lamps?
The rain blowing growth to rot? Lives passed beneath a ritual
That tears men's ghosts and bodies; the few healers
With their weak charms, moving here and there among the lamps?

A Thousand Killed

I read of a thousand killed.
And am glad because the scrounging imperial paw
Was there so bitten:
As a man at elections is thrilled
When the results pour in, and the North goes with him
And the West breaks in the thaw.

(That fighting was a long way off.)

Forgetting therefore an election
Being fought with votes and lies and catch-cries
And orator's frowns and flowers and posters' noise,
Is paid for with cheques and toys:
Wars the most glorious
Victory-winged and steeple-uproarious
...With the lives, burned-off,
Of young men and boys.

Suburb Factories

White as a drawing on white paper
The architect built the tall
Suburb factories,
Compact as a liner admired from the littered beach
Gaunt like the ward of a hospital.

And when he sunk their roots among
The places of spare trees
The huts and the wastes,
To stare down the polished arterial road,
And to peer across the chimneys,

Made the big concrete mushrooms grow,
Towers with gland-heads;
He edged to the cliff
The doomed life of the villas; fastidious streets,
Men signed with their fathers' manual trades,

Their faces curiously primmed and clenched
If perhaps they can leap above the memory
Of those scorned trades.
Stamping, the concrete brushes down their fences,
It brings drilled crowds, small property.

Changes though; change is in the air; roofscape
Touches some nerve, and the lost
Sinking scream
Of electric trains touches it, and white masonry
Springs up like a fire, but strikes like frost.

Waiting

To sit in the heavily curtained, old ladyish, waiting-room
While upstairs the gloved surgeon operates on a loved one,
Imagined as candle-still and unlike life, in the brilliant
Gas-sweet theatre. To listen to the clock's 'Doubt, doubt', and to hear
The metal of the knives made ready; and not to know any news;
        That helpless fear.

Is it like that bad dream of knives, our counting the years
Our listening to rumours until the guns begin and our volted
Delight in creating, our love, our famous words, and the personal
Order of our lives is devoured when our streets become a furnace?
I think so in times of despair, and the good in our random culture
        Woundable as a man is.

Yet know that from our crisis leads no white stair to a shut
Door and the deftness of another's hands. What sickness threatens
Our freedom to lounge in the green world, to be happy beneath the
Clocks of its cities we largely know. If we live we have the pride
To be capable of action, to speak out plainly. The wise and passionate
        Are on our side.

How Must we Live?

'How must we live?' From the caress, the shadow
Of that mother-Peace giver of our tongues, our eyes,
We advance, the sowers of cities. Back there
                    We see rise

Her image, the firm-footed, as men have used
Over harbours, seen the first and last. Now
Built up the sky by the old philosophy
                    The stone breasts, stone brow.

Blood is unquiet; 'From that nature we were born.'
When we look forward, knowledge will not serve;
The immense only is seen, as who from a height
                    Views the globe's curve.

Faces arrest us and the particular pity;
Wings, water, move us. But a deeper way
'What have we to live by?' beats back into brain
                    And cannot be frowned away.

My Sister

The old man bearded with illness weakens upstairs.
My sister who is great with child
Speaks of our early long days
In the house with the fig tree in the garden;
We speak of what the nurses taught
And the schools that teach our class,
Of what friends we had,
Of theatres, difference that money made.
My sister great with child, and the old man dying upstairs.

Across our stroke-by-stroke built-up picture
And, since, our eating with new friends
And turning upon new living-ways
As if exploring a turning stream,
Our laughing, travelling at different times;
Memory of gross South and North,
Making big slash and score
With asleep, hurting, and death and birth
Scrawls in comment which way the master-winds wear.

POEMS 1940 TO 1942

Aegean Islands 1940-41

Where white stares, smokes or breaks,
Thread white, white of plaster and of foam,
Where sea like a wall falls;
Ribbed, lionish coast,
The stony islands which blow into my mind
More often than I imagine my grassy home;

To sun one's bones beside the
Explosive, crushed-blue, nostril-opening sea
(The weaving sea, splintered with sails and foam,
Familiar of famous and deserted harbours,
Of coins with dolphins on and fallen pillars.)

To know the gear and skill of sailing,
The drenching race for home and the sail-white houses,
Stories of Turks and smoky ikons,
Cry of the bagpipe, treading
Of the peasant dancers;

The dark bread
The island wine and the sweet dishes;
All these were elements in a happiness
More distant now than any date like '40,
A.D. or B.C., ever can express.

Greek Excavations

Over the long-shut house
Which earth, not keys kept under watch,
I prod with a stick and down comes rattling soil
Into the dug out room;
And pottery comes down,
Hard edges of drinking vessels, jars for oil,
Mere kitchen stuff, rubbish of red or brown,
Stubble of conquests

– And I suddenly discover this discovered town.
The wish of the many, their abused trust,
Blows down here in a little dust,
So much unpainted clay;
The minimum wish
For the permanence of the basic things of a life,
For children and friends and having enough to eat
And the great key of a skill;
The life the generals and the bankers cheat.

Peering for coin or confident bust
Or vase in bloom with the swiftness of horses,
My mind was never turned the way
Of the classic of the just and the unjust.
I was looking for things which have a date,
And less of the earth's weight,
When I broke this crust.

Salonika June 1940

My end of Europe is at war. For this
My lamp-launched giant shadow seems to fall
Like a bad thought upon this ground at peace,
Being the shadow of the shadow of a war.
What difference if I wish good luck to these foreigners, my hosts?
Talking with my friends stand ghosts.

Specially the lives that here in the crook of this bay
At the paws of its lionish hills are lived as I know;
The dancing, the bathing, the order of the market, and as day
Cools into night, boys playing in the square;
Island boats and lemon-peel tang and the timeless café crowd,
And the outcry of dice on wood:

I would shut the whole if I could out of harm's way
As one shuts a holiday photo away in a desk,
Or shuts one's eyes. But not by this brilliant bay,
Nor in Hampstead now where leaves are green,
Any more exists a word or a lock which gunfire may not break,
Or a love whose range it may not take.

Delos

Wealth came by water to this farmless island;
Dolphins with backs like bows swim in mosaic
Floors where the Greek sea-captains piled up money;
And the jagged circular patterns spin with the rush of
The impetus and fling of waves.

Steps go down to the port. And in this area
You could buy corn and oil or men and women.
Above on the windy hill Leto the human
Bore her birth pains, gave two gods to a legend
Glittering and loveless like the sea.

Slavery, we know, was not of the market only.
Here specially were rich and poor, priests and their pennies.
Imperial slavery we know. But the salt Aegean
Rolled waves of flame and killing, quarrels of aliens,
Till life here burst and was quiet.

In the boulevards of these dead you will think of violence,
Holiness and violence, violence of sea that is bluer
Than blue eyes are; violence of sun and its worship;
Of money and its worship. And it was here by the breakers
That strangers asked for the truth.

Base Town

Winter's white guard continual on the hills;
The wind savaging from the stony valleys
And the unseen front. And always the soldiers going,
Soldiers and lorries beating the streets of cobble,
Like blood to where a wound is flowing.

War took friends, lights and names away. Clapped down
Shutters on windows' welcome. Brought those letters
Which wished to say so much they dared not say.
The proud and feminine ships in the harbour roads
Turned to a North-East grey.

Curious the intimacy we felt with Them;
We moved our meals to fit Their raids; we read
Their very hand across each bomb-slashed wall.
Their charred plane fallen in the cratered square
Held twisted in it all

Their work, Their hate, Their failure. Prisoners
Bearded and filthy, had bones, eyes and hair
Like other men in need. But dead like snow,
Cold like those racing winds or sirens' grief,
Was the hate which struck no blow:

The fear of speaking was a kind of tic
Pulling at the eyes. If stranger drank with stranger
It seemed thief drank with thief. Was it only every
Night, the fall of the early and lampless dark?
I remember it so often. And the lie,
The twist of reason,
The clever rumour planted in the nerves,
The dossier infecting like a coccus;
All these became for us the town, the season.

These, and the knowledge that to die,
Some stony miles north of our wintering
Was a more ordinary thing.

Death of an Airman

Dancer's naked foot so earthly planted
Limbs tall and turned to music of drums; all growth,
Grass, fountaining palm exulting and vertical,
       Dance his fair hair, his youth.

For when you tread delight as if a wire
And when your roots in the dark finger earth's springs
Your strength has an understanding that includes
Those shot-down wings.

Letters

Letters, like blood along a weakening body
move fainter round our map. On dangerous wings,
on darkness-loving keels they go, so longed for;
but say no memorable things.

The 'dear' and 'darling' and the 'yours for ever'
are relics of a style. But most appears
mere rambling notes; passion and tenderness
fall like a blot or a burst of tears.

Now public truths are scarcer currency,
what measure for the personal truth? how can
this ink and paper coursing continents
utter the clothed or the naked man?

Libyan Front

Cratered the land, unploughed, unsown, unfamiliar as a star
        Libyan front
Routine and dirt and story telling are triggered to something far
Night is Death's day when he sees best and when his appointments are
        Libyan front
Sand, our metaphor for time and waste, is all the world and its springs
        Libyan front
Very distant the feet that dance, the lifted silver and the strings
Poets and lovers and men of power are troops and no such things
        Libyan front.

Egyptian Delta

Rhyme for the runnels feeling among the crops
like fingers stroked through hair:
rhyme for the floating bare-foot walkers at evening,
the upright women with burdened heads who wear
five thousand years like a dress:
water wheel, rope and harness, where
the powerful ox with dancer's step goes round,
and his lifted eyes bound.

Be glad for taps and nozzles and water flowering,
the sozzling gardens drunk:
blossoms catching fire like a match's flaring,
semaphore of madman flags from bough and trunk:
eyes from the mud, and laughing,
filth and hunger steady as the sun. And sunk
somewhere in all a patience of this ground,
like the blind ox's round.

Pulling through nations, fountained further than thought,
the river with a breeze on its back
suddenly lifts your hair with coolness. Be
measureless because of water. Move through lack,
through sands, prodigious harvest.
There is an excellence of losing track,
of being no longer a person or sad. Being drowned,
being water, hooves, and their round.

Acre

In Acre it wasn't simply the peeping alleys,
the cobbles and the grave and Frankish gate:
towers stone by stone surrendering
all their Crusading darkness up to the sun;
though these could touch or fascinate:
not squares chattering with colours,
the long and leaping boats heeled on their sides;
melons and nets, and under arches the Eastern
sea gay as a scarf:
then the Turkish mosque fountaining delicate
columns like sheltered thoughts.
                              But not these nor
the useful whitened petrol tins
tracing the metalled high-road, nor the Arab
cemetery grieving for a few decades
where the town flung its rubbish.
                              Any such symbols,
or the whole jangled argument of eras
and lusts and cries for justice, might set fire to
the poet's immoderate, promiscuous love.

Frontier

A turn in the road. The bare and echoing shed.
A few men armed. Long tables for the Customs.
And there in the country grass some chickens fed,
and children were making a private world with their calling
where there were trees and a house. A clerk
with reddened eyes,
slowly turned marriage, travel and birth to paper,
like indexing the dead:
released one waiting figure towards the bed
of a lover, so long starved for, morning and night;
others a hundred miles to an epidemic,
to power, to a famine, to be quite alone:

gravely would write, though some slipped by like spies
with wild thoughts in their head,
in columns for them; in columns too for those
who saw in absolute file, in moody gun,
a permanence, a being somehow right,
like rocks, like turns in the road, like children's cries.

Cairo Restaurant

Light thrown
such as to trace the bone:
the few electric lamps in the little room
examining the heartless things of a face,
brow or measurable fall of cheek bone;
digging a cave to lair the desperate lies
or urgent witness of the eyes:
falling elsewhere on objects with no grace,
the narrow restaurant, its glass and wood,
rough service and rough food:
the welcome that a little money buys
out of the hungry East.

Lights burning. Expectation of news. A thought
of a stable, of an inn,
an upper room.

Again in the Eastern province of an iron empire,
being is dirtied by a banker's thumb,
bread is once more the bread we merely use:
eye and instinct cannot choose;
we are also born for a message to begin,
a narrow room, a tomb,
a portent and a danger that may give
a grace and a meaning; our bread too must live.

The Ship

The simple beach and the sea. And separate things
lie on this openness as on a hand;
sea-coloured tents, a boat upon its side,
Scarlet of flags, a children's see-saw, swings,
like elementary shapes a child has drawn;
and the mind grasps them in a stride.

Very deliberate, like a mannequin,
a full-rigged ship goes South,
and lets you tell for half an hour or more
how hollowed sails and keen unhurried bows
can be so lucid and so brave,
poet nor painter find one jot to add,
not the hairbreadth of a line,
wing or turning wave.

No wonder mind should find this scenery bland
as lotions are to eyes;
our loves being mostly natives of a land
mountainous, hung with forests, loud with storms:
and our thoughts climb
to light like things the digger's spade has struck,
a broken dish, a ring,
confused with dark and roots and time.

Behaviour of Money

Money was once well known, like a townhall or the sky
or a river East and West, and you lived one side or the other;
Love and Death dealt shocks,
but for all the money that passed, the wise man knew his brother.

But money changed. Money came jerking roughly alive;
went battering round the town with a boozy, zigzag tread.
A clear case for arrest;
and the crowds milled and killed for the pound notes that he shed.

And the town changed, and the mean and the little lovers of gain
inflated like a dropsy, and gone were the courtesies
that eased the market day;
saying, 'buyer' and 'seller' was saying, 'enemies'.

The poor were shunted nearer to beasts. The cops recruited.
The rich became a foreign community. Up there leaped
quiet folk gone nasty,
quite strangely distorted, like a photograph that has slipped.

Hearing the drunken roars of Money from down the street,
'What's to become of us?' the people in bed would cry:
'And oh, the thought strikes chill;
what's to become of the world if Money should suddenly die?

Should suddenly take a toss and go down crack on his head?
If the dance suddenly finished, if they stopped the runaway bus,
if the trees stopped racing away?
If our hopes come true and he dies, what's to become of us?

Shall we recognise each other, crowding around the body?
And as we go stealing off in search of the town we have known
– what a job for the Sanitary Officials;
the sprawled body of Money, dead, stinking, alone!'

Will X contrive to lose the weasel look in his eyes?
Will the metal go out of the voice of Y? Shall we all turn back
to men, like Circe's beasts?
Or die? Or dance in the street the day that the world goes crack?

Yachts on the Nile

Like air on skin, coolness of yachts at mooring,
a white, flung handful;
fresh as a girl at her rendezvous, and wearing
frou-frou names, Suzy, Yvette or Gaby,
lipped by the current, uttering
the gay conversation of their keels.

Lovely will be their hesitant leaving of
the shore for the full stream,
fingering the breeze down out of the sky; then leaning
as a player leans his cheek to the violin
– that strange repose of power –
and the race will hold them like a legend.

Terrible their perfection: and theirs I saw
like clouds covering the Solent
when I was a boy: and all those sails that dip
ages back in the hardly waking mind;
white visitors of islands,
runners on the turf of rivers.

What these ask with their conquering look and speed
written in their bodies like birds,
is our ecstasy, our tasting as if a dish,
magnificence of hazard, cunning of the tiller-hand,
a freedom: and it is by something
contrary in being human

That I look for a distant river, a distant woman,
and how she carried her head:
the great release of the race interns me here...
and it may be, too, we are born with some nostalgia
to make the migration of sails
and wings a crying matter.

Olive Trees

The dour thing in olive trees
is that their trunks are stooped like never dying crones,
and they camp where roads climb, and drink with dust and stones.

The pleasant thing is how in the heat
their plumage brushes the sight with a bird's-wing feeling:
and perhaps the gold of their oil is mild with dreams of healing.

The cold thing is how they were
there at the start of us; and one grey look surveyed
the builder imagining the city, the historian with his spade.

The warm thing is that they are
first promise of the South to waking travellers:
of the peacock sea, and the islands and their boulder-lumbered spurs.

The Building of the House

The building of the house became a part
of all our lives; how old it looked at first,
like an anatomy dissected:
how some inverted surgery fleshed it, nursed
features from out of clay and eyes to see;
and how the builders worked and all their gear,
the bucket, brick and rubble and all the art
of ladder, hod or rope,
were the remoter touches, cool in feeling,
against whose background what was memorable
showed sad or smiling.

Then startlingly the house was finished, and stood
more weather-worthy than our bodies could:
and for two lifetimes' interval
no one would see exactly what we had seen,
towards the bridge and the wood.

Why was this something we had not foreseen?
By what sharp argument of brick or stone
had we now first to love even those hours
– and maybe find them worst to lose –
which, passing, never touched us to the bone?

Peasant Festival

All day they had worshipped at the Virgin's picture
and now they camped, their families and their beasts,
with harness and piled fruit and mothers suckling
around the little mountain church, or moved
among the stalls, where tradesmen cried.
The petrol flares lit light and dark; and starlight
and the blind peaks and resin bleeding forests
cupped them above the plain.

What brought them riding here were not our customs,
and yet it was good to share their food with them
– wine from the village and white cheese – and know them
across some hundred years with their high boots
and great moustaches. And their songs,
love songs and bawdy songs at fall of night,
said after-things which rang like that cold air
as, one voice sang
under the dark of the trees; 'If I entered Heaven
and did not find you there and your little breasts
I should understand nothing.'

Egyptian Dancer at Shubra

At first we heard the jingling of her ornaments
as she delayed beyond the trap of light,
and glimpsed her lingering pretence
her bare feet and the music were at difference:
and then the strings grew wild and drew her in.

And she came soft as paws and danced desire at play
or triumphing desire, and locked her hands
stretched high, and in the dance's sway
hung like a body to be flogged; then wrenched away,
or was a wave from breasts down to the knees.

And as the music built to climax and she leaned
naked in her dancing skirt, and was supreme,
her dance's stormy argument
had timid workday things for all environment;
men's awkward clothes and chairs her skin exclaimed against.

Passed On

Some of his messages were personal
almost as his lost face; they showed he knew
about their pets, the life that went on beating
in desks and scrapbooks, and each particle

of the family language: the young engineer,
who had put khaki on and died in the mud,
at times would almost touch them.
                                    Yet he was
(But how?) the sing-song spirit-gospeller;

the irrelevance, the baby-talk and spout
of 'Vera', the Control; and stagey things,
a bell, a violin, an Indian chief;
even what crashed the furniture about.

But then he was their son. That love, that birth
made the old couple blind enough to bear
the medium's welcome, taking no offence,
and haunt his room that opened clean off earth.

In an Auction Room

How many deaths and partings spilled
this jumble in an upper room;
and every chair or mirror filled
with elbowing and smell of lives:
the gloom
of this tall wardrobe stopped the sun
entering a home; the great brass bed
stood in its throne-room, and its springs
and shining arms are crammed like mines
with regal illness and with love:
the terrible settee
with worn red flowers, the table de nuit,
the picture with the little man
walking the infinite road
to a West of gold;
these have all been (and are to be)
loves truer than our human mould,
or desperate walls
flung up against the shock of things,
what has no name; or growing old.

Sarcophagi

Excellent ritual of oils, of anointing,
office of priests;
everything was paid before these dead put on
the armless dress of their sarcophagi,
lying down in Phoenicia,

pillowing their heavy sculptured heads, their broad
foreheads like rides of sand, the rock of the chin,
the mouth, the simple map of the face, the carved
hair in full sail.

Surrender of sunlight and market and the white
loops of the coast,
was simply a journey, a bargain rigid as stone:
though youth took passage.

Stretched by the salt and echoing roads to the West
twenty-six bargain-makers of Phoenicia;
twenty-six dead with wide eyes,
confident of harbour.

WITH LUCK LASTING

(1963)

The Beginning

Its pale walls partly clambered on by creeper,
it slowly disentangles to the sight
out of the hill as you drive past the Bosphorus;
the castle, where the straits veer narrowest.

That acre of turret and bow-slit was enough
to start a war with. When it once was built
Mehmet and Asia marched out to the conquest
of Constantinople, while the Christian West
dallied, debated, lost their cause.

It was the beginning. It sealed the narrows off.
But in the end the castle grew tremendous;
changed maps, slew thousands, put out like an eye
world-renowned mural work of crowns and thrones and wings,
realised an age-old nightmare,
and ranged along the City's dusty sky-line
the muezzins' pointed towers like lances lifted.

Delicate Grasses

Delicate grasses blowing in the wind,
grass out of cracks among tiered seats of stone
where a Greek theatre swarmed with audience,
till Time's door shut upon
the stir, the eloquence.

A hawk waiting above the enormous plain,
lying upon the nothing of the air,
a hawk who turns at some sky-wave or lull
this way, and after there
as dial needles prowl.

Cool water jetting from a drinking fountain
in crag-lands, miles from any peopled spot,
year upon year with its indifferent flow;
sound that is and is not;
the wet stone trodden low.

There is no name for such strong liberation;
I drift their way; I need what their world lends;
then, chilled by one thought further still than those,
I swerve towards life and friends
before the trap-fangs close.

Notes by a Foreigner

Their opaque, restless eyes,
the last place you will find a clue to this town;
eyes that face yours or hunger past you,
darknesses cut from a woman's evening gown.

Encounters with frequent phantoms,
women whose beauty lays a hand on your gut:
the sound of the impetuous language,
blurred as if the tongue still savoured fruit.

Your wish to build them all
into one vision, with traffic bells, the fine
knives of the whistles, and the blind,
tapping to the world like caught souls down a mine.

The shuffle of evening crowds
past cinema lights; each sixteenth-century square
where the bronze kings and heroes rein
their grave war-stallions back: and everywhere

Blocks without hope going up,
windowless brick down two gaunt sides, that back
on wastes of sand and dazing lion-light
through which walk women in their mourning black.

Illusion, your old failure
to see except as a foreigner. There is just
a sense in which your town never
was true, for all its trams and banks and dust

-doomed sunsets like the hell
over a town bombarded, and for all
that light that stays a half hour more
as though mad cocks had given the dawn a call,

The echo-light no town
(of this at least you are sure), can parallel;
when things mean more yet fade, like places
you half remember, a now-not-beating bell.

From my Window

Now when the University students have abandoned
their game of bowls in the garden, with their cries of 'Two' or 'Six'
and the evening sky goes soured milk,

There are left the brightening windows of the rich owners of flats;
their meaningless finny gestures, dumb departures and entries;
a deaf man's theatre twenty times.

And quite indifferent towards the students or the rich
there are left the children of the poor, playing tag on a sandy waste,
and miles off southward ring the trams.

Alone on a building site a watchdog stalks by the fire,
wooed and repulsed by the jump-away flames, or raises its head
at a barking that chips a hole in distance.

Mediterranean Suburbs

Sunset; the streets of flats, new and forbidding;
on the left in the vacant site a block is rising,
ground plan and girders like a giant doodle;
opposite, waiting for its history,
forty blank eyes, another stares, unfinished.

Here in their heavy homes there live the solid
such as those passing now, the Father strutting
with legs apart, Mama in her striped furs,
two woollied stubborn children dragging after.

Reject of neighbouring streets, then questioning ours,
the sad and stammering music of a pipe;
and now its tall and scarecrow player turns
the corner like the grotesque of some need
we had forgotten that we were starving from,
or promise we have broken. Empty houses,
houses for next year, evening, restless houses.
Dressed in a city's shabbiness he walks
under the wild guess of that new-starred sky.

Fluted Armour

Bored and humbled by every disintegrating day,
because, meaningless, the wine-glass and the storm-cloud stayed
particular things:
having, as everyone must, lost my way;
I went to the National Gallery to trade
a confusion of particulars
for what you might call a philosophy, for
the world-gaze of the great Italians and was not
disappointed returning by Charing Cross Road, dazed
by particular things:
the narrowed eyes and caught breath of the archers in
    Pollaiuolo's 'San Sebastian',
the smiling lips of Bronzino's 'Venus',
and in Piero di Cosimo's 'Florentine General'
the cold smite of the fluted armour my finger-tips had grazed.

Out of Sleep

Surfacing out of sleep she feared
voices in the sky talking
with thick tongues. Night flashed
brightening her eyelids. Yet as panic cleared
she knew those voices never spoke the harsh
brogue of the guns. And then the rain
sighed in the leaves; it was thunder.
The rain said, hush.

It has been peace in our world a year:
what worse-than-memories seep
to infect our nights with fear
up from the angers of that other war,
ours copy here?
What towns burn on what darker coast of sleep,
how many histories deep?

A Spring Wind

Spring shakes the windows; doors whang to,
the sky moves half in dark and half
shining like knives: upon this table
Elytis' poems lie
uttering the tangle of sea, the 'breathing caves'
and the fling of Aegean waves.

I am caught here in this scattering, vagrant season
where telephones ring;
and all Greece goes through me
as the wind goes searching through the city streets.
Greece, I have so much loved you
out of all reason;
that this unquiet time
its budding and its pride
the news and the nostalgia of Spring
swing towards you their tide:

Towards the windmills on the islands;
Alefkandra loved by winds,
luminous with foam and morning, Athens,
her blinded marble heads,
her pepper trees, the bare heels of her girls,
old songs that bubble up from where thought starts,
Greek music treading like the beat of hearts;
haunted Seferis, smiling, playing with beads.

And since especially at this time
statues and blossoms, birth and death require
we give account of manhood and of youth,
the wind that whirls through London also rings
with the bang and echo of the Easter gun,
as in days gone,

from where the pilgrims' torches climb
over a darkening town
to set that bony peak Lykahvetoss,
Athens, and all the opening year on fire.

On a Carved Axle-Piece from a Sicilian Cart

The village craftsman stirred his bravest yellow
and (all the carpentry and carving done)
put the last touches to his newest cart,
until no playing-card had brighter panels;
with crested knights in armour, king and crown,
Crusaders slaughtering infidels, and crimson
where the blood laves:
and took his paintpot to that part
around the axle where a Southern memory
harking back out of Christendom, imagined
a chariot of glory
and Aphrodite riding wooden waves.

So some tanned peasant paid his money down
and till the years
put a full-stop to him or his purchase, jaunted
half around Sicily with wood for the fire,
long muscat grapes
or tangerines for the market in the town.
Thus answering, as his fathers' fathers had,
those metaphysical gaps and fears
which drain the blood of the age or drive it mad;
the 'why are we guilty?' and the 'who must punish?'

– With a salty way of speech; with tasselled harness
with a cart to match the sea and all the flowers;
with Roger the Christian and Palermo towers;
and in between the dusty wheels
the Queen of Love in a yellow gown,
featured like a peasant child,
her three red horses rearing from the foam
and their carved manes blown wild.

The Boats

Five boats beside the lake,
pulling bows first up the shore; how hard it is
to draw them, from each angle changing, elegant:
their feminine poise, the 'just so' lifting sweep
of the light timbers round the flanks sucked thin
into the thirsty bows;
                     the same or nearly
as makes no difference, since men settled first
near these magnolias, lived the different life
that is always the same; fished, traded, hammered, gossiped
wanting their food and wine, appeased the Powers,
meditated journeys
or turned and turned in their minds some woman's image,
lost or distant.
                     Near this bench and the keels
someone has scratched in the dust the name ELSA.

At Courmayeur

This climbers' valley with its wayside shrines
(the young crowned Mother and her dying flowers)
became our theme for weeks. Do you remember
the letters that we wrote and how we planned
the journey there and chose our hotel; ours
was to be one 'among the pines'?

Guesses went wide; but zigzag past that ridge
the road climbs from the Roman town; there stand
the glittering peaks, and one, the God, immensely
tossing the clouds around his shoulders; here
are what you asked for, summer pastures and
an air with glaciers in its edge.

Under all sounds is mountain water falling;
at night, the river seems to draw much closer;
darling, how did you think I could forget you,
you who for ever stayed behind? Your absence
comes back as hard as rocks. Just now it was
those hangdown flowers that meant recalling.

In a Foreign Hospital

Valleys away in the August dark the thunder
roots and tramples: lightning sharply prints
for an instant trees, hills, chimneys on the night.
We lie here in our similar rooms with the white
furniture, with our bit of Death inside us
(nearer than that Death our whole life lies under);
the man in the next room with the low voice,
the brown-skinned boy, the child among its toys
and I and others. Against my bedside light
a small green insect flings itself with a noise
tiny and regular, a 'tink; tink, tink'.

A Nun stand rustling by, saying good night,
hooded and starched and smiling with her kind
lifeless, religious eyes. 'Is there anything
you want?' – 'Sister, why yes, so many things:'
England is somewhere far away to my right
and all Your letter promised; days behind
my left hand or my head (or a whole age)
are dearer names and easier beds than here.
But since tonight must lack for all of these
I am free to keep my watch with images,
a bare white room, the World, an insect's rage,
and if I am lucky, find some link, some link.

Regent's Park Terrace

The noises round my house. On cobbles bounding
Victorian-fashioned drays laden with railway goods;
their hollow sound like stones in rolling barrels:
the stony hoofing of dray horses.

Further, the trains themselves; among them the violent,
screaming like frightened animals, clashing metal;
different the pompous, the heavy breathers, the aldermen,
or those again which speed with the declining
sadness of crying along the distant routes
knitting together weathers and dialects.

Between these noises the little teeth
of a London silence.

Finally the lions grumbling over the park,
angry in the night hours,
cavernous as though their throats were openings up from the earth:
hooves, luggage, engines, tumbrils, lions,
hollow noises, noises of travel, hourly these unpick
the bricks of a London terrace, make the ear
their road, and have their audience in whatever
hearing the heart or the deep of the belly owns.

Letter Home

Walk on a fallen sky;
tread softer on a blue paste of dropped jacaranda petals:
that sentry's face and hands
are carpentered from the same dark wood as his rifle butt:
past gardens and armed men
is a street number to find, 58, 57, 56;
the heat follows me around
like an overcoat in a dream; a ship's siren from the river
trembles the air with sorrows and names of iron harbours.
City where I live, not home, road that flowers with police,
what in all worlds am I doing here?

Morning in Madrid

Skirmish of wheels and bells and someone calling:
a donkey's bronchial greeting, groan and whistle,
the weeping factory sirens rising, falling.

Yelping of engines from the railyard drifted:
then, prelude to the gold-of-wine of morning,
the thunderstorm of iron shutters lifted.

The Café with the Blue Shrine

You push the soiled door-curtain back
and there, short-sighted, is the little café
garish and dirty in the city way;
like walls its very nature seems to peel and crack.

Sometimes a plucked string vivifies
that cave, and here the woman sang beside us
one of those Andalusian songs that touch
on tears, with…'I am in love with you for your Moorish eyes…'

She had what offered for her stage,
where the blonde calendar pin-up with her smile
hung facing that blue shrine in which the Virgin
behind her Spanish iron-barred window like a cage

Inclined her crowned and childlike head
with mild uncomprehending country gaze:
these things seemed fitting. But one sombre listener
gaunt at his corner table, motionless as dead,

Black clothes, black beret, chin on hand,
alone, perhaps, heard that song down his bones;
and our eyes turned toward his speaking stillness
once more, when we had watched the knot of swaggerers stand

Dicing at the bar, the mirror flawed,
the squat black stove with curling python arm,
the girl's mouth shaking to that final blaze
of singing that we hammered on the tables to applaud.

Castanets

Back will go the head with the dark curls
and the foot will stamp:
but now she stoops beneath
her arms or, frowning, whirls
her skirt to lie out flat on the air
so the breeze is on
our mouths, and the smoke swings:
dry like a thirst the guitar rings.

Across her eyes drunk hair; the flower
that lodged there spins to the ground:
coolly in the barbarous dance
the wrists arch up, and now
the castanets, those fever teeth,
begin to sound:
then, gunshot through a veil,
blow the night suddenly mad with their pelting hail.

In Athens

Her hank and swing of hair
then – the whole face in a glance – the rounding line
of cheek, the childlike
mouth that is learning yet to be composed,
the chin, the joy of the neck; you know each feature
about this stranger
like things you have learned by finger-tips or drawing.

The knock inside your chest:
someone you loved was like her; there is given
neither name nor time, except it was long ago:
the scene, half caught, then blurred:
a village on the left perhaps, fields steeply rising.

A perturbation of pulse,
and a word your body is trying to make you hear
on a city corner. It is so much like
the twist in the plotting of things she should pass here
so near where they talked well on love
two civilisations ago, and found
splendid and jeering images: horses plunging,
that apple cut, the Hidden One.

           A wryness,
and a name your body is trying to make you hear...

The Rendezvous

I take the twist-about, empty street
– balconies and drapes of shadow
– and glimpse chalk slogans on each wall,
(now governments have done their work)
that the fanatic or the duped,
even children are taught to scrawl:
the patriotic, 'Tyrants', 'Vengeance',
'Death to', etc.

                    Hooped
the barbed wire lies to left and right
since glass crashing, cars on fire,
since the mob howled loose that night,
gawky, rusty, useful wire
with little dirty fangs each way,
(what craftsman makes this fright?).
Black on that chemist's lighted window
steel helmets, rifle tops. I sense
the full moon wild upon my back
and count the weeks. Not long from this
the time we named comes round.

                    And true
to loves love never thought of, here
with bayonet and with tearing fence,
with cry of crowds and doors slammed to,
waits the once known and dear, once chosen
city of our rendezvous.

The Lottery Sellers

Beneath a gun grey sky
– with a wind savage out of Tartar places
– he barks four words to hurrying, lowered faces
and shakes his tickets with their potent numbers;
fluttering fortunes.

Gaze lifted over roof tops,
she calls four words in out-of-nowhere tones,
nailed as though cold could no more search her bones,
and droops her tickets lucky past all longings
or strength of stars.

Perhaps it will snow tonight:
two voices still keep with you as you go:
Luck never saw the sky hang charged with snow;
Wealth trembles, hugs his rag suit to his chest,
on a cold hell's corner.

Train to Work

9.20; the Underground groans him to his work;
he sits fumbling a letter; is that
a cheque attached? He is puzzled, frowns
sadly, like Rhesus monkeys, like us. Above
the frown fair hair is thinning. Specially
I celebrate his toes turned in, his worn
shoes splashed with mud (but his hands
are clean and fine), the bottoms of his striped trousers
crumpled by rain.
                    In a little while his station
will syphon him out with others, along, round, away
as a drop goes with its Niagara.
                  And because
he bears the cracking brunt of things he has never willed
and has eight mean hours a day
to live at the bidding of the gods, and is gentle and put upon,
this blindfold bull-fight nag, endearing stranger,
and before long, like others who come to mind,
is condemned to sure death, he sits
(with his mackintosh belt twisted),
poetry roaring from him like a furnace.

At 'The Angler'

The apple trees were all 'salaams' of clusters
in those walled gardens where the mown
grass, what with rains and years, took dents like peaches;
the bent old roofs, the trees, that grass
went on so with their lives there, we alone
seemed to be short of time to pass.

The world was summer and a doze, that pasturing
country so lazily inclined
down to the willow-wept, the swan-sailed river
and the eighteenth-century villages;
quelled river voices seeped the back of the mind
fooling the ear with distances.

And if rain rattled all night on the leaves,
the great night-crescent of the weir,
swollen with rainfall, growling its white tons
seemed to call pardon on our crime
of parting, cause more deep than now or here
talking to our short from its long time.

Lovers, we had our share of the ideal;
again, next day, with end of storm
how swans curved near as if to bring good omens
to us and – so love made it seem
there and then certain – in their trance of calm
blazed a white Always from that stream.

The Administrator

Some student I look after from this desk,
because of words I write down here,
grasps apparatus he had never known
or, weeks from home, speaking a foreigner's English,
spades English turf above a buried town.
He finds, but these words steer.

I flip back through the file, their photographs
talk out; a humorous Roman glance;
a German's, cunning spectacles, square head;
an Arab's passionate lip; and in a flash of
liking I stretch a point, cut back my dead
official cant. And chance

To look up from the page: one slow doom-burden,
storm vapours with torn fringes rolled
on Polar missions dark as they, the dour
rain ruled in slants on all things, start hard questions
on the humane, the human and on Power,
human to ask, but cold. But cold.

Night-time: Starting to Write

Over the mountains a plane bumbles in;
down in the city a watchman's iron-topped stick
bounces and rings on the pavement. Late returners
must be waiting now, by me unseen

To enter shadowed doorways. A dog's pitched
barking flakes and flakes away at the sky.
Sounds and night-sounds, no more; but then I catch
my lamp burn fiercer like a thing bewitched,

Table and chairs expectant like a play:
and – if that Unknown, Demon, what you will
stalks on the scene – must live with sounds and echoes,
be damned the call to sleep, the needs of day,

Love a dark city; then for some bare bones
of motive, strange perhaps to beast or traveller,
with all I am and all that I have been
sweat the night into words, as who cracks stones.

Sud-Express

Our speed's perpetual howling like a strong wind
is a sudden snarl of lions as a bridge is torn by

     Fate does iron wedges drive

Objects silently collide; their sounds were somewhere dropped
leaving selected clatters, the booming voices behind me,
the plop of a cork, a fork tinkling, as heard through wool or water

     Going is a kind of treachery. I own it

Villages are caught asleep; they have no time to stir,
a man is lifting a latch, horse and harrow for ever
turn at the edge of a field, still as those fishermen
angling clouds and treetops along their shining river

     Even when I say 'I love you' it is tainted with goodbyes

We pelt the way we came with houses, saplings, flowers;
the middle fields swing, boil back and stream like lava;
forests of distance shake their necks and gallop with us.
Though the great wheel throws me southwards
keep those eyes for me still. If you can, love me

Boat Poem

I wish there was a touch of these boats about my life;
so to speak, a tarring,
the touch of inspired disorder and something more than that,
something more too
than the mobility of sails or a primitive bumpy engine,
under that tiny hot-house window,
which eats up oil and benzine perhaps
but will go on beating in spite of the many strains
not needing with luck to be repaired too often,
with luck lasting years piled on years.

There must be a kind of envy which brings me peering
and nosing at the boats along the island quay
either in the hot morning
with the lace-light shaking up against their hulls from the water,
or when their mast-tops
keep on drawing lines between stars.
(I do not speak here of the private yachts from the clubs
which stalk across the harbour like magnificent white cats
but sheer off and keep mostly to themselves.)

Look for example at the Bartolomé; a deck-full
of mineral water and bottles of beer in cases
and great booming barrels of wine from the mainland,
endearing trade;
and lengths of timber and iron rods for building
and, curiously, a pig with flying ears
ramming a wet snout into whatever it explores.

Or the Virgen del Pilar, mantled and weavy with drooping nets
PM/708/3A
with starfish and pieces of cod drying on the wheel-house roof
some wine, the remains of supper on an enamel plate
and trousers and singlets 'passim';

both of these boats stinky and forgivable like some great men
both needing paint,
but both, one observes, armoured far better than us against jolts
by a belt of old motor-tyres lobbed round their sides for buffers.

And having in their swerving planks and in the point of their bows
the never-enough-to-be-praised
authority of a great tradition, the sea-shape
simple and true like a vase,
something that stays too in the carved head of an eagle
or that white-eyed wooden hound crying up beneath the bowsprit.

Qualities clearly admirable. So is their response to occasion,
how they celebrate such times
and suddenly fountain with bunting and stand like ocean maypoles
on a Saint's Day when a gun bangs from the fortifications,
and an echo-gun throws a bang back
and all the old kitchen bells start hammering from the churches.

Admirable again
how one of them, perhaps tomorrow, will have gone with no hooting or fuss,
simply absent from its place among the others,
occupied, without self-importance, in the thousands-of-
millions-of sea.

Table Tennis

Because the heavy lids will not drag up
I am playing table tennis with eyes closed,
asleep, and striking at the sound;
with what a grovelling score may be supposed.

In my dream I am tired and long to stop.
Pit-ponies, sex-fiends, gypsies' bears have found
mercy, I hope, in sleep.

                    Each thump, each kick
or chastening of my day crowds back in this
unskilful ghostly tournament of poc-pic.

I know my Opponent; Who he is I miss.
The ordeal turns wilder than before;
now serve and smash must fly through a shut door.

The Leopards

One of them was licking the bars of its circus-cage
then gazing out sleepily round the tall tent splendid
just here and there with scarlet and brass,
till the bang of a whip

Brought the animals lolloping onto their chairs (a tail
hung long and twitching, talking its own thoughts.) Possibly
the threat was lies, it was not so much
the percussion

Of the whip, but instead some gipsy trick of the tents
won over these golden kittens to rise and beg
and flaunt their white, powder-puff bellies
(though at the report

Of a lash that curls too near, out flutters a paw
like a discharge from a fuse.)
                                    Now they were rolling
and cuddling with the bare-chest tamer;
now cowering at the whip-cut.

With humans one judges better; the tamed, the untamed.
It is harder with these pretenders – claws in, out,
– finally snaking off low to the ground:
yet there was a likeness, something stayed and haunted
as they bleared and snarled back over their narrow shoulders
at that whip banging.

A Sunday

A black Cordoba hat tilted
and the chin-strap
make it.

And she his white mare
with tail coiffured
coming in dancing
(her eyes of a tragedienne)
speak it.

Crowd-din like gravel falling;
an odour of expectation
and that odour

Which rounds her fastidious nostrils:
blood sweetening the air
of evening and October.

Cripples

On that kind island the brick-coloured earth
lavishes barley and pigtailed maize man-high;
olives lean heads together
(with the goat-flock under them some inkpot spills)
and half a mile of crack-car road will run
with surf of oleander flowers;
villas and farms are bleach and colour-of-sky,
and moderate, watered hills
spread harvests of grapes that the next hill will have outdone.

But fig and bean trees bear such heavy crops
that out of age or wantonness of fruiting,
their branches give and sink
and farmers stick poles under them for props,
five or six to one fruiter's use;
so the trees stand when summer enters its height
(bolt-shot with perfume, leaf and juice)
like cripples on crutches or men crazed with drink,
staggering and laughing, arms hung up to the light.

Watchers

Their faces are untenanted. These were once,
and will be again so,
a village grandma with thin hair scratched back,
a ploughboy with spud nose and ragged mouth,
a father rigged for the town in his stiff black,
the brass stud at his lifted throat on show;
all tilted up one way
some of these faces keep half-smiles,
yet those smiles never grow.

Theirs are like faces sleep has drained. The dark
communion of dream which holds them world-aloof
is splashed with light from an arc. All their dear care
goes whispering and yearning
high above the sweep of circus benches
there where two manikins under the great bell-roof
walk down a hair;
he, prancing and masterful in his red-slashed shirt,
and slight and hesitant
she like a twist of paper turning.

The Wedding Pictures

Bulky with mackintosh and scarf
against the autumn weather
a man of pith and force, with grizzled hair
my friend the photographer

Brings me a sheaf of photos from the reception
for last week's wedding. There
exchanging gazes stand the couple together
under the Napoleon-period painting. Tall
or squat, caught out or posed, the guests parade,
myself among these categories somewhere;
there figure all
the smiles and all the hands that lift champagne
and – there was some joke then now past recall
– the bride again, pulling a comic face,
eyes wide and splendid.
                                    Why is it today,
with his hands full of gladness and beginnings
he comes reminding me of gnarled old truths,
staying to pass the gossip of his trade,
a trade that thrives wherever people gather;
new from his morning at the graveyard
and on his shoes the crust of graveyard clay?

By a Breakwater

At Dover the wind came spotting rain and whirled
gulls in big Catherine Wheels;
no holidaymakers dawdled on the front or neared the loud surf at all.

A storm-glare on that Castle, hung in the sky;
smoke downward streaking
from a ship heading East, and the sea out there with its snowing look.

I said there was no one; a breakwater sheltered one couple
in their embrace tight-pulled,
they were plain, middle aged; with his right hand he was emptying

A hypodermic syringe in her bare arm
(I looked twice; fear of dreaming);
she leaned on him, quite reliant.
                                        It is to be remarked

This scene can be told for a laugh: at the hopelessness
of a summer; at the fantasy
of such an act and its setting; or at Medicine masked as Passion;

Also, for a shiver, the macabre.
                              Or again, not squarely
for a joke or a flinching away
but, as here, for a sometimes blurred, other times emerging query,

Almost recognition. So clutched to each other, sitting nowhere
                              and hiding from the wind.

Lop-sided

A pressure on the ears,
the explosion's stinging bang
jammed with that blinding nerve of flame torn down,
the houses jumping dark
rain grossly hose-ing;
rivers heading eagerly down the street hub-level
colliding at corners, trying to climb back into fountains,
revolving rubbish.

We had remarked few warning preliminaries,
having the day to get through, that's how it is;
lassitude indeed, and yawning, something strange in the movements
of insects or birds:
nothing to end up this way.

Not consciously
had we been aware of such massive disproportions accumulating
quietly and long,
calling for that smashing and flying of space-architecture,
globe-scale outrage,
august grievances to be dreadfully righted,
leaving a sniff of burning.

Donkey

He belongs under a blow-torch sky
as much as selling water, or carrying beds through the street
or endlessly standing around;
he with big dirty hearthrug head and gorgeous eye,
he with his stripe of vigour, who raging in the heat
and belly-ache of love throws bitter complaint out with the sound
of croup, of cars braking, of hinges, a last-ditch cry.

Ankling along the cobbles of a cliffside, breakneck street
or the tracks of the bald plains or spinbrain mountain-twists,
he has come to a peace with servitude and those by whom he is downed;
let us waive further pathos, as he would;
for him there is no defeat:
turds entice him, but mostly he dreams straight on (and his ankles
            are tiny like children's wrists).

Hung with cheap lines of pottery,
bashed milk-cans, brushes, prayer-rugs or kindling wood,
taken for granted, loved or merely used,
with the master piled amid,
he props the four-hooved beast-and-human pyramid
that though stone yielded has withstood,
and points up over the early bones,
relic and monument...
donkey on business, treading the weeds past side-pitched pillar-drums
– pillars of the lost, imperial, the earthquake-tumbled towns.

Full Moon

Doubtful-edged and almost daylight
on marbles and the blank page of white walls;
drooping the little flowered tree
along my street in Chinese-paintbrush falls;

Mocking unfootfalled streets with moonshine,
moonlight rubs meaning as the sea rubs stones;
and does Time's sum again; tonight is
tonight and the last moon that disturbed my bones.

Close the sun-torn shutters, step
back to the lampbulbs' poor barn-theatre glow
or the prisms and rage of Southern noon,
and grieve and laugh in roles you too well know:

snow-crater light will prove how false they show.

The Agents

Anywhere your agents search me out:
in stations at night as I am going from where
you are not to where you are not,
thinking of God knows what under all stars,
in that shouting twilight
a stranger hurries, intent like others; there
my body alerts as when a danger jars.

In a bank they walk, or instantly torn
past me in cars; or as a child some days;
a week ago on those stone
stairs winding up to my work – the identical
managing of a scarf;
or some old letter dropped about displays
your fierce script like glass jags that top a wall.

Let them keep startling us as before,
frequenters of half-lights, the improbable;
they have been my friends for
such long and earthquake years.
                              Do not now state
they have not your orders,
anyhow that you do not wish them well,
while you sit proud, in the North, and hug your hate.

Chestnuts

First the demure green handkerchiefs let droop,
(what comedy was I up to then?)
next, one remembers almost to the day,
all that short brilliance of stuck birthday-lights
that brought the summer forward in a bound
(did pleasures or the rough deals get their way?)

Now in this lane where otherwise you listen
to a distant tractor and harrow working round
– which you can't glimpse; the weeds wave up such heights
– slither and run,
falling through parched leaves like the tearing of paper,
the conker thumps down, bursts its capsule wide
and rolls haphazard to its rest,
grandly prolific, in the wheel-marked dust;
first time in the light (and meaning my goodbye;
I know, I will not delay)
conker with a piece of the sun
of a flaring autumn on one waxy side.

Blue Arm

A high pink wall; plaster in map shapes peeling;
socks on the dangle; a row of windows; and over
the pots of flowers a blue arm reaches out, feeling.

Into a courtyard white-collared children are turning;
talking hums up in light like days at the seaside,
sound is the sun-daze, voices fuse in a burning.

And it all is an answer, perhaps; last night, unsleeping
I fought with a problem of writing; how to liberate
a certain thought into words, its own and leaping
(comfortless X-ray bones, the hours crept weeping).

Perhaps I shall find out how. Above the laughing
animation the blue arm pushes a window; sunstabs
are shaken my way over tree-tops. Heliographing.

Near Aranjuez

Ungated fields of yellowish earth
that chalk and flint peer through:
alone on the left hand hill a whitewashed chapel
with four dark trees, like stilted, elegant birds:
presently a crumbling tower; there was once
something forgotten now to love, to guard.

Coral is not more gradual than that castle
becomes gold debris, loosening stone from stone:
past sixty windy miles the April mountains
slowly unwinter; plaid cape to his chin
a peasant eyes us as he rides
with bundled firewood down a dust-plumed road
the Roman vanguards found.

On the Road

Our roof was grapes and the broad hands of the vine
as we two drank in the vine-chinky shade
of harvest France;
and wherever the white road led we could not care,
it had brought us there
to the arbour built on the valley side where time,
if time any more existed, was that river
of so profound a current, it at once
both flowed and stayed.

We two. And nothing in the whole world was lacking.
It is later one realises. I forget
the exact year or what we said. But the place
for a lifetime glows with noon. There are the rustic
table and the benches set; beyond the river
forests as soft as fallen clouds, and in
our wine and eyes I remember other noons.
It is a lot to say, nothing was lacking;
river, sun and leaves, and I am making
words to say 'grapes' and 'her skin'.

COLLECTED POEMS

(1965)

POEMS FROM VIENNA

The Empire Clock

Muted wood-wind is one noise of the traffic, and there is a second
when trams manoeuvre the bend, the muffled grinding and wail
of steel turned on steel.

The River drifts its ice under no stars towards
the Black Sea (and what winter cities?). The long-silent
Empire clock with its pediment

Abruptly intones once. Rather than a chime, a stirring,
a gruffness. And instantly I am conscious of the young man
from the war in nineteen-fifteen

Who cut on the back door in this house his 'goodbye'
to his girl, and the date.
                      Fifty-odd winters it stayed, that thought,

Which we painted out. Which we painted out.

On the 'Sievering' Tram

Square figures climb off and on;
mufflers, Astrakhan hats.
A wintry night for a ride to a clinic
to visit a new-born boy and his mother;
and the bell hurrah-ing.

Too many life-bullied faces
packed on the Sievering tram.
Yet a woman smiles at a baby near her
and beckons and beckons, as we run lurch
-ing, and sigh and restart.

That baby views the woman steadily;
(and the floor is mucked with snow.)
What do I bring to the boy and his mother
lying in the clinic? Daffodils,
bewilderment and love,

Ready money, a clock and a signature.
A Neon-light Pegasus glows in the sky
(Somebody's Oil) as we swing corners
past bakers' and laundries and snow, with the traffic
-gongs ringing like glory.

The Invaders

They would bar your way in the street
to grab your astounding watch;
that unknown thing, a handkerchief,
they would threaten you for, and snatch
to enrich a village wife
a hemisphere far off;
a firearm gave them right.

Girls wore soiled, frumpy clothes,
scrubbed make-up away, looked rough
when they hurried down to the shops;
that was the epoch's vogue.

Through a longing to look older
one woman put powder on her hair
– well-worn Occupation stories;
there is this which a few prefer:

The child asking for a tame rabbit;
some kindly foreigners who heard;
and her cry and her flight from the soldiers bringing
seven dead rabbits with blood
on their fur, and their necks swinging.

A Number

Looking up from her knitting, Anne said 'Fifty-three';
the number of stitches along her needle?
It could be the number of a wintry tram behind the house
whistling and howling across the meat-freezing bridge,
or digits of a crucial telephone number
or a friend's street door in London or in Vienna;
it might have been something of moment that took place in the year
one thousand nine hundred and fifty three, before
we raised those first drinks to each other in Gran Via, Madrid.

Knitting, she called to mind the women
knitting shawls by the scaffold in the French Revolution
– there were probably young faces seen there.
She reminded me also of the Fates at their woolly occupations.
'Was it the stitches?'
                    'No, today is your birthday.'
                                        Naturally
I had forgotten my birthday, and my age as fifty-three.
'I thought you meant the stitches in the row.'
I said 'Count them'; she counted. The number was fifty-three.

When she visited a clinic, later, her room was Fifty-Three.

Properties of Snow

Snow on pine gorges can burn blue like Persian
cats; falling on passers can tip them with the eloquent hair
of dancers or Shakespeare actors;
on roads can mute the marching of a company of infantry
(so that they seem the killed from a battle whispering by);
neglected, glues where you walk, a slippery black iron,
famous hospital filler,
proved friend of bandages and white hip-length plaster.
Decorative and suspicious: wine broken recently on snow...
Spaded with tinkles and grating
from a pavement, presently huddles in a heap blotched and disgraced,
a pedigree pet, now repellent.

On office, on factory roofs,
or stretching, severe, to horizons on trees, fields, fences,
with no way across except the way the traveller will plough;
nothing moving, and a sky the colour of grey trousers;
blanched snow, the Chinese colour of mourning, of death,
can rob the bones of their marrow,
turn a man's face towards home.

Clemente

The pride of Clemente was that the drinks he brought were fiercer
than those of Manolo, Rafael or Ventura, waiters at the Club;
he would linger and smile,
and watch you taste those drinks. (Clemente, and wouldn't you watch?)

Clemente died. One imagines strangers at the funeral, and foreigners,
bizarre, beside his family. He must have been very much mourned,
that man must have been,
by many who could never properly have known him, or dreamed his thoughts

When he was off duty. Kindness, a look in the eyes, a few stories;
what does it mean, to be 'known'?

                            Abroad, I dwell on his boast,
(whatever text was cut into his headstone)
echoing so strange a death, yet holding to its old grandeur:
'Clemente who wangles you the cruel drinks.'

You

Subways have similar gunbarrel perspectives
to those which, furlong laid
after furlong, you now thread.
If there were a friend
he might take the next man for you, or the one preceding
with his regular tread.
Aloft and on each side
hands and fingers are staring at you,
whose vigilance you will not evade.

Tonight you swing past odours of cattle, the breath of grass;
then colder smells, brine and decaying sea-plant;
a star trails with you half your course.

Always, voyaging or clambering the rocks of the farther bay,
such is your infirmity
that your words have to be spoken for you by others,
and perhaps in a different country.
                              You on the way
The name of which appalls,
from the hope-withering corridors on the mainland
to the treeless island pinnacled with the never-broken walls.

Dr Karl Lueger

Frock-coated Dr Karl Lueger
– bronze hand to bronze heart –
on his plinth in front of the cafés
where the morning shoppers sit
has exchanged his snow-tippet
and his middle European
busby of snow
for ribbons and runnels of pigeon-shit.

On the road below where the Doctor stands
I am watching a sparrow entirely absorbed
in eating a crust without help of hands.
With so much whip and flap
either the crust or the head
or both will be landing on someone's lap.

To Piers Spencer, five months old

You form and feel words over on your lips
mutely; for you words still are shapes of mouths.

If you become a poet, and short of pence
(your father's son even in this plight),
you will also mumble away, and citizens,
whose own words tumble out, and never a hitch,
will cower, when you compose, in fright.

Though others you will find throw looks of greed;
less daunted by your mimic speech:
So much your fellow-human-beings they are,
they will edge your way, and speculate
how if they could get closer somehow and overhear,
they might learn something that would make them rich.

Traffic in April

Returning West from our visit to the Embassy
– with four files on my knee – the car turned right;
there was chaos, then; we needed at once to turn left
but cars from that street were swinging (their left) across us;
and cars from opposite advanced; there were neither lights nor policeman.
A car nosed forward, clinched the jam. The Austrian
driver lifted his hands from the wheel and sat guffawing.
All those cars hooted; it was April, the snow just melted,
stone angels on roofs in sunlight, and the church towers;
the golden hands of the clocks glittering.

A quarter of a mile farther, a car fled by at fifty;
its front axle broke; it tilted, tore the road up,
continued, tried to bury itself in the road.
No one was hurt; that axle glowed with the glow
of furnace steel spilling from a great spoon in a factory.
It was sunset and lightning together; the road burned,
the axle burned. We had little
German or English for communication,
but the two of us, clambering out to gawp,
on that fine particular day
had the kind of language needed for a screw-loose world, and for laughing.

UNCOLLECTED AND
UNPUBLISHED POEMS

EARLY POEMS 1929-1932

The lights with big elegant fingers...

The lights with big elegant fingers
moulded and twined together and parted
the dancers' pliant bodies of pink plasticine:
the slim young man was whipped by the music like
      a top round the stage,
        ringing the cymbals with each kick of his feet.
but when the music was water rising in a lock
    you entered buoyed on the froth of the chorus' dancing
        whose smiles you alone could unstick.
    you alone the perched electrician in the wings
      forgot to hold caught in the net of his lantern
        and slid to his desire down the plank of the light.
for you alone above the plump knees of the chorus
the spirit of the audience stretched from the velvet tiers
    pursuing round the stage your elusive limbs
with tenuous arms of tobacco smoke.

Schedules

The urgent ringing of the electric alarum
   brought forth a Spring of gold station masters;
out came the waistcoated porters like bees;
   the telegraph posts had passed down the word,
and the signals on their stilts had seen it a long way off
   the soundless threading of the smoke,
as if a burning finger were drawn through the landscape,
   and they stood waving their arms in excited semaphore;
the clock, an experienced patron of sport,
   with the face of a judge ticking out the seconds;
and the people tinkling pennies at the slot machines
   seemed to be taking bets with robot bookies;
now the tremors of the sound coming
   made ripples on the sea of cloth caps and bowlers;
up and down went officials stemming the overflow;
   the bosomed woman sprouted hands
multitudinous as an Indian goddess,
   and in every hand was a child;
each man clutched his prospects, his future,
   packed up in his handbag;
each man for himself!
   the last bend was turned;
round went the faces like blown leaves on a tree
   and in came the train
chasing the expectation of itself,
   sweating and panting,
wiping its face with a large white pocket handkerchief.

Collection

A lukewarm, trouser-treasured, sixpence for God,
A penny for the marriage of the curtain and the rod,
A penny, a penny for the pitching of the pine,
A penny for the innocence of John the Divine
Sitting in the window, immaculate though stained;
A penny for St Michael the lectern, explained
Just like the Deity, existence without form;
A penny to keep our convictions warm;
A penny for the honesty of the kitchen chair;
Accept, O Lord, our offering and receive our prayer.

Festa

Because it was the Queen's birthday
we had all run up our spirits' pennons to the top of our flagposts
and skimmed about on the surface of our lives
like little flies on water:
No one knew what to do
but they were all sure they were doing it:
the motor-bicycles went round in circles
arguing at the tops of their voices,
and the clapping started up
and tried to drown them
with a thousand clattering cylinders:
the slim young jockeys
balanced on the handlebars
and they and the paper hats and painted bladders
chased each other in and out through the forest of the smoke.

The mouth-organ man
with his shoulders over his ears
    rhapsodised.
'Grass all over our trousers,
    patterns of grass on our hands
our pleasure crowns the day's gold cornet
    and fills the embrace of our demands.'
'Fête champêtre by the marquees:
    the only death O Lord
is when the roundabout leaves the ground,
    the halfpenny leaves the board.'

Then they cleared away the sun
and up went the fire balloons
carrying with them the burning by which they climbed
enthusiasms cut loose
never looking down
till the fire went out from under them
and left them lying about all over the sky.

The rockets said 'Ah!'
leaping like gold fish
from a white splash of upturned faces
and arched their swan necks
to join point to point
in a suspended electrical kiss;
their broken passion sparkled down the sky
like downward champagne bubbles.
But the continuous roundabout music
which was the engine that drove the day's excitement
stopped: and the fiery porcupines
pursuing each other nose to tail in mid air
stopped: and our spirits' last rockets were fired
and our eyes full of ashes:
and the moon came up
to sweep away the crowds and the rocket smoke
with a mind soured like a domestic servant's
who only sees the morning's broken bottles and dirty glasses.

Above, the fingers of the tree...

Above, the fingers of the tree;
high above, the arched sky
stood immense, grave with cloud:
her eyes, turned to me
by her aliveness were made quick.
Between deliberate sky and slow river
for a glance, amazed, I held as tenant
more than was owed to them and their summer,
where their live world
ends, beyond this, alive.

Departure

The hills begin their march again; Pauline
admired, untouched, is drowned out by their waves;
the old lady, whose sick bed, never seen
unearthed soon-silenced voices from the graves
now treads the night-waiting stars: and Destiny
takes moods and manners from the breathing one
unbodied now in brain; from the dead lady
her dying, and with some small leaf upon
a hedge, seen carelessly, shuts them up all
for good into the cupboards of the mind.

At loss, the mind grows older in this school
holds harder to life, if that's what is designed.

Those near and dead who think there is another...

Those near and dead who think there is another
Death to pray against, claim their memory –
thoughts that I believed three nations' frontiers
and a sea stretched to hide.
Mountains now blue over earth's rim
wished for, be near, big gods,
outbulk our small thinking
for fear these thoughts and my loathing,
strong acid, burn away your shadows
while distance still promises, untrusted,
while they are strangers
on the skirt, there, of the sky
still, and the people crowd to the carriage windows.

After Love

His absentness, his evading
Of her fierce identifying love
Was not self-prisoner's,
Marked him rather as one

When the fire fell who gave
Self as a thing most precious.
This the worse lover
In giving but counting...

At rare after-meetings
Now is the disappointed,
Wounded with self given,
Apartness once given.

Her easy talking, quick
Child's confidences, the cool
Hand given make irony
Of the natural images

He had matched her with – of birds
For her changing moods, new trees
And all swift creatures' kind
For her body.

Of Nature so, who drew
Her blood from Earth's heart, gave
Love unreflectingly,
She, changed so easily.

Wondered, is again natural,
By the young of animals
Is imaged, whose eyes forget
Late pain, by this hour's

Young sky new out of clouds
Printless of all Time's past.

Poem

After the wheels and wings of this intense day
Evening makes the sky big; as harvest's end
Final, the fields of strong hands empties.

In day, in the tide's, in the great flame's reaching
My hard want of you would have been easier to bear
Companied by men's and creatures' need, roots' thirst.

The hour that unstrings the world, horizons tilting
Blind into dark, earth undressed of life,
Stone, moon, point moving on sky map,

Holds all bitterness, littles the will so imperious,
Shows to will's self its dream-weak feet and hands, giant
That clock and sheer machine by which it starves.

Clouded, Still, Evening

Breathing in leaf only
And in quick stem earth lies.
Known hills and the first star
Day's hot breath misted out.

Eyes left from need's service
See world too enfranchised;
Fearfully hands touch
Grass, trees, strange, not ours.

Men's ways in this silence
Seem far, and men's business;
Fine sense thought-distance sent
To left and right reports

Dominion of blind hills
And a world of close leaves.

Though I feel each tree's burden,
Earth's sap and strength,
To my pride and my doubting
I know no echo here,

By sympathy too exiled:
To this dark state, my source,
As man not native, even
Among men's corn stranger.

Poem

White factories lancing sky
As the city grew near
Were symbols of changed state,

Pulse and strength of steel arms
seemed hammering out new world
Not by you informed. The road

Led through the large morning
From that landscape, witness
Of Love's strange life, hard dying.

Absent, yet in loud street
You were, and in café,
And but wore her and her.

The cheating eyes, blood's tumult,
Wrote you more sure than those
Of senses' no and yes,

Whom place and minutes kill.
And when I thought you changed,
As hill and leaf for stone,

I thought out you who stand
On the inward side of sense –
Leaf, stone, are of your substance
And these ghosts whom I see.

Two Poems

I

My pulling on of shoes
My opening of doors
Speaking – the hundred acts
That serve my hourly use

Are then not disparate
Are nationals of one blood;
Closer, the raiding eyes
The thoughts around each gate

Are surely dyed the same;
In these, too, lover is,
And I, since I have loved you,
In everything I change
On the world must write your name.

That for sense enough keen
Within a street I must
From the rest show different;
And though I walk still here
I breathe, from what I had been,
Your love's whole air distant.

II

Her hands waking on her lap
Let out in me a prisoner,
Her hands' unclasping fired the train
That lit my mind with her:

I saw her limbs were a well full
From the same source that moved the day's
Swift over heart of slow; she was all
Desires walking their natural ways.

(Suddenly I saw this. Surprise
Was yet such sort as understood
How long this truth, she being near,
Had housed in bone, run in the blood.)

Also, though to no coward mind,
She was healing, and of Sleep's nature.
I saw that in her love I would find
Sharpness to cut the sun into
This sensual tent in which I am blind.

Poem

Who sees the rain fall into the Spring land
And the sun's attack from hill to hill behind,
Who in the wind, from a new quarter blowing,
Smells the year turning, the new hungers preying;

Who feels at pulse the general advance
And each defence marched down by suns and rains,
Now on him too the hands strong above choice
Pressing to strange streets, promising no ease;

Young, may he have his wish, have from the start
A credit of pride to overtide first doubt;
Success on his first making or ordering
Shine down remembered failing, stammering.

From friends through various disguise may he tell
The close spies weaving against will
Urging to give place to an admired one,
Be blunted with kind names, or use caution.

Sometimes with lover feel that unique force
That makes the 'I' all things and every place,
For lover is new, lover is from outside,
Stronger than the tower where the man is tied.

Fused in these hours to all that has world's name
Into one circuit with them with no break,
– World run the rivers of its strength through him,
World that he nerved himself against, and was weak.

For seeing whole I had been too near my friends...

For seeing whole I had been too near my friends:
When we drank or drove I came near to one,
Near to another in speaking of a woman:
What could I hold back, using their blood, their brain?

In part only I saw them. Then in the train
I crossed fields that had never known their fire;
An evening country turning, hedges and trees
Not leaved with their words and laughter, as those were.

The brow of Summer matched against their quickness
Made them seem far and overshadowed them.
They must spill apart and change whom I thought firm;
I saw them draw like green things to their time.

Such height of corn, so many miles...

Such height of corn, so many miles
Of Summer's uncountable heads held up,
One standing mane, to the dusk lights
Lit on the hills –

Suddenly held all my mind. Earth
Smelled, and was the wealthiest table laid.
Earth, like a precious grain-ship, sailed
With its cargo's worth.

'There I must change,' 'there was denied,'
'There failed.' Dark as the cloud I saw ride
West above the fields, was the thought;
'Wanting what men do, from what plenty
I must go wide.'

UNCOLLECTED POEMS 1935-1946

Most things having a market price...

Most things having a market price
My ears are full of the buzzing of the price.
Money dances in front of the page. I rise
And go to live as my money buys.

I've food to suffice. But out of day
Height doom and delight are narrowed away;
Anxiety takes what I wish to say;
Invention winters a worm's way.

I, Jack, walking on the hill's shoulder...

I, Jack, walking on the hill's shoulder
Arm me to me, prevent myself becoming
Barky trees becoming earth that earth
Today hard under my heel as a boulder,
Forged with frost: trees that soon a bolder
Month will send fountaining with leaf, earth
The crops are going to crumble and dance through. Hold
Myself as man from re-earthing, the drift to be homing.
I having to remember who I am when I am. Hang
To friends scattered across England; but having
To remember how long there is to remember; long
To be living when there is place, not difference and wring;
But having in a given time to hunt like gold
This: the singly achieving some thing.

The Runner

As a trained racket hand's sweep
As breasting air a swallow-diver's
Liquid fall; straight straight homing
No other boy can pace him, he is a greyhound, makes them creep
Laughing out for him is another act of running.

Wounds like raw iron fed to the wheel,
The people's drugged sense of injury,
If these must grind, then thrust out killing edge;
Feet hungry for ground, lounging ignorant good will
Can stay loved, no straws be drawn, have a neutral's privilege.

Winter Landscape

The spiky distance was the town; spires,
Factories, gasworks, shrunken in the telescope of blue.
If there was any sound
Across that giant nerveless palm of ground
– Work from the rail – its action was long done,
And it came limping late on lame feet
Past the tiny horses among the steel floods.
Brush over the sky with endless weeping clouds
Ascending towards us from those thorns; the town.

Near the bridge an aeroplane was perched.
I saw the pilot square in his padded coat
Smoking, chatting to friends.
He mounted, waved to the three waving friends;
Turned the plane, jolting, on to even ground:
Then she ran up wind with an excitement of engines,
poised her bird's tail, was in air now, swept about
As a sower throws, a waker stretches, and
Strong up some sky-scent followed, glad as a hound.

The House

There that terrible house, those corridors
Fluffed with sound-proof material
Where a glove is drawn over feel of good and evil:
And men move whom wages move, but without belief.

Wages and hum-drum made the thin, forbidden,
Mouth of this young girl. She admires a man
Who has not seen her. How she smiles at her hands
In secret, as if sharing a joke with someone.

A simpleton claws at money across my mind.
A speed-king hunches in his cockpit. Lovers
Go spry to the pictures – it is Saturday. Marchers
Sing, furrow the fountained square: Whom fanaticism,

Hunger, hunted; speed to crumple distance
Or any lust electrified to burst bound
From that terrible house; them I stand with outside.
That house I know; I live now: therefore love them.

Going to the Country

Now ranging cracker-brilliant areas
Where the higgledy shops shout each other down
And cinemas carved as mosques sell to the humbled
An evening as the hero who breaks all bars,
Our bus rolled towards country wood and down:
Now less lighted stretches; residences whose
Stony outside – porches for knees, severe
Shuttered windows under eyebrows of stone
Suggested councillors, business men of mark,
Or seated Egyptian dead. Through these we were
A horn of light butting through straits of twilight...
Now wealth, now the market. At last, open and dear
To drivers a world made simply of road, and stark,
Where sky and earth were one coalmine of dark.
Fingers jabbed North and to the coastal towns.
In Town we had many friends, and of confidence,
Who didn't need us to reckon or be stilted,
Good company at drinks, enquiring and witty
At the play or in the street. They would have lent their sense
To explore or ignore a public life disordered
As a photograph from a war with a steeple tilted.
They would be up. Country was early to bed.
But far from them, with colder air to breathe,
Lying under a country roof we were content
To hear – we would have given each other voice
– One trudging step which crossed the yard beneath:
And because nothing else moved, that one noise spread
At least to the cirrus cloudlets overhead,
That top of ceilings. We were pleased with our choice.

Picked Clean from the World

Picked clean from the world by the speed of our train
We lay the uneasy night
Seeming to lurch through cloud
To drop like an aerial jumper
To explore at random the cisterns of the rain
The deafening workshops of the thunder.

In the morning, the sunny plateaux, shrubs
That claw up fierce from an earth baked dry
And writhe black arms like a fire's stubs,
Feathered olives, and the rolling maize
Dangling its carter's whips,
And the vine, knee-high.

To enter alertly a new town-square,
To cross the equator of shade and glare,
To smell and touch snow;
New adjustments to a new life shaped
By female harbour or river's flow
– Mind needed these as body bread.
At home, in an industrialised country
No other wish will do instead
Of that ancient disruptive wish, springing naked
Like a dream whose sense we are made to know.

Just as at Pont du Gard
Where the river is broad across the gravel,
Grateful because of the shade, and level,
Bathers who look up are
Hit with astonishment,
Seeing suddenly the Roman viaduct,
Its trampling arches of yellow stone,
With its stilted valley-stride
Fill all the sky one way,
Enduring and monstrous in its image of travel.

They Tell a Lie

Parted, the young and amorous touch tragic hands by letter.
The world between is a factory of fear. It is thought better
    Not to admit why.

Active men are chucked like slag to waste or at length
Given such work they can use the mere half of their strength;
    It is dangerous to ask why.

Many died spilt from air, in deserts or in the sea's
Murdering lanes, or boxed in the trap of cellars. These
    Should not have been told a lie.

I walk between walls of war and mark in a gesture or an eye
Sure as alkali and acid, those who would deeply deny
    What we are fighting for and why.

The weather beats and blows, and the scene will not keep still
And some must die but the water has got to go down the hill,
    Though today they tell a lie.

In Memoriam

The earth slumped in
and through successive empires those two stayed,
tomb-thieves, splendid beyond their title, free
of a King's palace. Round the walls there swayed
forms of beast-cowled, bird-pinioned deity;
corn in a precious bin
stood there with wine beside the treasure load
to tend the Soul on its tremendous ways
and from a nearness still uncrossed-to glowed
long buried Pharaoh's visored golden gaze.
Scholars, the second stir
since that first burial year
found them where the earth held them in its cramps,
finger-bones hooked to Alexandrian lamps.

The ciné-camera pointed
and the tall hatted Frenchman stands through Time
next to the boulevard 'pissoir' he has left
buttoning his trousers. Anger starts to climb
into his face. Outmoded passers, reft
decades from their appointed
age, throw a glance or pause to stare our way;
dead eyes alive from a dead Paris day.

By the cold church wall
stern on their knees the Tudor couple pray
starched into wood with those great ruffs they wore
and in descending scale of small array
sharp upward handed all their family score.
If we asked at all
impertinent questions of their loves and fears
or when they smiled, be certain this is how
they would face Time. Some gold and red adheres

upon their angular draperies even now
once from the wet brush new.
But as mortals dead
and honoured, haughty red
and gold their burial due.

The Top-Storey Room

Above London sailed my room
with clouds and evenings.
Tidied from day to day
by the woman with the low voice and the sad mouth,
its emptiness assumed by character
and watched me like my portrait.

To blind my room
I lived the disorder of London
hoping that in some bar or entrance-way
among the years of brick
a face would suddenly flare into the truth;
but there were only the faces.
              Then at night
it was good to unlock my room, to find
my papers, the cheap desk, my books
waiting by the bed.

              Yet sometimes
potent with memory, on the morrow of storms,
morning grew wings, the seagulls came
blown across dreamed of waves and miles to visit
the flagposts, or to wheel
across my window pane, and dazzle
the air like juggler's knives.

UNCOLLECTED POEMS 1947-1963

Pino

Pino, a hill-top village, slanting street
and at the corner a wall where gossips sit
in a row at sunset, like migrating birds,
backed by the sky and forty miles of plain.

Buses heading for somewhere else; the words
cart wheels grind and jerk or a peasant cries
as the white oxen lift their swinging throats,
somnambulists with long Egyptian eyes.

The 'National' inn, the sleepy, smiling maid,
the queenly, fat Madame in a dress of spots;
simple kindnesses like that harsh strong wine;
and two weeks blank of great events. In fine

A time of waiting. Most of our life is that.
But waiting sometimes vivid with the sign
of things amazingly connected; whether some
day of thunder or night with the Plough slung over
the road of foreboding and of dreadful hope,
the road to the towns and what there was to come.

The Clock

When the great convent clock strikes
up there from its facing tower
there is no shield between us, and the swell
enters my house like a wave and my rooms are bell.

I wonder what chimes mean to those
wing-hatted hidden nuns,
(linen and wood and nails); the rolling;
quarter to the hour; the hour. The planets tolling.

And I tangle out with the back of my mind
– looking across the deserted
walks and the low long roofs of their entombing
– my own reflective affection for that booming.

Which is that is grimly faithful,
that lead and iron friend,
and lends a touch of theatre or of rhyme;
one is Prince today and Clown the other time.

Yet, joke of fate to send me here
in sound of such a watchman;
the hour is ill although the night be prime
for me who abhor a watch through dread of Time!

I, wishing, hating refugee
from Time, who love his medium:
and at my hand, as that wry voice discloses
Time's creature too, this brimming wine, these globed and lolling roses.

For Signorina Brunella Mori

Tell me, you Romans, who but the dark Brunella,
    giovane, bella,
could ever give such a startling twist to the hoary
    'memento mori'?

A Ward

A ward dim like a wagon-lit; quick footsteps,
commotion of whispers; one bed curtain-bright;
shadows of the doctors bowing and straightening,
small, huge; small, huge. Methylated-ether tang.

Next day the air still keeps its eyes averted
when he has gone, with the gentle
rumble and clink of wheels. All fitting comment
seems to have crept away, too.

Young nurses tiptoed pulling curtains round
along the way he took, a decency
(if for our sakes, not his)
for which we are grateful. Blinding us was human.

Whatever knowledge we are capable of,
on a reckoning it will take a little while
of the kind, brisk, brittle hospital routine
to numb a memory, perhaps of only
a head drawing hard breath still, tipped back, eyes closed, chin fallen,
an arm flung from the sheets;

Or thoroughly needed to cleanse
this new taint of our general heritage
from a shining ward that neighbours
well-built Knightsbridge and lordly Hyde Park Corner.

Black Cat

Black cat
sleepily narrowing his eyes at me,
putting up a thick tail like smoke from a steamer,
speaking in a small rusty voice;
then trotting ahead, making short
friendly runs half sideways;

Cat in a garden of tawny and crimson
great still unfolding roses;
lawns smudgy underfoot after the downpours,
air tangy, bonfire raging,

Cat in a garden with roses in the September evening,
birds alert on the trees, worms like corkscrews sprouting,
fish in the pond plopping rings;

Myself thinking through roses, Autumn, pools and fire,
at the end of an episode in my life,
on the edge of a journey,
the auguries good;

And circling out from these paths paced along
tomorrow's or next year's passions, railroads, gardens...
and – with dear famous promises, and lies
– mountains, amazements, what new cities rumour.

Castille

Smouldering moon and stars like flaming crosses,
midnight the hour,
Spain; lovers walking past my balcony
and the clock banging out from the convent's pointed tower.

I sense the historic plain, the olive orchards,
and whatever it is that tries
past roofs and starlight to be understood,
as the answer tries to speak from a peasant's or a statue's eyes.

Such nights or noons I start to know this people,
how within they carry the sear
of Summer and blizzard and the short brash Spring,
gaunt valleys with the crash of water falling sheer;

How all their gentleness must root in soil
sterner than ours:
boulder and scrub and mountains shaped like pain;
hearts that ferment with gold and dust, dead bones and crowns and flowers.

This Day

Though passion for her is my life's mere commons
some days, and this, stand clear – but the rendezvous,
the impersonal, busy bar, the City morning,
her looks, her voice, were only those I knew.

There have been so many days, so many rooms:
yet from that very noon with the light streamed in
around the curtain's edge, and the darkened bed,
after two years I drink her breath, her skin.

Witness

You play the tape-recorder back;
there is yesterday again and the known and urgent voices;
there too (it was never in your yesterday)
is the gear-crash of a lorry moving up towards the mountains.
Paper chattering,
a bell ringing, a door that bangs,
a clack of glass on a table come shouldering among your voices.

You handle photos taken at a party;
exquisite and impertinent among the faces triumph
intruders you never noticed: electric fittings,
the grin of a useful ashtray, the splashy veining on marble.
An irruption?
What in the name of all that is Thing-born
did you expect? You were genial or fervent; and there was present,

Loyal to its loyalties, that Box
with the mad face and the whirling features to eat and spue you;
or when there were Lais, da Vinci and Socrates,
Byron and Catherine of Russia at your humdinger party,
then
all goggles and windows like a fly
the camera, soapy and cold to the holding fingers, blinked at it.

Written on a Cigarette Packet

Bloody lonely without you.
                               Stilettos;
your light voice locked in the tape recorder,
                                                  batteries run down.
Rum-drumming of motor-bikes
and under the arc of Jupiter
the summer-night balconies talking to each other
and the bar 'El Tenis'
                         to the bar 'Juan'.

That cloth folded on the radio is probably
folded just as you left it folded.
(Jupiter South-East about its purposes)
Perhaps I am also away;
my jacket I tossed across that chair
seems to have a ghost recumbent inside it.
'Stiletos'. You wrestle with Spelling.
                                        'Stiletoes'.

Jupiter topple to blazes;
                         for lack of you
I stare at your card propped on the mantelpiece
with your spelling, 'Stilletos'.

From the Military Academy

At evening from the Military Academy
bugles blow up red clouds west of my apartment,
bugles with the bell-notes and the
tingling ones blow white stars
up, the big first kind;
nail gold leaf on skyscraper windows
Eastward; and citizens
at the hour of the bugles rumble their shutters up
and dogs bark, nervous.

And because these bugles fidget for attention
to matters in the past or hazards of sometime
(it seems the future),
but with imprecise meaning,
I write about bugles to be hell-rid of the
worry and recurrent itch of bugles
when corners of the streets belong to the young,
boys and girls who join them,
creatures of an early noon.

The Train Window

Stroked like a reflection high up on the train window,
an apparent trick of sight, they haunt up into
snow-mountain tops right above you hours away,
hazed, with a wet flash of the sun on them
and, lower, a faint hatching
of rock-strata;
                          they wear the authority of
all-there-is-to-be-said about a problem, or
are like something you wanted to make.
                                    Are also
what you need presently to turn your eyes from.
Whatever it is up there, extreme to endure,
you encounter enough of it
in the look of that torrent, down on the level
on which we say goodbye to someone, or return to her:
its darkness racing the train wheels,
bare branches of winter saplings reaching over it,
and its white foam-breaks tumbling over backwards.

OCCASIONAL AND UNFINISHED POEMS

from **Conducted Tour after Edward Lear**

Said the larger and fatter of two police
To the harlot of Alexandroupolis:
'What satisfies me so
Is a fuck από πίσω;
But don't loop the loop as you stoop, Alice.'

A misanthropist living in Giza
Had a stand like the tower of Pisa:
That night it was flat
And the cat on the mat
Had a smile not unlike Mona Lisa.

A research student living in Mahdi
Wrote a book throwing new light on Hardy,
He maintained with effrontery,
Hardy hated the country
And lived near St Paul's with a guardee.

From Cairo this: scorn upon verse from Alex...

From Cairo this: scorn upon verse from Alex,
whether in long hand, short hand or italics.
Item: we think the verse of Williams (Gwyn)
is dissonantal druid, twittering, thin
like seven Welsh devils dancing on a pin.
As for the verse of Edwards, the dark doctor,
we think it like a privy waste-pipe blocked or
an Eno-drinker hammering on a locked door.
What epigrams so lacked an end or middle
as those of Sodom's blond historian Liddell
– so quick to foul an English nurse's idyll?
But oh what startled Muse would not miscarry
when in the swollen verse of Durrell (Larry)
pornography and Greece and gaga marry.

For madmen, darkness whip and chain…

For madmen, darkness whip and chain
was the sharp cure, and for migraine
by the Blue Nile a red hot rod
pressed to the nape in praise of God
and hope of health: and so I shiver
with ice bags balanced on my liver
or drink such potions as must ooze
from Port Said harbour's fetid glues
or – ghoulish and obscene as these –
from Jaffa's, close in to the quays;
fouler than rubber burnt, or hair.
Here pap is all my bill of fare;
in beastly childhood I recline
foe to all noble food and wine
and view my medicine-bottles, each
designed to cast out retch with retch.
Such, till all peptic days are sent
my homeopathic punishment;
for, as in old times, this strong devil
goes not out except by evil.

I met you, George, upon a refuse dump...

I met you, George, upon a refuse dump,
Cursed by Mahomet and his camel's hump
Where Nile ran urine-coloured through the squalor;
And now – God bless me! There's my friend John Waller.

– Now what a change! you're knocking back your noggin
With me and Tambi in the pleasant Hogg Inn,
And heading (after certain patter said
And seven and sixpence) for your marriage bed.

I wish you all the beer you need and more,
Safety from most relations, and each bore,
A little touch of Bloomsbury in the air
And anniversaries thick as Tambi's hair.

Casa di P——

The bell and the parade of winking girls,
the writhing and the shifting foot from foot
were invented by Harry the American, who cheats
the world in rice from a seat at the Palace bar.

That evening was created from our guts,
the allurements, the suggestion of disinfectant,
from things we had dreamed, feared, wanted. There were many
threw slivers in the cauldron that it steamed from.

That frowning man-at-arms, the enormous Bawd
brown-jumper-armed, was made by my headmaster,
the Puritan one who died of drink, whose sex-talks
each red-faced boy was sworn to silence over;
She was the avenging nightmare of those warnings.

John invented the room hung full of knickers.
And I invented the whore waiting for her client,
reading *La Mujer Vencida* (paper covers).

The prints in the stained hall of classical scenes
– rotund limbs of Muses, shaded columns
– were my art-mistress', who robbed the life from
the Red Indians that we drew. Where is she now?

Someone – perhaps a rich invalid at Worthing
– imagined the elderly aproned servant woman
whose hopeless tired eyes stare through this poem.

It is clear, of course, the evening never existed;
that what seemed flesh, that blonde, the gleaming Arab,
were dust or grass, mere hallucination
for which in a way we were all responsible.

And a gossiping Protestant clergyman from Athens
seemed to descend with us the ill-lighted stairs,
stone by stone with all their doubts and turnings,
to the watchman fumbling keys and the empty street
and all that the moon regarded with such eyes.

The girl in the black mantilla with the ink splash eyes...

The girl in the black mantilla with the ink splash eyes
is leaning and singing some warm and throaty tune
about two lovers (slant of the guitars)
and 'the rays of the moon'.

Dusty from the same door extends the plain
centuries of poverty and war have torn
and the great road with never a turning
to the iron cold of the jagged mountains, the real
the quieter moon hacked clear through the sky and the Spanish stars
like shaken knives or distant bonfires burning.

Look at my suit...

Look at my suit
my tie (called quiet)
new shoes, new shirt
wine (fiasco) or the table
                    new pen
the cigarettes (50) on the table
Spain coming in through the window
what do I owe all this to?
what was I before?
My maid cleaning the pipe from the basin
about to lay lunch

Rocks like a Dürer landscape torn and hacked...

Rocks like a Dürer landscape torn and hacked,
goat path ascending; tiny flowers, shrubs and boulders
with blindest eyes, with tongues and lions' paws
Ledges on hanging ledges and beyond

– Words and more words can tire one; here 'montagna'
meaning the pitiless bruising splendid Love in
Death of Castille and meaning
'Mountain'; yet from that legged peninsula where Monte
Meant the white crown that dwarfed the midday steamers
scratching the frosted glass of Lake Maggiore;
'Mont' is the grim obverse of all our choices
Hanging its field of snow above
Terraces of *tourist hotels* or watching
The evening lights burn out from sanatoria.

The Greek word Vouni; fed with all the winds
Sleeting through Balkan passes down from Russia
Clattering the blackened ikons on the walls
These nights when all the Aegean ghosts are talking.
'Vouni' or 'mountain': meaning 'far from home'
meaning the sense of power for climbers seeing
the pencilled road the shrunken aqueduct
that spans a valley; all a reservoir
flashing like a window; many words to say
how clouds come smoking down between two crests
as from a fire, the words that partly say
The stubborn irreducible stony miles
not plough nor word can rule; where it is bad
to be when night, as now, comes on, and mountain
speaks a wild language made of mists and stones
of animal skulls like staring tribal masks
Oh – meaning 'mountain' – by the small white flower
shed adder skins turn slowly into dust.

The story is of battles and of conquest all the way...

The story is of battles and of conquest all the way
if not the language, still she conquered Greeks
and conquered little Greeks, which is much harder;
delinquent children welcomed her with shrieks

From names, dear me, she sometimes took a beating
Shopkeepers ran and poured her extra brandy
(with mice she fought, but only drew the battle)
but men and women bared their hearts to her
she conquered both the happy and neurotic
unlikely people told her their life-histories
and both would keep her sleepless with their prattle.

She conquered boredom, wantons, drink and people
but as we snuggled down to occupation
took herself off and left us, (as she had warned us)

to sense the pains of self determination.

TRANSLATIONS

GEORGE SEFERIS: *The King of Asine and Other Poems*
translated by Bernard Spencer with Nanos Valaoritis and Lawrence Durrell

Part I: Myth of our History (1935)

> 'Si j'ai du goût ce n'est guères
> Que pour la terre et les pierres.'
> ARTHUR RIMBAUD

1

The messenger,
For three years intently we awaited his arrival
Watching very closely
The shore the pines and the stars.
Joined with the blade of the plough or the keel of the ship
We were searching for the first seed
That the primeval drama might start again.

We returned to our homes, crushed
Our limbs sick our mouth ravaged
From the taste of rust and brine.
When we awoke we journeyed Northwards, strangers;
Plunged into the mists,
By the fleckless wings of swans which wounded us.
In the winter nights – the strong East wind maddened us
In the summer we were lost in the agony of the day which could not die.

We brought back
These carvings of a humble art.

2

Still another well within a cave.
Once it was easy to draw up effigies and ornaments
To please the friends who still remained faithful.

The ropes have snapped; only the grooves on the lip of the well
Remind us of our past happiness:
The fingers on the rim, as the poet said.
The fingers sense for a while the coolness of the stone
And the warmth of the body passes into it,
And the cave stakes and loses its soul
Every moment, filled with silence, without a drop of water.

3 *Remember the Baths by Which You Were Slain*

I woke with this marble head in my hands
Which tires my elbows and I do not know where to put it;
It was falling into the dream as I was rising from the dream
Thus our lives joined and it will be hard for them to disentangle.

I look into the eyes, neither shut nor open,
I speak to the mouth which keeps on trying to speak,
I hold the cheeks which have outstripped the skin
I can do no more.

My hands vanish and come back to me
Mutilated.

4 *Argonauts*

'The Soul too
If she would know herself
Must look within a soul.'
The stranger, the enemy, we saw him in the glass.

Good lads were the companions – did not grumble
Either at toil or at thirst or at the frosts
They bore themselves like the trees and waves
Accepting wind and rain
Accepting night and sun

With the change, not changing.
Good lads they were; whole days
They sweated at the oar with downcast eyes
Breathing rhythmically
And their blood reddened submissive skin.
Sometimes they sang, with downcast eyes
As we passed the island with the barbary figs
To the west, beyond the cape of dogs
Who bark.
If she would know herself, they said,
Into a soul she must look, they said.
And the oars beat the gold of the sea
In the setting sun.
Many capes we passed, many islands, the sea
Which leads to the other sea; gulls and seals.
Sometimes luckless women who wept
Keening for children they had lost;
And others raving called for Alexander
And glories buried in the depths of Asia.
We have moored on beaches full of the night scents,
With songs of birds, waters which left on the hands
Remembrance of great happiness;
But the journeys had no end.
Their souls became one with the oars and rowlocks,
With the grave face of the prow,
With the trace of the rudder,
With the water which fractured their image.
The companions finished, each in turn,
With downcast eyes. Their oars
Mark the place where they sleep on the shore.

No one remembers them. Justice.

5

We never knew them.
                    Deep down it was our hope that said
We had known them since our childhood.
We saw them twice perhaps and then they took to their ships;
Cargoes of coal, cargoes of grain, and our friends
Lost for ever beyond the ocean.
Dawn finds us by the wearied lamp
Clumsily and painfully scribbling on the paper
Boats, mermaids and sea-shells.
At nightfall we walk down to the river
Because it points us the way to the sea
And we pass the nights in cellars which smell of tar.

Our friends have gone
                    perhaps we never saw them, perhaps
We met them when sleep
Was still leading us near the breathing wave
Perhaps we seek them because we seek the other life,
Beyond the statues.

6 *M.R.*

The garden with its fountains in the rain
You will see it only through the low window
Behind the blurred pane. Your room
Will be lit only by the flame from the hearth
And sometimes the distant lightning will reveal
The wrinkles on your forehead, my old Friend.

The garden with its fountains which were, in your hands,
A rhythm of the other life, beyond the broken
Marbles and the tragic columns
A dance among the oleanders
By the new quarries,

A misty glass will have severed it from your days.
You will not breathe; the earth and the sap of the trees
Will leap from your memory to strike upon
This window beaten by the rain
Of the outer world.

7 *South Wind*

Westward the ocean melts in the range of mountains.
To our left the South wind maddens,
A wind making naked the bone from the flesh.
Our house among pines and carobs.
Big windows. Big tables
For us to write the letters we have been writing to you
These many months, which we drop
Into the separating void to fill it.

'Daystar, when you lower your eyes
Our hours were made sweeter than oil
On a wound, more joyful than cool water
On the palate, more peaceful than the cygnet's down.
Our life lay in your hands.
After the bitter bread of exile
If we remain nightly before the white wall
Your voice creeps by like a fiery hope.
And once again the wind strops
Upon the nerve a razor.

'We write to you each of us the same things
And each remains silent to the other,
Looking, each of us, separately at the same world,
The light and the darkness on the mountain,
And you.

'Who will lift this sorrow off our hearts?
Yesterday evening, tempest, and today

Again the weight of the sullen sky. Our thoughts
Like the pine needles of yesterday's rain
At the door of the house, heaped up and spent,
Try to build us a collapsing mansion.

'Among these decimated villages,
On this cape naked to the south wind,
With the mountain before us, hiding you,
O who will measure this decision of forgetfulness?
Who will accept our offerings and at this end
Of Autumn?'

8

What do they seek our souls as they travel
On decks of decayed ships
Crammed together with sallow women and weeping infants,
Unable to attain forgetfulness in the sight of the flying fish
Or the masts which point to the stars;
Worn out by the gramophone records,
Committed unwillingly to vain pilgrimages,
Whispering broken thoughts from foreign tongues?

What do they seek our souls as they travel
From harbour to harbour
On ships with rotting timbers?

Shifting broken stones, inhaling
More painfully every day the coolness of the pines,
Swimming in the waters here of this sea
And there of that sea,
Without the sense of touch,
Without men,
In a country which is no longer ours
No longer yours.

We knew that the islands were beautiful
Somewhere around where we are groping
A little higher or a little lower
A tiny distance.

9

The harbour is old, I cannot await any longer
The friend who left for the island of pines
Or the friend who left for the island of planes
Or the friend who left for the open sea.

I stroke the rusty cannons, I stroke the oars
So that my body may revive and decide.
The sails give only the salt
Smell of the late storm.

If I wished to remain alone, I sought
For solitude, I did not seek such a pining
The scattering of my soul to the horizon,
These outlines, these colours, this silence.

The Stars of night bring me back to the longing
Of Odysseus for the dead among the asphodels.
Here where we moored we wished to find among the asphodels
The valley which saw Adonis wounded.

10

Our native place is enclosed, all mountains,
Whose roof is the low sky day and night.
We have no rivers, we have no wells, we have no
Springs. Only a few cisterns, ringing hollow,
Which we adore.

A sound standing hollow, identical with
Our loneliness, identical with our love, our bodies.

Strange we were once able to build
Our houses, huts, byres. And our marriages,
The dewy coronel and the marriage fingers
Have become enigmatic, insoluble to the soul.
How were they born, our children, how grew up?

Our native place is shut in. They enclose it
The two black Simplegades. When we go down
On Sunday to the harbours for a breath of air,
We see, lit by the sunsets,
The shattered wrecks of voyages unfinished
Bodies no longer knowing the art of love.

11

Your blood sometimes froze like the moon
In the unfathomable night your blood
Spread its white wings over
The black rocks the shapes of the trees and the houses
With a glimmer of light out of the times of our childhood.

12 *A Bottle in The Sea*

Three rocks, some burnt pines, and a deserted chapel,
And further above
The same landscape copied starts again:
Three rusted rocks in the shape of a gate
A few pines burnt black and yellow
And a square house buried in whitewash;
And further above, again and again
The same landscape climbs like a stair
Up to the skyline, up to the sunset sky.

Here we moored the ship to mend our broken oars,
To quench our thirst and sleep.
The sea which embittered us is deep and unexplored
And spreads unending calm.
Here in the pebbles we found a coin
And threw dice for it;
The youngest won it and disappeared.

We re-embarked with our broken oars.

13 *Hydra*

Dolphins banners and the sound of cannon.
The sea once so bitter to your soul
Bore the bright ships with all their colours
Blue with its white wings it rolled and swayed them,
The sea once so bitter to your soul
Now bursting with colours under the sun.

White sails and sunlight and the dripping oars
Beat with the rhythm of drums on docile waves.

Your eyes would be lovely if they could look
Your arms would be splendid if they could stretch
Your lips as once they did, would live
At such a miracle;
You were seeking it

        what were you seeking by the ashes
Or in the rain in the mist in the wind
Even at the hour when lights grew dim
And the city faded and from the pavement flags
The Nazarene showed you his heart
What were you seeking? Why don't you come? What were you seeking?

14

Three red pigeons in the sun
Shaping our destiny in the sun
With colours and gestures of people
We once loved.

15 *Quid πλατανων Opacissimus?*

Sleep, like the green leaves of a tree, wrapped you round.
Like a tree you breathed in the calm light,
In the lucent source I discovered your form:
Eyelids shut, eyelashes brushing the water.
My fingers in the smooth grass found your fingers,
For an instant lay on the pulse,
Sensible of the heart's pain in another place.

Under the plane, near water, amongst laurel
Sleep removed you and made fragments of you
Around me, near me, never touching the whole,
Joined to your silence:
Seeing grown larger or smaller your shadow
Losing itself among the other shadows, in the other
World which grasped and released you.

The life which was given to us to live, we lived it.
Pity those who attend such patience,
Lost in the black laurel, under the heavy planes,
And those whose solitude speaks to cisterns and wells,
Who drown among the voice's circles.
Pity the companions who shared our loss and our sweat,
Who, like the crow flying beyond the ruins,
Were swallowed in the sun, hopeless of enjoying the reward.

Now give us, the other side of sleep, tranquillity.

Into the track, into the track again, into the track,
How many laps, how many rounds of blood, how many dark
Tiers: the people watching me
Who were watching when from the chariot
Splendid, I raised my hand, and they applauded.

The foam of the horses spatters me, when will the horses weary?
The axle grinds, the axle glows, when will the axle catch fire?
When will the reins snap, when will the hooves tread full on the ground
On the soft grass, among the poppies where
In spring you picked a daisy.
They were beautiful, your eyes, but you did not know where to look
Nor did I, I without a country
Who am struggling here, so many laps
And my knees fail me above the axle
Above the wheel above the cruel course
The knees fail easily when the gods wish it,
None can escape, strength is in vain, you cannot
Escape from the sea which cradled you and which you seek
In this hour of struggle among the panting of the horses,
With the reeds singing in autumn in the Lydian mode,
The sea which you cannot recover although you run
Although you circle in front of the dark bored Eumenides
Unforgiven.

17 *Astyanax*

Now that you are going, take with you the child
Who saw the light under that plane tree
On a day when trumpets rang and weapons glittered
And the sweating horses lowered their heads to the fountain
Touching the green surface of the water
At the trough with their moist nostrils.

The olive trees with the wrinkles of our fathers
The rocks with the wisdom of our fathers
And our brother's blood quick upon the earth
Were a mighty joy a rich pattern
For the souls who knew their prayer.

Now that you are going, now that the day of retribution
Dawns, now that no one can tell
Whom he is to kill and how he is to die,
Take with you the child who saw the light
Under the leaves of that plane
And teach him to study the trees.

18

I am sad because I let a broad river flow between my fingers
Without drinking a single drop.
Now I am sinking into the stone.
A small pine on the red soil
Is my only companion.
All I loved has gone with the houses
Which were new last summer
And collapsed under the autumn wind.

19

And if the wind blows it does not cool us
And the shadow remains narrow under the cypresses
And all around slopes rise to the mountains:

They weary us
The friends who do not know how to die.

20

In my breast the wound opens again
When the setting stars are kinsmen of my body
When silence falls under the footsteps of men.

These stones sinking into the years, where will they drag me?
The sea, the sea, who shall exhaust it?
I see the hands which beckon each dawn to the hawk and the vulture,
Bound to the rock which sorrow has made mine,
I see the trees which breathe the black calm of the dead
And then the smiles, which do not move, of the statues.

21

We that set out on this pilgrimage
Looked at the broken statues;
Our minds wandered and it seemed that life is not lost so easily
That Death has its unexplored ways
And a justice of its own;

That while we are dying upright on our feet
Sinking into the stone's embrace
United in hardness and weakness
The ancient dead escaped the course of doom and rose again
Smiling in a strange silence.

22

Now when so much has passed before our eyes
That our eyes have seen nothing, but beyond,
And memory following like the white screen one night in a walled place
Where we saw strange visions, stranger than you
Pass and vanish in the motionless foliage of a pepper tree;

For having known so well this destiny of ours
Wandering through broken stones, for three or six thousand years
Digging in ruined buildings which once, perhaps, were our homes
Trying to remember dates and heroes;
Shall we be able?...

For having been bound, for having been scattered,
For having struggled with unreal, as they put it, difficulties,
Lost, then striking again a road full of blind regiments
Sinking in marshes and in the lake of Marathon
Shall we be able to die according to the rules?

23

A little further
And we shall see the almond trees in blossom
The marble shining in the sun
The sea rippling.

A little further
Let us rise a little higher.

24

Here terminate the works of the sea, the works of love.
Those who shall exist here some day where we end,
If the blood should overflow to darken memory,
May they not forget us, the weak souls among the asphodels.
May they turn upon the mysterious darkness
The heads of the victims.
We who owned nothing shall teach them peace.

Part II: Ancient Dances (1936)

Santorin is geologically composed of pumice-stone and china-clay; in her bay islands have appeared and disappeared. This island was once the birthplace of a very ancient religion. The lyrical dances of a strict and heavy rhythm performed here were called Γυμνοπαιδίαι.

THE GUIDE TO GREECE

1 *Santorin*

Stoop if you can to the dark sea forgetting
The sound of a flute on naked feet
Stepping on your sleep in the other the sunken life.

Write if you can on your last shell
The day the name the land
And fling it in the sea that it may sink.

We stood naked on pumice-stone
Watching the islands rising,
Watching the red islands sinking
In their sleep in our own sleep
Standing naked here
We held the scales that were falling
In favour of Wrong.

Instep of power, unshadowed will, disciplined love
Plans that ripen in noontide sun
Avenue of Fate with the clapping of a new hand
On the shoulder;
In a land that crumbled enduring no longer
In a land that once we possessed
The islands are sinking ashes and rust.

Ruined altars
The friends forgotten
Palm-leaves in mud.

Let your hands travel if you can
Here on the curve of time with the ship
That touched the horizon.
When the dice struck on the slab
When the lance struck on armour
When the eye discovered the stranger
And love grew dry
In pierced souls;
When looking around you see
Feet reaped in a circle
Hands dead in a circle
Eyes dark in a circle;
When there is no choice any longer
Of a death which you seek for your own,
Listening to a yell
Even the yell of a wolf
Your own justice;
Let your hands travel if you can
Unfasten from treacherous time
Let yourself sink,

Must sink who carries the great stones.

2 *Mycenae*

Give me your hands, give me your hands, give me your hands.
I saw in the night
The sharp peak of the mountain
I saw the plain flooded
In the light of an invisible moon
I saw, on turning my head,
Black stones huddled
And my life stretched like a cord
The beginning and the end
The last moment;
My hands.

Must sink who carries the great stones;
These stones I have carried as long as I endured
These stones I have loved as long as I endured
These stones, my destiny.
Wounded by my own soil
Tortured by my own garment
Condemned by my own gods
These stones.

I know they know not, although
I have often followed
The path from killer to victim
From victim to vengeance
From vengeance to another crime
Feeling my way
Over the unexhausted purple
That night of homecoming
When the Furies started whistling
In the scarce grass
I have seen snakes coupled with vipers
Woven over the fated generation,
Our destiny.

Voices from stone from sleep
Deeper there where the world darkens
Memory of toil rooted in rhythm
Striking the earth with feet
Forgotten
Naked bodies buried in foundations
Of another time. Eyes
Concentrated, concentrated on a sign
You can no longer discern
And the soul
That strives to become your soul.

Even the silence is no longer yours
Here where the millstones have halted.

Part III: Poems from *A Book of Exercises*

1 *Five Japanese Poems*

I

Empty chairs
The statues returned
To the other museum.

II

What a job to gather
The scattered bits
Of every man.

III

What's wrong with the rudder?
The boat makes circles
And not a seagull in sight.

IV

Naked woman.
The pomegranate that broke
Was full of stars.

V

Whether it is dusk or whether it is dawn
White is the flower
Of the jasmine.

2 *Epitaph*

The lumps of coal in the mist
Were roses rooted in your heart
And the ash covered your face
Every morning.
Plucking shadows from the cypresses
You departed last summer.

3 *Epiphany, 1937*

The flowering sea and the mountains towards the waning moon
The great stone near the barbary figs and the asphodels
The pitcher that would not go dry at the close of day
And the shut bed by the cypresses and your hair
Golden; the stars of the Swan and that star Aldebaran.

I have kept my life I have kept my life travelling
Among the yellow trees with the slant of the rain
On silent slopes piled with leaves of beech;
No fires on their crest. Dusk falls.
I have kept my life; on your left hand line,
A mark on your knee, do they exist
On the sand of the summer gone
Do they exist where the north wind blew, while I hear
Around the frozen lake the strange tongue?
The faces I see ask nothing, nor the woman
Who walks bent above the child she is suckling.
I climb the mountains; darkened vales; the snowy
Plain, the snowy plain stretching, they ask nothing
Not the time shut in dumb chapels
Nor the lands that stretch and seek, nor the roads;
I have kept my life whispering in the vast silence
I no longer know how to talk or think; whispers
Of the sea at night on the pebbles like human speech
Like the memory of your voice saying 'happiness'.

I shut my eyes searching the secret meeting of the waters
Under the ice the smile of the sea, the locked wells
Fumbling with my veins those veins that escape me
Where the water-flowers end, where ends that man
Who walks blind on the snow of silence.

I have kept my life, with him, seeking the water which touches you
Heavy drops on the green leaves, on your face
In the empty garden, drops on the motionless cistern
Aiming at a swan dead among its white feathers;
Living trees and the gaze of your eyes.

This road has no relay, it never ends, however much you try
To remember your childhood days, those who went away
Those who disappeared into sleep, into marine tombs,
However much you long for the bodies you loved to stoop
Under the hard branches there of the plane trees
Where halted a bared ray of the sun
Where a dog shivered and your heart beat.
This road has no relay: I have kept my life. The snow
And the water frozen under the horses' footprints.

4 *In the Manner of G.S.*

However far I go voyaging, still Greece wounds me.
At Pelion among the chestnuts the Centaur's shirt
Slid through the leaves to cover my body
As I climbed the hillside, and the sea followed,
Mounting like a thermometer's mercury
Until at last we struck the mountain waters.
At Santorin touching the islands which foundered
Hearing a flute play, somewhere across the pumice,
An arrow suddenly shot
From the confines of vanishing youth
Nailed my hands to the deck.

At Mycenae I raised the great stones and the treasuries of Atreus,
Lay down to sleep beside them at 'La Belle Helene',
Losing them only at dawn when Cassandra shrieked
With a cock hanging at her black throat.

At Spetsai at Poros and at Mykonos,
The barcaroles sickened me.
What do they want, all those
Who imagine themselves in Athens or Piraeus?
One comes from Salamis and asks another
If perhaps he is just 'coming from Concord Square'?
'No from Constitution' replies the other blandly,
'Ran into John and he stood me an ice.'
Meanwhile Greece is travelling onwards.

We know nothing, hardly even know ourselves
As beachcombers, all of us,
Knowing not even the bitterness of the harbour
When every ship has gone
And those who experience it we jeer at.

Strange people who declare themselves to be
In Attica, and yet are nowhere:
They buy sugar almonds for their weddings,
Hold hair tonics in hand, get photographed;
The man I saw this morning sitting
Before a background of pigeons and flowers,
Let the hand of the old photographer smooth out
The wrinkles left on his face by the birds of the air.

Meanwhile Greece travels on, unceasingly travels
And if one sees 'The Aegean flowering with corpses'
It is those who tried to swim after the huge ship and catch it,
Those who wearied waiting for vessels which never seemed to start,
The 'Else', the 'Samothrace' and the 'Ambrakikos'.
They whistle now as night falls on Piraeus,

They whistle again and again but no capstan
Stirs; no wet chain
Flashes in the sinking light of the sun
And petrified in gold and white the captain stands his ground.

However far I go voyaging still Greece wounds me,
Screens of mountains, archipelagoes, bald granite
The ship which journeys onward is called AGONY 937.

Part IV: Poems from 'Log Book' 1 and 2

1 *Mathias Pascalis among the Roses* (1937)

I've been smoking since morning without a break
If I stop now the roses will curl round me
Smother me in thorns and shed petals
They all grow crookedly but with the same red tone,
Staring: they expect to see someone: nobody passes;
I watch them from behind the smoke of my pipe,
Scentless, on a dropping stem;
In another existence a woman was saying to me 'you can touch this hand
And this rose is yours, it is yours you can take it
Now or later, just whenever you wish'.

I descend the steps still smoking
And the roses descend with me irritated
And in their manner there is something of the voice
At the roots of the cry, down there where man
Begins to shout: 'Mother' or 'Help'
Or of the little white cries of love.

It is a small garden full of rose trees
A few square yards which go down with me
As I descend the steps, skyless;
And her aunt was in the habit of telling her
'Antigoni you forgot your gym today,
At your age I didn't wear corsets, in my time.'
Her aunt was a wretched creature with varicose veins
Wrinkles around her ears and a moribund nose
Yet her words were always full of wisdom
One day I saw her touching Antigoni's breast
Like a child stealing an apple.

Will I perhaps meet the old woman as I thus descend?
When I left she said to me: 'Who knows when we'll meet again?'
Later I read about her death in some old newspapers

And about Antigoni's wedding and the wedding of Antigoni's daughter
Without the steps coming to an end or my tobacco smoke
Which gives me the flavour of a haunted ship
With a Mermaid crucified to the wheel when she was still beautiful.

2 *Our Sun* (1937)

It was yours and mine, this sun. We shared it.
Who is suffering behind the shot silk? Who is dying?
A woman was shouting, beating her dry breasts 'Cowards
They have taken my children and torn them to pieces, you killed them
With your strange stare at the fireflies in the evening
Lost in your blind contemplation.'
The blood was drying on a hand made green by a tree,
A soldier slept grasping a lance which shone against his body.

It was ours, this sun, we saw nothing behind the gold embroideries
Later the messengers came breathless and dirty
Stammering unintelligible words
Twenty days and nights across sterile lands
And nothing but thorns
Twenty days and nights and the torn bellies of the horses
And not a minute's pause to drink the rain water.
You said, let them rest first, then let them talk,
The light had blinded you
They died touching the rays of the sun saying 'We have no time'
You were forgetting that no one ever rests.

A woman was howling: 'Cowards' like a dog in the night
Once she must have been beautiful like you
With a moist mouth, the veins alive under the skin
With love –

It was ours, this sun; you kept it all and would not follow me
And then I learned these things behind the silk and the gold;
We have no time. The messengers were right.

3 *Morning*

Open your eyes and unfold
The black cloth full and tighten it.
Open your eyes wide and fix your eyes
Rivet, rivet your eyes, now you know
That the black cloth is unfolded
Not in sleep nor in the water
Nor when the wrinkled eyelids fall
And sink aslant like shells,
Now you know that the black skin of the drum
Covers your whole horizon
When you open your eyes refreshed, thus.
Between the equinox of spring and the equinox of autumn
Here are the running waters here is the garden
Here the bees hum among the branches
And ring in the ears of an infant
And the sun, there! And the birds of paradise
A great sun greater than light.

4 *The Return of the Exile* (1938)

'My old friend what are you looking for?
You have returned from years of absence
With images which you have built
Under alien skies
Far away from your own land.'

'I am looking for my garden;
The trees come only to my waist
And the hills are low as terraces
And yet when I was a child
I played among the grass
Under the great shadows
For hours I used to run
Breathless across the slopes.'

'My old friend be patient
Slowly you will become accustomed
Together we will climb the hills
Following your familiar paths
Together we will sit and rest
Underneath the plane trees' dome
The garden and the slopes you loved
Slowly will come back to you.'

'I am looking for the house I knew
I am looking for its tall windows
Darkened by the ivy
I am looking for the ancient column
Landmark of the mariner.
How can I walk into this hutch?
The roof comes only to my shoulders
However far I look, I see
Men on their knees
Men in the attitude of prayer.'

'My old friend can't you hear me?
Slowly you will become accustomed
Here is your house in front of you
And at this door will soon come knocking
Your dear ones and your friends
To welcome you and wish you well.'

'Why is your voice so far away
Lift your head a little higher
That I may grasp the words you say
When you talk you seem to shrink
As though you sank into the ground.'

'My old friend reflect a while
Slowly you will become accustomed
Your dreams have built
An unsubstantial land with laws
Alien to the world of men.'

'Now not a whisper comes to me
The earth has swallowed my last friend
How strange from time to time
Everything gets lower here
Around me whirl and sweep
A thousand scything chariot wheels.'

5 *The King of Asine* (1939)

’Ασίνη ν τε   ILIAD

All morning round and round the castle we were searching
Beginning from the shadowy side where the sea
Green and without reflection – breast of the slain peacock –
Accepted us like time, with never a gap in it.
Veins of rock came downward from on high,
Twisted vines and naked, many branched, reliving
At the touch of water, which followed by the eye
Tried to escape the tiresome cradle-swinging,
Losing its strength by small degrees.

From the sunny side a long beach wide open
And the light splashing jewels on the great walls,
No living thing about, the wild doves having gone,
And the King of Asine whom we had searched for these two years
Unknown, forgotten by all, even by Homer.
Only one word in the Iliad and that uncertain,
Dropped here like the gold sepultural mask:
You tapped it once – remember the echo? Hollow in the light
Like a dry jar in the dug earth,
And the same echo in the sea with our oars;
The King of Asine a void now under the mask,
Always with us, always with us, underneath a name
’Ασίνη ν τε...’Ασίνη ν τε...
                    And his children statues
His desires the beat of bird's wings and the wind

233

Between the spaces of his meditations, and his ships
Anchored in an invisible harbour:
Under the mask a void.

Behind the large eyes, the curving lips, the ringlets,
In relief on the gold cover of our lives,
A shadowy point travelling like a fish
In the dawn-blue waters of the sea, when you see it,
A void always with us:
And the bird which flew away last winter,
With a broken wing,
The ark of life,
And the young woman who went suddenly away to play
With summer's dogtooth,
And the soul which searched the underworld chirping,
And the country like a great plane-leaf dragged down
By the torrents of the sun
With the old monuments and the contemporary sorrow.

And the poet lingers, looking at the stones, wondering:
Does there still exist then
Among these broken lines, points, edges, hollows and curves,
Does there still exist
Here where rain and wind and all decay in passing meet,
The motion of a face, shape of a tenderness,
Of those who diminished so strangely in our lives?
Who remained wave-shadows, thoughts in the sea's limitlessness?
Or perhaps not nothing, but only the weight remains,
The nostalgia of a weight of a living being,
Here where we live unsubstantially, bending
Like the withes of horrible willow
Heaped on the lengths of hopelessness
While the yellow streams bring down
Rushes uprooted with the mud,
Image of a face petrified in a decision of bitterness.
The poet himself a void.

Shieldbearer, the warring sun comes up,
And from the depths of the cave a frightened bat
Strikes the light like an arrow on a shield
'Ασίνη ν τε...'Ασίνη ν τε.
                    Might it have been the King of Asine
We hunted for so carefully on this acropolis,
Our fingers touching, sometimes his very touch upon the stones?

6 *Stratis the Mariner among the Agapanthus Flowers* (1941)

There are no asphodels, no violets, no hyacinths;
How then will you talk to the dead?
For the dead know only the language of flowers
That is why they keep silent –
They journey and keep silent, they endure and keep silent
In the assembly of dreams, in the assembly of dreams.

If I start to sing I would cry out
And if I cry out
The agapanthi admonish silence
Raising the small blue hand of an Arabian child
Or the footprint of a goose into the air.

It is weary and difficult, the living do not suffice
First because they cannot speak, and then
Because I need to ask the dead
Before I can advance any further.
There is no other way. As soon as I fall asleep
The companions cut the silver strings
And the sack of the winds empties
I fill it; it empties, I fill it; it empties
I awake
Like the gold fish swimming
In the furrows of lightning,
And the wind and the flood and the human bodies
And the agapanthi nailed like the arrows of fate

Into the thirsty earth
Shaken by spasmodic gestures
As if loaded on some antique cart
Rolling down broken roads on ancient cobbles,
Agapanthi – asphodels of the negroes:
How can I master this religion?

The first thing God made is love
Then comes blood
And the thirst for blood
Which goads it on
The sperm of the body like salt.
The first thing God made is the long journey,
The house is waiting,
With its blue smoke
And an old watchdog waiting
For the returning traveller to die.
But the dead must show me the way.
It is the agapanthi that hold them speechless
Like the sea's depths or the water in a glass.
While the companions drag on in Circe's palace
My trusty Elpenor! My poor fool Elpenor!
Or, can't you see them?
– 'Help! Oh Help us!' –
On the blackened crest of Psara?

7 *Calligraphy*

Sails on the Nile
Songless birds with one wing
Seeking the other in silence;
Fumbling in the absent sky
The body of a marble youth;
Writing with invisible ink in the blue
A hopeless cry.

8 *Old Man on the River Bank*
(to Nani Panajiotopoulos)

And yet we must reckon how we advance:
It is not enough to feel to suffer to move,
Nor that your body be in danger in an old embrasure
When the hot oil or molten lead furrow the walls.

And yet we must reckon whither we advance,
Not as our pain would have it and our hungry children, and the chasm of
        companions' cries from the opposite shore,
Nor in the way it is whispered by the dimmed light in a little hospital,
In the clinical light which flickers on the pillow of the youth operated upon
        at noon,
But in some other way: I may wish to express it as
The wide river flowing from the great lakes deep-buried in Africa,
That was once God, and then became a road, a gift-bearer, judge, delta,
Who is never the same as the old scholars taught,
Nevertheless the body remains, the same layers, and points,
The same orientation.

I want only to speak simply, to be given this grace,
Because the song has been loaded with so much music that little by little
        it is sinking,
And we have decorated our art so much that its face has been eaten away
        by the gold,
And it is time for us to say our few words because tomorrow the soul will
        set sail.

If pain is the human lot we are not men merely in order to suffer,
That is why I think so much these days of the great river,
That great advancing meaning among the herbs and weeds,
Among the grazing beasts which drink, men who sow and reap,
Among great tombs and small habitations of the dead –
That current which goes its way, not so different from the blood of men,
And the eyes of men looking directly beyond without the fear in their hearts,
Without a daily tremor for the small or even the large things,
When they look ahead like the wayfarer, used to measure his road by stars,

Not like us the other day looking at the shut garden of a sleeping Arab house:
Behind trellises the cool small garden changing, becoming larger and smaller,
Changing, as we watched, the shape of our desire and spirit,
In the dropping of noonday we the patient dough of a world which,
       expelling, kneads us,
Caught in the sumptuous nets of a life which was right and went to dust,
       foundered in the sands,
Leaving behind it that indefinite cradle-motion of a tall palm, making us
       giddy.

9 *Stratis the Mariner on the Dead Sea*

> *In the chapels built on legendary sites one may read the*
> *appropriate passage from the Bible in English, and beneath it:*
>   'THIS IS THE PLACE GENTLEMEN.'
>
>   Letter of Stratis the Mariner from Jerusalem – 22nd July, 1942

Jerusalem derelict city
Jerusalem city of refugees.

At noon you sometimes see a mass
Of black leaves scattered
Swept on the asphalt road
It is the birds migrating under the sun
But no one raises his head.

Jerusalem derelict city!

Unknown tongues from the tower of Babel
Without relation to the grammar
The chronicle or the book of psalms
Which they taught you to read at Autumn
When the fishermen moored their boats to the jetty;
Unknown tongues glued
Like cigarette-ends to decayed lips.

Jerusalem city of refugees.

Yet always their eyes utter the same word
Not the word that became Man – the Lord forgive us –
Not journeys to see new lands, but
The dark train of escape where the infants
Feed on the dirt and the sins of their fathers
Where the middle-aged feel the chasm
Growing between the body
That drags on behind like a wounded camel
And the souls with the endless courage, as they say;
It is the ships that carry them
Standing erect like stuffed bishops in the hold
Only to end one evening, lightly
On the sea-weed of the deep.

Jerusalem derelict city.

Three monks from Mount Athos
Sailed to the River Jordan
And moored on the banks
Their little red Caique;
Three months they journeyed
And moored to a branch
On the banks of the River Jordan
The offering of a refugee.
Three months they hungered
Three months they thirsted
Three months they were sleepless
They came from Mount Athos
They came from Salonica
The three enslaved monks.

We are all like the Dead Sea
Many fathoms deep under the surface of the Aegean.
Come with me and I will show you the place.

In the Dead Sea
There are no fishes
There are no sea-urchins

There is no sea-weed
There is no life.

No creatures live there
Creatures with a belly
To suffer hunger
With nerves to feel,
And suffer pain.

THIS IS THE PLACE GENTLEMEN.

In the Dead Sea
The wares of contempt
belong to no one;
Who cares?

Heart and thought
Stiffen in the salt
That is bitter
And fuse with the mineral world.

THIS IS THE PLACE GENTLEMEN.

They are all in the Dead Sea
Enemies and friends
Wives, children
And relatives;
Go, and seek them there.

There they lie in Gomorrah
Down in the depths
In perfect happiness
For they await
No message.

And now we continue our journey
Many fathoms deep under the surface of the Aegean.

ODYSSEUS ELYTIS: *The Mad Pomegranate Tree*
translated by Bernard Spencer with Nanos Valaoritis

The Mad Pomegranate Tree

In these whitewashed courtyards where the South Wind blows
Whistling through arcaded rooms, O tell me
Is it the mad pomegranate tree
That darts into the light scattering her fertile laughter
With whims and whispers of the wind
O tell me is it the mad pomegranate tree
That shakes with newborn foliage at dawn
Opening all her colours high with shudders of triumph?

When the naked girls awake in the plains
Reaping the clovers with their fair hands
Tossing the depths of their slumber
O tell me is it this mad pomegranate tree
That slips the lights in their fresh baskets
That overflows their names with songs
Is it the mad pomegranate tree
That fights the shadows of the world?

The jealous day adorns herself with seven glowing wings
Surrounding the eternal sun with a million prisms
O tell me, is it this mad pomegranate tree
That grasps a horse's mane with a hundred lashes
In her runaway race
Sometimes sad and sometimes grumbling
O tell me, is it the mad pomegranate tree
Shouting the dawn of a new hope?

O tell me is it this mad pomegranate tree
Rejoicing in the far-away
Shaking a handkerchief of leaves and fresh fire
A sea pregnant with a thousand ships
With waves that run and roll for ever
Towards untrodden shores, O tell me
Is it the mad pomegranate tree
That creaks her rigging high in the lucid air?

In the grape-blue heights feasting and flaring
Defiant, dangerous, tell me
Is it the mad pomegranate tree
Smashing with light clean in the middle of the world
The tempests of the demon
Spreading from end to end
The yellow mane of dawn
Embroidered with crops and songs
O tell me is it the mad pomegranate tree
That swiftly unfastens the silk dress of the day?

In April's petticoats and the cicadas of August
O tell me, she who plays, she who works, she who drives us crazy
Shaking from Menace all his bad black shadows
Pouring drunken birds into the sun
O tell me she that opens her wings in the breast of things
In the breast of our deep dreams
Is it the mad pomegranate tree?

The Lemon Trees

Listen, the poet laureates
move only among plants with unfamiliar names:
box or acanthus.
For me, I love the roads which find their way to grassy
ditches where in half dried pools the boys
catch a few famished eels;
the tracks which follow the slopes
descend between tufts of reeds
and end in the back gardens among the lemon trees.

Better if the clamour of the birds
vanishes swallowed in the sky:
clearer sounds the murmur
of the friendly branches in air that hardly moves
and the touch of this smell
which never quite leaves the earth
and fills the heart with a restless languor.
Here like a miracle the war
of the torn passions is silent
here to us poor falls our share too of riches,
the smell of the lemons.

See, in these silences when things
yield themselves and seem about to betray
their ultimate secret
sometimes the feeling comes
of discovering a flaw in Nature,
the dead point of the world, the link that does not hold
the thread to unravel which finally lands us
in the centre of a truth.

The eyes fumble round
the mind searches, tunes, parts asunder
in the scent which spreads like a stain
when the day gradually tires.
The silences in which one sees
in every human shadow that draws away
some disturbed divinity.

But the illusion fails and time brings us back
into loud cities where the blue shows
only in scraps high up between the eaves.
Rain tires the earth; the tedium
of winter thickens on the houses,
light becomes a miser – the soul bitter.
When one day through a half-closed doorway
among the trees in a courtyard
shines out the yellow of the lemons;
and the ice of the heart melts
and in our breasts peal
their songs
the golden trumpets of sunlight.

Don't ask us for the word which cuts and shapes...

Don't ask us for the word which cuts and shapes
our formless spirit, there are letters of flame
to utter, nothing to shine like a crocus
lost in the middle of a dusty field.

Fortunate he who walks serenely
on good terms with himself and others,
indifferent to his shadow the glare of summer
prints on a flaking!

Don't ask us the formula to lay worlds open,
there is only some twisted syllable dry like a twig.
Only this today we can tell you,
the thing we are not, the thing we do not want.

Bring me the sunflower so that I can transplant it...

Bring me the sunflower so that I can transplant it
into my soil burnt with brine,
for it to show all day to the sky's mirroring blue
the anxiety of its amber face.

Things that are dark lean towards clarity
the bodies of things flow out and empty themselves
in colours: colours in music. Vanishing
is therefore the luckiest of chances.

Bring me the flower which leads
to the springs of transparent gold
where life like an essence turns to vapour
bring me the sunflower crazed with light.

To shelter, pale and preoccupied...

To shelter, pale and preoccupied
in the shadow of a burning garden wall,
to listen among the plum trees and ivy tendrils
to the clucking of thrushes, the rustling of snakes.

In cracks of the ground or on the vetch
to watch the files of red ants
now breaking, now entwining
from the tops of tiny hillocks.

To watch between leaves the far-off
pulsing on the spangled sea
while a tremulous shrilling of cicada
rises from the bald peaks.

And walking in the sun which dazzles
to feel with wonder and sadness
how all life and its pain
is in this following a wall
crowned with sharp splinters of bottle.

The Mourning Girl

You sat on the rock waiting
as the night came on
and the pupil of your eye showed
how much you suffered.

And your lips were drawn in a way
exposed and trembling
as if your soul were whirled like a spinning-wheel
and your tears were pleading.

And you had in your mind the thought
of yielding to tears
you were a body falling from its bloom
back to its seed.

But there was no cry from your heart's breaking:
that breaking became
the meaning, scattered upon the world
by the sky, all stars.

Denial

Upon the hidden beach
white as a dove
we were thirsty in the mid-day heat
the water was bitter.

Across the yellow sand
we wrote her name.
Marvellously the breeze blew:
scattered our writing.

We were daring then, we were brilliant,
full of longing and passion:
we snatched our life. What fools!
Life has changed now.

SELECTED PROSE

The Exhibition of Dutch Art at Burlington House

For the criticism of this article from the literary and artistic standpoints, and its complete condemnation from both, I am indebted to my dear friend, Carel Ramsay Jones.

The British Public has long been the target for the witticisms of its neighbours, who saw fit to attack it for its alleged lack of sensibility and appreciation of art. From the immense attendance at the recent Flemish exhibition, I gather that it has triumphantly freed itself from this stigma. This evidence has been amply supported by the success of the Dutch exhibition.

I suppose that the phrase 'Dutch Art', in the first place, inevitably conjures up in the ordinary person's mind a medley of the homely sunlit interiors of Vermeer, de Hooch, and Terborch.

To take these three at random and run them rather unfairly together, I should give as their virtues a very clear knowledge of what they want to do, an admirable technique, a sense of colour, and a sense of space. I should then go on, in my sweeping way, to say that their ambitions were very limited, and no great strain, consequently, was put upon their technique. That their sense of colour was apt to be that of the fashion expert rather than that of the artist, and their sense of space was too often cheaply secured by a mere insistence on perspective.

When they look at these pictures (I am generalising again) the feelings of most people could be put under the headings of: 'Domestic', 'Restful', and 'Cheerful'. I leave out the people who went round with notebooks recording those pictures which they recognised as hanging in their own houses or their friends'. Or rather I will make a fourth heading for the feelings of 'Recognition'. No, this is not inclusive enough: 'My dear, here is a picture lent by the poor dear King. We *must* come and look at it!'

These minor Dutch artists could take an interest in the ordinary. That is, in itself, a good thing. The trouble is that it was not a painter's interest. It was an ordinary interest. Cézanne's and Van Gogh's apples did not come from the same tree as theirs.

This is not roundly to condemn Vermeer and his fellows, for they are not in any way pretentious. Their little domestic idylls have often a certain literary charm. Their fault is that they are inclined to bore.

The cheap-jack oratory of Frans Hals drove me for refuge to the small room of primitives. It is interesting to reflect that the smile of the 'Laughing Cavalier' will go down to posterity in company with that of 'Mona Lisa' and of 'the World's Sweetheart', Miss Mary Pickford. 'Mona Lisa' deserves better.

The primitives were there, it seems, to show how far from grace Dutch art had strayed since its childhood.

Then there was Rembrandt, the *pièce de résistance*. It was a temptation to shirk the issue and confine myself to a quotation from *Masterpieces of Dutch Painting*, for sale in all book shops. 'Rembrandt, the supreme painter who revealed to the world the poetry of twilight and all the magic mystery of gloom.'

To talk, after this, of Rembrandt's chiaroscuro seems quite a bathos.

Rembrandt, a man of genius and bad taste, was not at his best in his portraits. I hate the 'Man in the Gold Helmet'. But sometimes his portraits, too, have a really plastic greatness, for example the 'Architect' and the 'Jewish Bride'. Rembrandt's dramatic sense often leads him into danger. In comes the Scissor-Man of the literary and snaps off the fingers of the artist.

His etchings were more consistently good than his paintings.

And Van Gogh. It is no good to argue that Van Gogh was not a good artist because he was mad. He was a good artist but not a great one. He was not great because he had not sufficient form, though his line is sometimes magnificent. He was not great because he often forgot himself and became a poet. But I was nearly arrested as an incendiary for trying to light a torch at the flames of Van Gogh and with it kindle a Promethean fire in the 'Ideal Homes' of de Hooch.

I noticed particularly 'The Artist's Room', ('My dear, is the window open or shut?') but some of his best were not exhibited.

It is an exhibition to which you can take your parents, or indeed anyone. I saw two members there of the Cock House of my old school.

February 1929

Note on Auden

Auden doesn't go soft and sermonise. Because our pity is appealed to so much, an emotion you can't live with for long at a stretch, sermonising is a particular fault of contemporary poets. He succeeds in brutalising his thought and language to the level from which important poetry proceeds.

November 1937

Ideas about Poems

Folk poetry, both ancient and modern, shows a remarkable callousness (e.g. 'Och Johnny I hardly knew you...' and 'A handsome young airman lay dying...'). And J. Synge, a writer who was consciously basing his art on the life of the common people, said that poetry must become 'brutal'.

That is to say that more sophisticated poetry, if it is to have any force, has also to be rooted in the uncivilised layers of the mind, where what is ugly and what is beautiful can both be contemplated and do not exclude each other.

Nowadays, through living in a more urban and controlled society, a poet starts off with a tenderer heart and a weaker stomach than, let us say, an Elizabethan. To write poetry he has to brutalise himself back out of his upbringing. His dangers are that, faced with injustice, violence and squalor, he may either get numb, frigid, over-intellectual, or soft, sentimental.

The capacity for pity and the capacity for scientific detachment may both be valuable to him in the rest of his life but they are dangerous to him as a poet. Pity and disgust and the scientific attitude are all attitudes of separation, not of joining. (Though pity or disgust might provide the necessary impulse to begin writing.) True poetry is a dance in which you take part and enjoy yourself.

This is the real meaning of the old definition of poetry as giving 'pleasure' (where we are inclined to say 'truth'). This, too, is what Yeats meant when he said, 'passive suffering is not a proper subject for poetry', and when he said, 'The Muses are women and love the embraces of the "warty" (sexy) boys'.

1942

Keith Douglas: An Obituary Note

We wish to express our profound regret for the death in action, during the battle of France, of Keith Douglas who had contributed to several numbers of *Personal Landscape*. As a captain in a tank unit he took part in the Allied advance which followed Alamein, and in the course of it was wounded.

It was in North Africa that he wrote the poems we were fortunate enough to be able to publish, and which are among the small amount of successful verse written by soldiers from the battlefield during the present war. His most remarkable qualities as a poet are his economical use of language for statement (metrical and sound effects are rare), the surprise and force of his images (c.f. 'Cairo Jag', and '*Vergissmeinnicht*'), and the maturity of the 'pity' (as for instance in 'Enfidaville'). He regarded himself as being in the tradition of Wilfred Owen.

A volume of his poems and his journal of the North Africa campaign, with his own illustrations, are being published by *Poetry, London*.

1945

The Wind-Blown Island of Mykonos

If you look on the map to the east of Greece you will see the islands which are called the Cyclades. They hang like a necklace across the south of the Aegean Sea. All Greek islands are different. I am here concerned with one called Mykonos, where I would rather spend my summer than anywhere in the world.

The ship, as ships often do, brought us into Mykonos at six o'clock in the morning. But since the arrival of the ship from Athens is a great occasion, the whole population was down at the little harbour to meet us. And what I saw was more remarkable even than I had been told. Above are the tawny, lion-coloured hills scribbled across with rough stone walls such as you find in the English Cotswolds. At the foot of these hills lies the little fishing harbour, so small that you could hold a conversation across it. And every house in the little town is white, with a flat or a domed white roof. It is like one of those towns made of white sugar in the fairy stories. In the shady white lanes which twist like a maze among the houses even the stone flags of the pavement are white. The windmills and the little chapels scattered across the bare hillsides are gleaming white. The fishermen wear sashes of white, or white and blue, around their waists. Even the cats, I observed – and very well fed, happy-looking animals they were – were white or had white shirt-fronts.

Before the war you could get a room for a shilling a night; a very clean room with ikons or holy pictures on the walls representing, in ancient dark colours and tarnished silver, the Virgin Mary or the victory of St George over the dragon. The island proudly boasts that it never came under the power of the Turks during their occupation of the Greek mainland. Indeed, there is a statue to a local lady who financed and personally led into battle a squadron which fought against the invaders.

In Mykonos there is nearly always a wind. If you are one of the people who hate wind, as I am in principle, this may sound uncomfortable. But it is because of this wind, which blows down from Thrace, that you are cool in Mykonos at a time of year when you would be roasting in Athens. In the end, you come to like this wind, as it scours through the town as though it would leave nothing that was not white and speckless, and blows the extravagant blue of the sea into white flecks of foam. Rather the incessant wind by day, and, by night, the wind sighing like a ghost around the town and stirring the black ikons on the walls, rather that than the flat sea and everyone biting their nails and getting short-tempered, as they always do on the sultry, calm days.

Mykonos, like the other islands of the Cyclades, is bare and rocky, and supports very little agriculture. In summer, the population lives by the tourists, to whom they sell their gay woven materials, and by fishing. In winter a number of men and women go to get jobs on the mainland. In common with other Greeks, the islanders are very friendly, and in conversation your landlady or the old woman in the shop may address you as '*matia mou*', that is to say, 'my eyes', or, as we might say, 'ducks' or 'dearie'.

This friendliness and hospitality is sometimes embarrassing. I was once taken to a village wedding up in the hills. My host, a fine-looking fellow with a handlebar moustache and a shaven head, gave me glass after glass of the excellent village wine. But with each glass of wine, as is the custom, I was expected to eat a small piece of bread on which was balanced some goat-cheese so strong that a single taste took the skin off your tongue and palate. I found it wise to accept the wine and drop the food on the sandy floor, until I stood in a little circle of bread and cheese, which I hoped was not noticed in the general litter.

Mykonos is not only a beautiful island, but a very strange one. When the wind blows at night through the white moonlit streets, you find it easy to believe some of the ghost stories which the islanders tell you. One of the figures who haunted the island was no ghost. He was Nicola, the madman, whom you would sometimes come across engaged in his strange ritual of measuring. Nicola, driven by some obsession, would spread his arms in a doorway or at a window and measure it – so many arms' length up and so many arms' length across, looking, as he did so, like a man signalling in semaphore. Then he would move with his strange crouching run to the next doorway and measure that in a similar fashion. Sometimes, when the moon made the white streets look more ghostly than usual, Nicola would be induced to abandon his strange geometry and take, instead, the part of Hamlet. From goodness knows where he had acquired a skull, which people said belonged to a woman he had once loved. Holding the skull at arm's length, he would talk to it and make court in wild whirling phrases which would not have sounded out of place in a play by some melancholy Jacobean dramatist.

There were other strange things on Mykonos. There was a type of large lizard which was reputed ungallantly to attack women on lonely paths, but always, it was said, would run away if a man or even a boy child came up. And then there were those priests, a couple of grand old men with long beards and hair done up in buns under their stove-pipe hats, whom a friend of mine tried to photograph as they sat on a bench outside the church. The old men were apparently unwilling to be photographed, and made signs of protest. But my friend, a journalist who is an experienced photographer, begged permission and took two exposures of them. When the film came to be developed, there was the church, there was the bench, but there were no priests, nobody was sitting there at all.

One day I went to Delos, that island across the water from Mykonos where in ancient times there was a famous oracle. The city has been largely excavated and it is a strange experience to walk in the streets which died nearly two thousand years ago, and in the market, the harbour district and the residential area, where you can still see the fine mosaic floors laid down in their houses by the rich merchants. The only people who live on Delos are the coastguard and the manager of the little hostel with its small museum. As it happened, there was a storm, and the steamer was unable to fetch us again, so for three days we lived at the hostel. As the food got short we were very sadly reduced to eating the manager's tame rabbits. At last the storm went down a little and we were rescued. I have a vivid picture in my mind of the little steamer being tossed about on waves each of which seemed to me as big as an island.

But you will be wondering what you do as the daily round of holiday life. The answer is, you bathe, you sit in the unfailing sun on sand more soft and silvery than I have every known elsewhere, and you sail. A lot of people have a weakness for islands. I confess to this weakness, especially for the beautiful and hospitable islands of Greece. Once you have visited them, in peace time, they will hang in your mind like a fantastic dream of happiness. A well-known Greek poet, George Seferis, has written a poem which expresses this island symbolism. Some travellers are asking what they are looking for in life. They reply:

> We knew that the islands were beautiful
> Somewhere around where we are groping
> A little higher, a little lower,
> A tiny distance.

September 1946

Dialogue on Poetry

by María Alfaro and Bernard Spencer

The following dialogue, undertaken by our collaborator María Alfaro with the English poet Bernard Spencer, was recently broadcast on a special programme of the BBC. Bernard Spencer, a professor currently at the British Institute in Madrid, is a notable young English poet, whose works, though few in number, have been very well received by critics.

MA: What is poetry? The question is not easy to answer. In the poetic universe, there is space everywhere: for the lyrical and the everyday, for clarity and fog. Poetry can, and has to be, on many occasions, enigmatic, because man is the source of enigmas, and there is no object, no being, no moment, that doesn't turn out to be impenetrable. On the other hand, more than from happiness, the poetic soliloquy is born from misfortune.

BS: So, do you believe that the poet has to be, inevitably, obscure and enigmatic?

MA: Obscurity also has its limits. At times, what can happen is that the poet, drawing down the curtain between himself and his readers, conceals the universe from himself.

BS: Do you believe that intelligence plays an important part in poetic creation?

MA: The music of verse and the magic word can vanquish the intelligence of the poet.

BS: I believe that emotion has to dominate over all the other sentiments.

MA: Yes, emotion, the mystery and literary beauty of language. Mallarmé said that one should 'extend the cloud, precious, floating over the intimate abyss of each thought'. Speaking is, usually, to throw bridges over life. The poetic mystery, in general, is justified by the foolishness and lowness of the multitude. From here the exile of the poet among the people. Beginning in 1850, at the height of romanticism, the isolation of poetry comes to dominate more and more, stimulating powerfully a pessimism that will later seem inseparable from the poetic vocation. The romantic hope of a communion between the poet and humanity evaporates, giving way to an obsessive and bitter negation, and, then, in general, the poet feels this inversion of attitude as a very painful trial. At the same time, the poet's solitude breeds ambition. From the mixture of these two, there results a curious duplicity of attitude towards this humanity, from which they feel separated. A separation tinged with nostalgia... Now, the poetry of the young – at least in Spain – is exploding in cries of disdain and desperation which eventually, logically, will disappear in the work of the mature man, because, to the extent that the poet confronts, with more earnestness, the mediocre intelligence of people, his anger disappears. And now, Spencer, let me ask you a question. Does English poetry tend more to lyricism, to ecstatic contemplation, than to the habitual imprecations of Latin poets?

BS: Modern English poetry has two tendencies, one of which is noted in Dylan Thomas and certain poets on whom he has had an influence – Welsh and Scottish above all. This tendency goes towards the fantastic, the rhetorical, and the violent. The other is, to put it plainly, a poetry of the streets. These popular poets feel a curiosity to know the lives of others and have an interest, for their own benefit, in the description of a landscape, of a street through which the crowd circulates, in the furniture decorating a house. Without doubt, in them, objectivity predominates. Examples of these poets are Auden and MacNeice, who became known around 1930. Yeats, the Irish poet, aficionado of magic and oratory, remained, despite the qualities of the other group. Hardy, who had so much influence on poetry, allowed his voice to be heard more in confidential tones than with a lyrical accent.

MA: Let me interrupt you. Do you believe that the English poet responds, with greater intensity, to nature rather than conflicts and human passions?

BS: Our nature poetry is magnificent and has a great tradition. However, Hardy, who among the moderns was a passionate interpreter of nature, frequently referred to human beings, as did Lawrence. I believe that this happens with the best known and celebrated poets of today. Andrew Young, a great modern nature poet, deals with the countryside theme in which sparrows and the whole of nature abound.

MA: And, speaking of death as poetic theme, the Spanish poet tirelessly responds to it. In Spanish poetry, both ancient and modern, the word 'sangre' (blood) is a *leitmotiv* repeated to satiety.

BS: Probably, the Spanish attitude towards life depends, with a lot more intensity than in England, on the life/death dualism. This, at least, is the idea that we English have. This is what the travellers who go to Spain believe they see, not only in the ritual killing of bullfights but also in certain religious symbols. On the other hand, the Englishman who dedicates himself to fox hunting pretends that his interest doesn't consist in being present at the death. As for the dualism I referred to earlier, it is clearly expressed in Spanish painting. We have the example of the skull as symbol in pictures by Zurbarán, El Greco and such like, in many drawings and paintings by Goya. Also, in the seventeenth century, we had our period of obsession with death. The playwrights Webster and Tourneur can stand as examples. And not to mention Shakespeare, both in *Hamlet* and in *Measure for Measure*. The obsessive idea of death is one of the characteristics of romantic literature, as can be seen in Keats and the Brontë sisters. I believe that truly deep poetry ought to be dominated by the idea of death to the same extent that it should be by life, its opposed side. And this also means that poetry bears the inquietude of the times. Among modern poets, T.S. Eliot in *The Waste Land* and D.H. Lawrence in *The Ship of Death* have frequently chosen the theme of death.

MA: And now, I'd like to know your opinion about the life of English writers. In Spain, many men of letters live in public, frequenting 'tertulias' (circles) and cafés where they expose themselves to the curiosity of the public. Don Ramón del Valle-Inclán met in a popular café with people who turned up only for the pleasure of hearing him talk about everything human and divine. The majority of these people did not belong to the literary world. The tertulia at the café de Pombo, headed before the war by Ramón Gómez de la Serna, was famous and its celebrity travelled beyond the borders of Spain, and there wasn't a visiting personality who didn't drop in at the old café. Now, the café de Gijón – which you know – is the base, not only for young writers and poets, but also for others recognised over time. Our novelists – and in general the intellectuals – are easily available. An example of this is don Pio Baroja, who receives all those that go to visit him with exquisite and traditional Spanish courtesy. Our writers lead a private life where their personality stands out strongly, as much as – and at times more so than – in their books.

BS: To what you're telling me, I have to reply that in eighteenth-century England the writer regularly attended the Coffee Houses. At the end of the nineteenth century the poet Yeats used to make appointments with Lionel Johnson and other poets at the Cheshire Cheese. Currently, certain groups of young writers can be seen meeting regularly in certain special pubs. But the continental tradition of the literary café doesn't exist in England. We shouldn't, nevertheless, forget: first, that London is an immense city and that poets may live at distances such as Hampstead and Chelsea; secondly, that the pubs (what you call *tabernas*), where you have to stand because they have few seats, are open only at specific times of day. For this reason, it's not pleasant to be chucked out into the street at the very moment in which a new theory about romanticism is being expounded. For all these reasons, the English poet tends to isolation, given the impossibility of belonging to determinate literary groups. And, now, to finish, let's go back to Spanish poetry. Don't you think that when we're dealing with love poetry, the poet, in Spain, looks for his love with more passion and in a more direct way than the English poet? I think that English poetry tends more to what I would call the human condition than to have an interest in the personal fate of the lover and, for this reason, is more metaphysical, has a greater social content, and as a result, comes out as less egoistic.

MA: On this last point you're right, for in Spain individualism reaches as far as poetry. Perhaps today we tend to make the love theme a more abstract matter. The Spanish, in general, go directly towards things, without putting a brake on impulse, with the violence that characterises them, whether to obtain what they desire or to express, without ambiguous words, their desire in the passion of love. And this is, in my opinion, the essential difference that exists between English and Spanish poetry.

1951

Madrid Journal

May 2nd

They are going to sack the traditional Madrid dustmen. Anyhow, they are going to install dust-cars, big shiny vehicles with trodden-down backs, to replace the donkey-carts and mule-carts of the 'traperos' [rag-and-bone men] or 'basureros' [dustmen]. And I don't imagine the same people will operate the new cars as did the carts. As you came back at five or six after a night's drinking you would meet them, sometimes walking by their donkey's head or sometimes riding on the baskets of rubbish; some of the girls very handsome, dressed in faded reds or pinks, their heads tied in a scarf and riding proudly, a slight and not unbecoming pallor of dust on their skin. This to the sound of the harness bells, exhortations to their animals and now and then the creaking, windy love call as one donkey came in sight of another. I sometimes hear one dustman who walks past my house and speaks to his mule in deep, dignified Spanish tones, addressing it, personally, as 'mula'!

So well known is this morning dust-army, that I have known someone say to his friend, 'I know I have had a real party when I see donkeys,' a remark which in other parts of the world would be interpreted differently.

One of these warm, windless nights. Over a beer at 'La Concha' he told me about the excavations at Paestum. Since I have never seen them I countered too quickly with those at Delos. Stupid. I might have found either an informed archaeologist or a fellow-spirit, someone to whom dug-up towns give the same mysterious, romantic, ignorant excitement as they do to me. The long, empty, roofless boulevards of Delos, with the wind blowing, a few pillars standing; nobody.

He had been in Naples for a couple of years. Confessed quietly to having made fifty or sixty visits to Pompeii. Yes, he said, he had travelled a good deal; Madrid was a very noisy town. No comment. In careful English he observed that his French and German were as good as his Spanish, but he wanted to improve his English and Russian. In England he had been asked in Lancashire if he came from Cheshire. Looking at his mild, brown, appearance, I said that he might easily be taken for an Englishman. 'No, you are saying that to flatter me.' Damn, I didn't mean when he *spoke*.

Back away, get out of that one.

He is a dealer in antiques. When he went to America and was asked the object of his visit, he said it was 'to look at the antics there'. 'So they were distressed,' he added 'by my wrong stress; and so was I.'

He was fond of the Liverpool area, where by the way the best Victorian antiques are to be found. He would like to go back to Liverpool. Liverpool! In his determined Spanish way he paid the bill, leaving me protesting, and wandered off among the shadows under the acacia trees.

A dog asleep on the pavement, smiling.

Shapes of Spanish clouds. This evening it is windy and the sky from my terrace looks like a hairdresser's experiments as he tries to invent a new coiffure, some brushed up, some curled round an imaginary cheek or neck.

On other days there are cigar shaped clouds, perhaps one drove the other, as regular as cigars or cheroots in a box. Or fish-clouds; some like swordfish.

Then a corner of the intense blue sky is striped with clouds, as though a piece of striped material had been dropped there, or in an empty sky there is one small cloud shaped like a star. Unpleasant reflection; the burst of an anti-aircraft shell, but white.

The distracting lusciousness of the girl in my class this morning who has only turned up four times in two months. 'Are you Sita Soler Lopez?' 'No, I am Sylvia.' She was not attending to the lesson, but kept on pulling down the low neck of her jersey still further and sleepily scratching the upper slope of her breast. What is it all for, this terrifying biological engine of Spanish girls' sex appeal? Couldn't the necessary ends of Nature be attained less prodigally? It is as if trees should need to become greener or flowers to have a stronger scent, or glow worms to shine like head-lamps.

Half the people who drank with me in my flat last night were strangers and probably will stay so. Who was the quiet, serious woman in black on the divan? Who was the other one with the silver pattern round the neck of her dress? I imagine a sort of statistical parade of my drinks lined up on a table before I start one of these evenings. This time I happen to remember what they were: six gin-fizzes, something like a bottle of wine at the restaurant with dinner, two anis (one on the house) and four brandy and sodas. And since they were Spanish drinks, a good inch of gin or brandy in the tumbler each time. By the drinks, on my imaginary table, is a packet or more of cigarettes to be smoked before dawn. Is it the same in every capital city?

How strange the foreign wish for hot food appears to the Spanish! It comes – and so does the coffee – just as it comes, cold or lukewarm. The plates are cold, and evermore shall be so. We open a tin of my precious English kippers brought from Gibraltar. My maid has a passion for them. 'What is this fish, señor?' 'Smoked herring.' 'Then it is a large sardine.' 'No, it is not, it is a fish called a herring.' Then tonight: 'Maria Cristina, I have helped myself, won't you come and take your half before it gets cold?' Presently she re-appears; 'Señor, do you like that fish hot?' 'Yes, in England we always eat it hot.' 'I find it so much better cold. I make a sandwich of it with bread, the bread soaks up the grease, and in that way it is very rich.'

This is the season of swifts. They are making black flashes across my terrace every morning and evening. I have just discovered that some of them are nesting in my roof, in the holes in the walls where at one time there must have been supports fixed for an awning over the terrace. Somehow flattering to me to run a swifts' hostel. A swoop at full tilt, a fluttering sound, a blink of wings and they are in. (Question: can they turn round inside, or must they come out, tail first, at the same speed?)

My best taxi story: We were coming fast round the corner into El Barco and nearly carried away a rag-and-bone man, who, with the traditional sack over his shoulder, was just stepping off the pavement. My driver had been making pungent comments on everyone and everything throughout the journey. Here was a target for his scorn. He began in the formal Spanish manner, 'Rag-and-bone man, what were you thinking about?' The answer that snapped back, whatever it was, for I couldn't hear it, shook my driver visibly, but he recovered himself, and, as he accelerated, leaned through the window to retort, 'That is what I married for!' (!por eso me casé!)

Memo: Frances' story of the taxi-man who proposed to her after taking her across the town. 'I have never seen a woman whom I liked better than you, señorita. You need have no doubts about me; I am a serious man. Will you give me six months in which to court you?'

Hammering; one of the typical noises of Madrid. At the bottom of my seven flights of stairs there are two workmen beating away; in the narrow space the noise is nearly unendurable. They are making a cut in the upper part of the wall with chisels. The blonde on the fifth floor wants to put in an electric oven and they are installing the cables. Pieces of plaster fly all over the stairs and the hall, though sometimes the men notice you and stop to let you pass. Why are they always hammering here, whereas in other countries things can often be done by screws, wrenches and twisting? I wonder why Madrid is not lower than it is, in the process of being hammered into the ground.

I wake up and it is a wonderful morning, already heavy with the heat of the day to come. Some smoke hangs in the air, in the direction of the mountains too lazy to go up to the sky. The snow on the mountains is nearly melted. On the road to Toledo, at midday, half-a-dozen labourers are sitting in a field having lunch in the shade of black umbrellas, as sheep in hot weather stoop their heads together to keep cool. Miles and miles of Castille without any trees at all, and the crops coming up thick. Peasants in the fields with floppy Van Gogh straw hats. A tractor in brilliant red and blue, and two hoopoes with black-barred wings flying up. In the village, when we arrive we ask the way of a shepherd who is carrying a sheep round his neck, held by front and back legs and kicking like clockwork. Instead of the normal sheepdog, there is a greyhound following him. A storm of swifts round the old church. A plaster Virgin over the entrance of the house where we are to have lunch. During lunch an unidentified insect rolls its egg across my knee. When menaced, it flies with it to the table.

Maria Cristina has a friend in to help her and they are washing the blankets. Up go the wet ones, dangled plump across the terrace and my view. During lunch, the expected; the cord comes away and down they all come on the floor of the terrace. I have coffee and watch Maria Cristina and Maria Luisa putting them back, making a game of it, giggling, their ear-ringed heads bobbing about against an immaculate June sky which goes milky with haze down towards the roof tops. In the corner, against wall and sky, a bang of red geraniums.

'Señor, Mr Harrison will give himself tonsillitis. He keeps on drinking cold water from the refrigerator!' 'I will tell him so, Maria Cristina.'

House Porters

My first house had a woman as porter. 'A disaster,' said the man I rented my flat from. She was very dirty and very drunk, and on some whim once re-directed some letters of mine, though they were clearly addressed, to Aranjuez. Sometimes, in a drunken fit, she would run screaming round the 'patio' complaining that she had been robbed, and all the heads of the residents would pop out of the windows and a many sided argument would go on in shrieks.

My second house had a suave, correct porter who successfully kept out beggars. My third, a porter who seldom appeared at all but lived noisily and squalidly in his room under the stairs with a large family. One day we all received letters from the landlord telling us that the porter was on a charge of stealing the equivalent of £111, collected from the tenants to pay for the central-heating. On no account were we to entrust him with any money. Some months later he was still in his job, though as a presumed thief and a notorious drunkard (for I was told he stole the money, poor chap, to pay for his continual debauches) it seemed curious that he was still considered suitable. One of my neighbours asked him why he was so cheerful, since he was due to appear on a serious charge. 'There is only one ill that cannot be mended,' he replied, 'and that is death.'

My present porter: a wrinkled, kind old man, very deferential, who likes to sit outside the porch playing with children. His wife came up to the flat the other day – Maria Cristina is on very good terms with her, and they do shopping for each other. I renewed my complaint that the gas-pressure was very bad. 'Ah,' said the old lady, 'It has never been right since the war. Everything is different since the war (the Civil War).' 'But it can't be that there is less gas in Madrid, for the new block next door has flames from the gas stove a foot high and roaring! You must send for the gas men again!' 'Patience, we must have patience,' she replied. 'No, señora, not patience; effort, insistence, and things will get done. I hear the word "patience" too often!' Here I ended my rant, for I observed that she and Maria Cristina were looking at the Englishman with embarrassment and pity.

A hot day at Aranjuez. Past the terrace of the 'Frog' restaurant the river moves sleepily, smelling of green. In the shade of the tall plane-trees we find a table and loll there drinking a cool white 'wine of the house'. Across the road they are selling strawberries. Boats called 'Isobel' or 'Paloma' drift up and down.

Presently we ask the waiter if there is anywhere in the town where, in return for ordering some wine, we can eat our picnic lunch at a table. 'Why not just where you are?' says the waiter. Well, England?

[*from* **Madrid Notebook**]

Standing at the window 9.30 pm 'mist' across the stars, still visible. Radios, the warmth, stir. Light from inside the film flat. Know who they are. Voices from the dark balcony above – girl, man? Chuckling, throaty. Girl reading with wireless below.

Opposite, the black dog which barks. Woman having dinner, speaking to someone invisible. Light on (why?) in the Colegio – desks. Cars parked along the street, some moving.

The group around the street lamp outside provision shop. Some chairs. A children's group further down. Loungers. El Tenis.

So many windows & scenes opposite. A chair someone is going to sit on. The relief, the sociable hour.

What are they thinking? Girl with beautiful hair looking out. I have no secrets. Windows all open. A book of poetry on the sofa. A glass of wine.

Am absolutely lost. Hope for more evenings like this.

New Poetry
Introduced by Bernard Spencer

I want to start with a book of poems by John Holloway, which is called *The Minute*. Now Holloway is associated with the poets of what has been called 'The Movement', but I wouldn't say that he is very typical of them. The texture of his lines is richer than what you would expect of the other supposed members – less metrically flat lines, like counting on your fingers – and there is a more emotional build-up behind what he writes. What he has in common with them is a certain suspicion of the world, a dourness which this group seem to regard as a suitable modern attitude; what, at its worst, is a You-won't-catch-me-bending manner.

Here is a poem which illustrates some of his best qualities, a power to make a memorable, haunting, line and a profound and exact observation of Nature; in this case, I suppose, Nature as encountered in North East Scotland, where he had lived. The poem is called 'Warning to a Guest'.

I expect you noticed that that poem, mostly perhaps on the surface, had the suspiciousness of the world of which I was speaking. The guest is warned not to let himself go, not to expose himself too far to the influence of Nature and to the mysterious, the 'fabulous things of the moon's dark side'.

What I thought good was the organisation of the verses, in which the sense often ran over the end of one line into the next, so that the rhyme-scheme, although important, was not too insistent. And then there were the effective 'resting' lines, shorter than the others, like the fourth and the sixth in each verse, and their contrast with the longer 'moving on' lines which preceded and followed them. And I very much liked the observation and sensibility of 'Keep to the wet streets where Mercury and sodium flood their sullen fire' – with the sound play on the 't's and 'm's and 'f's. And again, about the small birds, 'Down the soft fog. So sharp their pulse / Trills, and their dram of blood burns up so clear, / Each minute, in their bright sight, makes a year.'

The next poem of Holloway's I want you to listen to is about a chase and pursuit in a dark house at night. As a theme it reminds me of a story by Henry James called 'The Jolly Corner' in which a man, after fearful tensions in a dark house, finds the self he might have become. And I suppose in Holloway's poem too the second of the two figures is in some sense the narrator himself; but in any case the poem is a real good weird one, and it ought just to get inside you and flap and bump round and explain itself. The language is the vernacular, and there are no commas, but there is a moral, which is drawn with some alarm! The poem is called 'In the Dark'.

The next book is an anthology, which is called *Mavericks*, meaning 'unbranded steers', edited by Howard Sargeant and Dannie Abse. The sensible idea of the editors was to show that there were other youngish poets, all born since 1920, outside the so-called Movement, who were worth publishing. Though they say in their Introduction that these writers don't form any school of writing as such, they also say that they are not afraid to show strong feelings, and one of the editors quotes approvingly the words of Browning – 'Let us be unashamed of soul'. Reading this anthology I wished that strong feelings were more often communicated to me by the poems in it. I sometimes wanted to apply to the writer of one poem or another the remark of Dr Johnson about Addison – 'He thinks justly, but he thinks faintly.' When the poems were unsatisfactory, the trouble often seemed to me a certain 'Daddy-Wordsworthism', that the poet had chosen some normal activity, such as having a bath, and had laboriously applied symbolic treatment to it, as it might be, 'I turned on the tap – and see how modern man is able to control the enormous powers of Nature!' or 'I take off my clothes – we are all forced to be unadorned and honest sometimes!' Of course there is nothing wrong in everyday things as subjects for poetry; a poet may write about cheese if it excites him sufficiently and in the right way.

It is hard to anthologise an anthology, to select poems from it which represent it. I have liked poems by several of the writers represented here, for instance Vernon Scannell, Michael Hamburger, David Wright and Jon Silkin.

Here is a poem by J.C. Hall, which exploits the symbolism of the Island, or if you wish, Innocence, the Garden of Eden. It is called 'The Island'.

In contrast to the innocence of the Island in its first state is the classic predicament of the human being who knows that he admires one thing and chooses another, that his hate and his love may have the same object. 'Odi atque amo'. This predicament is expressed with passion by Dannie Abse in a poem called 'Duality'.

That was the predicament of the duality of man's nature. There is another classic predicament; of man's loneliness, his essential separation from other human beings, his fear in the face of the Not-Self, of infinite Space, of Night; even, as this next poem says, 'the exhausting fear of Death and Mystery... and fear of Nothing.' That is the subject taken by David Gascoyne in his long poem, specially written for the radio, called 'Night Thoughts', which was performed on the Third programme in December 1955. The same title was used for a long, elegant, improving, and stuffy poem written in the mid-eighteenth century, but I can find no important connection between the one poem and the other.

I am very conscious that I cannot do real justice to Gascoyne's poem by picking out bits of it. Also, it was written specially for the radio, it has been served up cold in book form, I am now offering scraps from it, warmed up – and I am even inviting you to go back to the cold dish tomorrow. I say this because I think it must in general be more effective heard than read with the eyes. The technique used, the slow building up of effects by the accumulation of simple words, without many surprises, and the repetitions, is aimed more at the ear than the eye.

The poem has three sections, the Statement, then Man's search for happiness in the pleasures of the City, and finally the scene in a garden where Man's fears are dispelled. I think the first section and the third are the best, for Gascoyne is not the sort of poet who shines in satire. In a good sense his mind is an innocent one. And it is perhaps in the middle section that the reader of the published text will especially miss the music that was part of the performance.

There is certainly a lot in this book, with its changing verse-rhythms and sometimes its prose-poetry, which show his familiar qualities, his moving earnestness and his sense of compassion.

The scene is Night. Here is the complaint of the Three Moral Souls, as they are called, with the other voices joining in [recording from *Night Thoughts*].

And now from the last section, in the Garden, when Man finds 'a profound serenity...something vastly fundamental, self-effacingly withdrawn, that has been lying there and is there all the time' [recording from *Night Thoughts*].

It is a far cry from that to Aegean Greece, the scene of most of the poems by Constantine Trypanis which appear in his new book called *The Stones of Troy*. Here is one of these amazing Greeks who dares, since his

273

own language is not widely enough read, to write in English and compete successfully with English-born writers!

What are the characteristics of these poems? An irony and a tenderness, all held in a certain formality, almost reserve, of manner. These, with an intense awareness of the landscape of Hellas, and of man's life set against the passing of history, have been the great qualities in the work of some of the best modern Greek poets. My own guess is that the formality of such poetry arises from the wish to steady and control the ebullient Greek national temperament. And then a strong consciousness of the ancientness of the Greeks as a people, and of the landscape of their country, are some of the means by which the Greeks have kept their identity and survived their troubled history.

England and Greece are well brought together in this half-humorous, half-serious tribute to the lady who, one supposes, was the author's English teacher. It is called 'Miss Fitzsimon'.

And here is a poem of childhood, of horror and fascination. The children are the same, I think, who listened to Miss Fitzsimon's stories. It is about a beggar, and is called 'Winter Afternoon's Walk'.

For me the most striking thing in that poem is the way the fear is shaken off and put into perspective in time and space by the images of the last verse, leading up, with the repeated sound of 'w' to the enormous distances of 'The ripe marble and oak of the Genoese / Villas wrestling always with the wind.' And, to end with, a short poem on a rustic picture of the Nativity. You may think this is the sort of poem, however good, that has been written before, until you come to the force and truth of the surprising last lines ['Picture of the Nativity in the Church of Krena in Chios'].

1957

I Will Abroad

The expression 'travel book' has a great many shades of meaning. One of the approaches to writing 'travel' literature is that of the man who has lived for years in the country concerned and moves with confidence in its society. For good measure let him be a bit of a botanist and geologist and know all about the relevant history and literature. Gerald Brenan is that sort of a writer. He is of course well known already for his studies of Spanish literature and for *The Spanish Labyrinth* and *The Face of Spain*.

In *South from Granada* (Hamish Hamilton) he describes how he turned up in Spain after the First World War, supported only by a small bounty from the Army – he admits that his choice might just as well have been Italy or Greece – and, weak from dysentery, wandered around Andalusia till he found some rooms he wanted to rent in Yegen, a small village on the Southern slopes of the Sierra Nevada. There he lived for six or seven years, and it is Yegen and its valley that this book is about, though Brenan has in fact lived in the South of Spain, with a few interruptions, ever since.

Typical of his down to earth, unemphatic but vivid style is the picture of his maid: 'All her movements were quick and lithe, and under her dingy black clothes – in our village married women who were past twenty-five dressed in black – her body wriggled about like a snake's and sometimes in sheer exuberance seemed on the point of slipping out of them altogether. She danced well with a sort of suppressed buoyancy and after some exciting evening, when the gypsies had come in and, well plied with wine, she had joined in one or two "malagueñas", she would collapse on a chair in a state of complete torpor. Her tragedy was her face. Although at this time she was scarcely past thirty, it was lined and worn like that of an elderly woman, and when I had been a year or two with her I discovered the reason. She never let water touch it, but every morning and evening washed it with a strong aniseed spirit which burned and shrivelled the skin till it looked like the side of a Spanish sierra.'

There is a fascinating chapter on local beliefs and rituals: 'Opinions differed as to whether they (white witches or "hechiceras") anointed themselves with fat prepared according to a secret formula and took off naked from the roof tops or whether they launched themselves without pharmaceutical aids in short white nightdresses…' One old lady asserted that 'In her mother's time it had also been common for a girl who had been initiated into the "hechicera's" arts to give her young man a drink which turned him into a donkey, after which she mounted him naked, or rather with her skirts bundled round her head, and so rode about very pleasantly through the air all night.' In a discussion of innate powers possessed by more normal individuals it is revealed that the captivating qualities of a good singer are described in that part of Spain as due to an 'indwelling sprite', which is identified with the common tapeworm. Readers who are quite unfamiliar with Spain may also be startled to learn that Protestants have tails.

Accentuating the Spanishness of the rest are chapters describing visits from Virginia Woolf, Bertrand Russell and the portentous Lytton Strachey (who nearly disintegrated from the journey) and an interview with a morose and eccentric Scotsman who had lived in the neighbourhood for years without ever learning Spanish or coming to terms with the inhabitants.

Whether he is writing of superstitions, the customs of courtship, the country fairs, the landscape, the people of the village or their festivals, Gerald Brenan puts the real Spain before you and, in particular, that 'yellow, ox-hide' valley where he lived, and there will be still less excuse now for anyone to believe in that romanticised, operatic Spain of which the silly traditions still linger on. This is a wise, loving, deeply observed, beautifully written book which will become a classic.

Another of the authentic types of travel-book is illustrated by Peter Mayne's *Saints of Sind* (John Murray). The author, who also wrote *The Narrow Smile* and *The Alleys of Marrakesh*, is equipped with stamina, inquisitiveness almost beyond the reach of man, wit, good nature and a couple or so of the useful languages (about his learning he appears modest). What ostensibly drew him on his journey was a precise aim: to find out more about the 'saints' or holy men who are numerous in the Sind, a district of the lower Indus, in West Pakistan. These holy men inherit their title and position and they range from the humble spiritual teacher with one or two disciples to the recluse at a shrine and again to the well-to-do landowner with his modern cars.

One of Peter Mayne's expeditions led him to a tea party with a number of reluctant 'faquirs' or dervishes, and I cannot imagine anyone else who would, in the interests of pure enquiry, have the stomach or the persistence to force his company on such hosts and in such circumstances.

'They were obliged by Pathan tradition to receive me as a guest, now that I had come in. This was no moment for begging. On the contrary, they should bestir themselves and offer me a cup of green tea, though God knows I didn't much like the look of the crockery hanging from the bony fingers of the tree...Someone handed me a dirty-looking cup with tea in it. It must have been from an earlier brew, because the present kettle was still a long way from boiling and my tea was tepid. Someone asleep in his rags with a bit of sacking pulled over his face awoke and looked out from his lair. He was very old, with a mad face and a cap covered with bright woollen bobbles...'

On another occasion, while he is enjoying the hospitality of a rich and progressive holy man, he is, against his will, given a massage by a wrestler. This is one of the set-pieces of fun in the book, and very funny it is. There is an old man who watches the author's agonies and provides comments: 'When I was young...everyone would look at me because I was so beautiful, and they would call me "soldier", or "Pathan" or "Pinkie" because of the fine pinkness of my skin. Not red like that', he explained, indicating me, 'I am pink. Look!'

'Yes, look, Peter sain,' Akbar said. 'He is not very pretty now because he has gone so old, but his pinkness remains like before...pink, like a parrot.'

Once or twice it appears as though the Ackerley world is going to dissolve and the author is going to be in the presence of something really numinous, and especially when he is taken to see what promise to be esoteric mysteries. But, no, the mysteries turn out to be someone playing a harmonium, others smoking and chatting, a burlesque of a parade-ground scene, everyone laughing.

Finally Peter Mayne dogs down and forces an acquaintance with a very minor holy man, who is more of the spirited adviser or teacher class, and a prolonged hunt for this man's last disciple and cook ends up with a hilarious hashish party.

Peter Mayne needs no excuse; he is so urbane, so readable, at times acceptably facetious and at times extremely funny. But one reflects: with all his scholarship and his knowledge of history and languages, with all his persistence and enthusiasm, was this slapstick and weirdness all there was to find? And in one of his serious moments he asks much the same question. If, after the giggles, we have a feeling of frustration, so did he, and Europeans have often felt frustrated in the Orient. Is it that we seldom really *get* there? If so, what is the reason?

The Brass Dolphins (Secker and Warburg) by Christopher Kininmonth is an account of Malta and its subsidiary islands. The author (such are the stern demands of modern travel literature) is equipped historically, architecturally and, it seems, linguistically too, to deal with his subject. He already knew other parts of the Mediterranean – he is the author of books on Greek islands and on Rome – hoped to like what he found, and in fact settled down in Gozo, one of the northerly islands. This book is required reading for all of us now that Malta is increasingly in the news. I must myself confess to having been very ignorant about the place, because of a sullen prejudice, dating from childhood, against garrison areas which quite left out of account what I knew of the importance of Malta in the last war and the gallantry of its inhabitants. In fact the book reveals Malta as most attractive and makes its long and varied history absorbing to read. Malta had a megalithic culture around 2000 BC, was perhaps – or rather, Gozo was – the island of Calypso in Odysseus' wanderings, had a Greek colony, was fought over by Rome and Carthage, was occupied in turn by the Arabs, the Normans and the Spanish, and entered its grandest period when it was given as headquarters to the Sovereign Order of St John of Jerusalem by the Emperor Charles Vth in 1530.

The history, the architecture and the topography are all set in their proper places in this book among the author's house-hunting, the acquaintances he made, the pleasant boozy evenings and the drums, bells and bangs of the festivals. There is a good map and quite stunning photographs.

1958

Ankara Notebook

Ankara, Feb 10th

All night and a lot of the day there is a yowling of cats, mostly heavily coated Ankara cats, dirty white and dirty light brown with small, mad, dolls' faces. This time I looked out into the scrubby gardens outside my window because there was a movement. Almost hidden by a wall, a brown & white cat was on the back of a cat that seemed to be mostly 'white'. In ten minutes or so, I looked out again. The pair of them must have moved up a low wall, along it for a few yards, under some barbed wire and down into my garden. From time to time the female cat was moving a little forward, carrying the other, like someone struggling under a heavy load, often stopping. The cat on top had its forelegs around the shoulders of the lower one and was working one of its hindlegs in spasms down the other's side and rump. Sometimes the under-one cried out sadly, but not loud, as it was bitten in the neck. It had no expression except pathos. Now and then this strange procession crept a little onwards. What a Via Doloris! No coitus was apparently happening while I looked; the top cat kept on losing its grip on the hind quarters of the lower one. Their two tails were thrashing in the dust. To remember this when an English clergyman talks of what God is like.

Istanbul, Feb 12th

The sharp smell of the lavatory on the ferry, crossing from Asia in the fog. Unlike what I thought was human; oppressive like burned paint or hair, or like acid; not just the usual ammonia – plus.

Istanbul, Feb 15th

Behind Aya Sophia. Some soldiers were parading on a piece of flat ground below me, where there were lorries. When the young officer saw something wrong in their dress or equipment, he struck the offender with a stick. Two men got beaten on the hands, being made to hold them out. The sound came clearly up to where I stood. Perhaps this was hearty fun – he was showing his stick to a friend. Anyhow, a number of the men stood badly, one leaning forward as though he were about to jump; another with his hands joined in front of him, though the group were supposed to be 'at attention'. In the background, evening, the Bosphorus, Asia. And a little way from the soldiers, the Seraglio of the Sultans, which looks over the water. The water where they would throw, tied up in sacks, women who had behaved scandalously.

Morning: the ship's sirens in the fog between Europe and Asia, anxiously yelping and baying.

Evening: the ferry between the two continents coming in towards Europe, tall and lighted up like a birthday cake.

Ankara, March

A little man with a growth of beard, the ragged remains of an army coat, patched trousers and gaping shoes who was walking up the street, bowed under the springs and metal framework of a double bed. The great Oriental sight, the moving to and fro through the streets of beds. The continuation of the Race.

J.R.'s gardener in Ireland, speaking of a salmon he had seen caught: 'It was a foot between the eyes, with a back like a donkey's.'

(Again: 'with a head too big to go in the bucket.')

Young Turkish soldier with the number A. 4755 on his shoulder, sitting on the stone staircase leading to the second floor of the Faculty of Letters, Ankara University, overlooking a football field with some students kicking about. As I pass, he is not looking at the football, but reading *Great Expectations*, in English.

A man with unusual blue eyes passes me in the main street and addresses me roughly and demandingly in Turkish. I spread my hands, meaning 'Don't understand'. We pass. I turn round to look at him again. He has turned round to look at me.

The barber (called Barber here) and I have not a word of any language in common, except 'shampoo'. Very well, I have one. Sure enough, as in all the Levant, he washes my forehead and nose and, worse still, drives his fingers into my ears. I struggle; he seems to apologise.

When I was a child, my nurse used to roll a corner of a handkerchief round one of her hairpins, push it into my ear hole and revolve it like a drill.

April

My Turkish does not improve. The fare should have been two lire. I gave him two and a half and refused the change (innocently). The taxi man offered to give me a half lira. I waved it back. He was highly delighted:

280

'Gurgle-in-church!' he said (I swear it was that) and grinned all round his head.

In the Wagon Lit

Morning. What a show of wide-waisted trousers! What belts round what great bellies! Beautifully pressed trousers of rich and strange materials! 'Co-respondent' shoes. Cuff links, silk shirts with initials under the heart, and buttons, buttons everywhere. Signet rings. Powder over blue chins, pene-trating scent of toilet-water. Signet rings. Watch-straps. Key chains leading into side pockets. Key-rings. Stamped leather wallets, no doubt, special belts with purses for strapping money and other valuables to the body. Trusses for hernia, sock suspenders. Men: the artificial sex. Cf. The old armour display in the Wallace Collection. (My father's and uncle's leather hair-brush cases, stud boxes with initials, sets of razors, razor-straps, tie presses, tie pins etc).

Z. Bey is really rather handsome, with a long, droopy, puffy face like a hound, and sad brown eyes. Tall, carefully dressed (*English* material, my dear Mr Bernard.) Thinning grey hair carefully combed back. Retired naval captain, aged 48.

Met in the weird bar of the Modern Palas where he comes nightly for two hours 'raki' drinking before going round the corner to the Journalists' Club of which he is Honorary (?) (?) Associate Member.

Liaison officer with the British Navy before and during the War, and so wildly Anglophile. There are many stories of Captain B and Commander E and others, and even of Admiral C, a great hero who gave his daughter a 'signal' to call for Z. Bey at his room with her car and to bring him to dinner and to dance with him afterwards!

Perhaps it was our second meeting when he said to me, 'Your physiog-nomy and your pronunciation of English give me great pleasure!'

Z. Bey divorced his first wife and chose a woman lawyer for his second. Regrets it. Their main quarrel is her seventeen-year-old son by her first marriage, whom she spoils.

The other day Z scolded the boy for not doing his homework and told him to turn the radio off. After abusing his father the boy seized a knife and attacked him. Z forced him on to the floor, pinning the knife hand behind him, and called for Mrs Z to come and look.

1958

Anatolia Notebook

Road to Konya, April 1958

The plain, grimmer than Castille, became less eventful; grimmer, under grey skies, than the Egyptian desert. Areas of green (startling) crops very occasionally. Where are the villages that sow them?

Villages, every 45 minutes or 1 hour of driving. Houses are cubes of clay, flat roofs one (or two) tiny windows. Plain flat, no trees, straight road. T. Hardy's Egdon Heath cannot match this. The loneliest place. If there was a storm. No shelter at all.

Passing a lake. No building. No boat. No fishing? Someone said: 'the unloved country; they don't know what to do with it.' Nomads, who have not learned to live in a country? Mountains, some snow, overhanging.

Flocks of lambs, white as breadcrumbs on the dark land. Dramatic light on two sides of clay houses. A blue door. A modern silo, organ pipes, a collection of cylinders, tall, airship-silver.

Sometimes wells. Apparatus like a leaning ship's mast, leaning oblique against a horizontal bar supported between two uprights. The foot of 'the mast' weighted with heavy stones. A rope from the top of the 'mast' supports a bucket.

A pillar-box red Westinghouse tractor with huge wheels.

The plain. 'On whom the rain came down'...

The road at intervals becomes a rutted track where they are re-making. Piles each side of gravel, clay, earth. Tractors. Pools of water. Cars go by flinging up muddy water ships.

A shepherd with a flock, white on black. Knitted wool cap or draped material like a turban on his head. Puttees round the shins & ankles. A staff in his hand. Long khaki coat? In one place they wore felt capes like a great envelope or sandwich-man with great broad exaggerated shoulders, wool-capped head and feet only protruding.

Big sheepdogs like wolves, like huskies, off-white or tawny, fling themselves at the car or chase it, barking and showing long fangs. They are disconcerted by the dust flying up behind us. Hard to bark, hard to take breath for running, in the dust-cloud.

Sometimes little shepherdesses with white head-dress, veils, and baggy flowered trousers.

Towards the Taurus mountains. Low hills with no soil left, only flat plaques and slabs of slanting stone.

In the villages, women favour the captive balloon silhouette.

In the mountains, pine trees, fantastic jagged, pinnacle rocks like a Dürer background: Grey, silver rock, dark green of pines. Big mountains with snow – (brindled with snow) mist-hidden tops. (Life doesn't belong up there). The relief of trees. The red road always.

Most beautiful: lanes with evergreens, and fresh young green leaves on other trees. Mountains behind, blue and violet. After hours and hours, a soft misty flashing horizontal in the distance. The sea. When we come down, my first view of the Mediterranean for several years. Big white breakers and their distant sound beyond startling green, green fields. Groups of camels, free along the roads and in the fields. Storks in flocks, white & black plumage, some settling uncomfortably into unsafe nests in small trees.

One camel down by the beach. Afraid to bathe but wanting to?

Banana plantations, no fruit at this season, the broad blades of their leaves slashed short. Warm Spring evening weather along the coastal strip. Storm-clouds over the mountains we had come from. The patches of road being built between the popular seaside resorts, Alanya, Antalya, etc. The wrong turning taken. Notices of dynamite-blasting which we did not see.

As we drove into Alanya, 8.00 pm, the great rock over the town with its belt of Seljuk walls & battlements drooping around it. A spray-mist like smoke above the white, breaking waves.

Accommodation the Alanya Palas. Accommodation to be expected by a lighthouse-keeper or a good-conduct prisoner. Refugee-camp? But sanitation? The public wash-basin?

1958

Poems by Bernard Spencer

BBC Third Programme

The poems I want you to hear this evening may mostly be described in a technical sense as dramatic; they present a scene in a city or in a landscape and tell a story about what is happening to people there. I have sometimes heard comments on the amount of trouble I take to show the scene in which events are happening. Well, to the extent that one writes poetry to understand better what is going on in life, I find that for this understanding of some incident or moment which I feel to be important I need to get the background and, so to speak, the furniture in, even some small details. There are perhaps inanimate things which belong to the drama and demand in a very clear voice to be included. I hope I avoid the merely topographical by having a wider and in any case more human aim.

Most of the poems are in an incidental sense autobiographical. For me, poetry begins very much at home, wherever home may be, and I have not myself, however much I may admire it in others, much inclination to turn to mythology, folklore or the events of history for a theme, although, as you will gather, since I have been working near the Mediterranean for a good many years, the historical references of that area do crop up in my poems.

The first poem, which happens to have been written before any of the others, has a setting in France, at a place along the River Loire. The theme is the possibility of entirely perfect and happy episodes in life, although the title implies that they do not usually last very long. ['On the Road']

The next poem has a similar subject. It was written many years later; the river is the Thames, and here the threat of the passing of Time and the necessary separation of the two lovers is prominent, although there is an insistence on the essential timelessness of love. The title refers to a pub in the Thames valley. ['At the "Angler"']

Here is a poem which turns on the familiar conundrum, the question of which comes first in artistic appreciation, the feeling or the implications, the thought. Or rather it is about the impossibility of separating the two. The title, 'Fluted Armour', comes from the elaborate suit of armour worn by the subject of a certain portrait in the National Gallery.

I have said that my poems are inclined to be autobiographical and to follow the events of my life. The title of the next one, 'Notes by a Foreigner', is rather a bleak and angular one, but the phrase 'Notes by' was suggested by the fact that I was writing a prose journal at that time. I am trying to explore the feeling, very familiar if you live abroad, of being a foreigner even in a place which you love and think you know well. It must be an experience common to many people, especially since the War. But, after all, everyone can have it, even in his own home town. The device of speaking to myself as YOU is also derived from the conventions of journal-writing. The town happens to be Madrid, but it might be a number of other places.

The next two poems you will hear now have Athens as a background. In the first one I refer at the end to the dialogues of Plato and in particular to the two horses, one of Impulse and one of Reason, which pull the chariot of human life in contrary directions, and to the myth of Cupid and Psyche, and to the myth that human beings, each like the half of a split apple, go around the world looking for the other half-apple. ['In Athens' and 'Full Moon']

Of the next two poems, the first refers to a very common sight in the streets of Mediterranean towns, the sellers of lottery tickets. The second presents a very contemporary scene; in a town which you know and love there is an outbreak of political feeling; mobs march through the streets rioting; soldiers are called in. Civilised values are forgotten in the excited satisfactions of the masses. ['The Lottery Sellers' and 'The Rendezvous']

The poem 'Sud Express' speaks of the parting of lovers when one has to go to another country. In this poem I have used the 'juxtaposition' technique, by which the thoughts of the lover are inserted among the impressions of a journey in a fast train.

Finally, here are two poems written recently when I was working in Turkey. In the first poem I speak, unusually for me, of historical events: the castle I mention can be seen some miles outside Istanbul, and I later refer to the conquest of Constantinople, as it was then, by the Turks in 1453 which formally ended the Byzantine empire. Of the second poem it only need be said that it was written after a journey South through Turkey. ['The Beginning' and 'Feathery Grasses']

1959

Lawrence Durrell

Bernard Spencer, author of a book of poems, Aegean Islands, *and currently professor at the British Institute in Madrid, is, like his friend Durrell, a great connoisseur of and enthusiast for the eastern Mediterranean world. For this reason, he is a person particularly qualified to introduce him.*

Lawrence Durrell – perhaps because of a persisting childlike quality – is one of those people who possesses the precious gift of creating myths. For them, what surrounds them, as much the country as houses or people, holds a dimension distinct from reality and appears invested with magic. He has himself spoken to us about this gift of his: 'All my favourite characters are beyond pattern and proportion...' The first of his books to see the light was *Prospero's Cell* (1945), in prose, full of the luminous atmosphere that came to be considered typical of his work. The title derives from the thesis, held half seriously, half jokingly, that the Greek island of Corfu, where he lived for some years, was visited by Shakespeare and constituted the inspiration and imagined background for *The Tempest*. The characters who populate the book, though some based on real types, are as enjoyably fantastic as the thesis: Zarian, the Armenian poet who 'walks as if he wears a heavy cloak', the Count, the tall and bearded Greek doctor Stephanides, 'Probably reincarnation of comic professor invented by Edward Lear'. His candle-lit dinners, and his memorable conversations, have a nostalgic aftertaste. The war bound to put an end to his Utopia in that 'everything is exactly as the fortune-teller said it would be' was not far away.

Lawrence Durrell, born in 1912, was educated partly in India, and it would be enchanting to have explained to us how for this and other reasons he avoided a great deal of the system of carrots and sticks, leading to decided moral attitudes, that is typical of an English schooling. After a period in a military academy, and another in Paris as a writer, he suddenly and abruptly moved with his mother, brothers and sisters to Greece. A characteristic fact: he took with him five volumes devoted to brain surgery.

Since then Greece has become a legend for Durrell. His second book of travels, *Reflections on a Marine Venus* (1953), the fruit of his stay on the island of Rhodes as press attaché, follows the same attractive formula as the first. In it there is the rich descriptive prose, the insight into a world of Greek speech and – contrasting with the lyrical and fantastic – a perceptive and animated erudition that allows Durrell to illuminate the history of the island and add – with an attractive touch – a calendar of Saints and Flowers. His latest book of travels, *Bitter Lemons* (1957), perhaps the best, is a report on the years that he spent in Cyprus, at first as a teacher in a country school, and later as a press attaché with the Governor. It contains an analysis of the recent political crisis, as seen by Greek speakers, and he felt in his element as much with Cypriot villagers as in the Governor's Palace. A difference between this book and the approach and tone of the first two is that Durrell gives vent, in the period before the crisis, to a tumultuous feeling of farce, in the feats of a love-struck and malicious pupil, and in the extremely funny scenes when the author looks for a house in a Cypriot village and is initiated by a cynical Turkish friend in the subtleties, laments and absurdities of the peasant contract, slow and deceitful.

Lawrence Durrell has been a government functionary in Cairo, Alexandria, Rhodes, Belgrade and Nicosia, and Director of the British Council in Greece and Argentina. ('I will go on from there,' as he says, 'wearing out countries'; however, as his humorous books *Esprit de Corps* (1957) and *Stiff Upper Lip* (1958) on life in the embassy show, he remains frenetically in love with the British Isles).

To those who admired his first two books of travels Durrell would snarl: 'They are no more than an embroidery of fantasies', and he declared his intention to write a novel that would shake up the public. As in a pirouette, and as much talked about abroad as in the British press, there appeared his trilogy *Justine* (1957), *Balthazar* (1958), and *Mountolive* (1958), a study of the life of Alexandria, the timeless city which was also the theme of the modern Greek poet Cavafy. A city in which Africa, West and East meet, and which has become another of Durrell's myths. The facts are observed through the eyes of a heterogeneous group of people of various nationalities and their different visions add quality one to the other. This difficult technique of 'many windows' – until from the dreams comes profit – employed with success, give such truth, plenitude and originality to his novels, which is one of the principal reasons why, by turns, they provoke and attract. Given that the author is a lover and admirer of Place, with the influence of Plank's and Einstein's theories, it is not surprising that the normal Time sequence ends by being shattered. The characters are dedicated to the search for, and the attempt to understand, love (sexual or not) and fidelity. When this or that doesn't prove convincing it's because in the process of looking back the myths have been inflated – whether jokingly or in all seriousness – until they achieve the dimensions of some fantastic Carnival figure. It is this artistic 'exaggeration' or stylisation that withholds our total sympathy from the romantic and fatal figure of Justine. Others, like Leila and the British diplomat Mountolive, are admirable types of flesh and blood. What is always definite, and attractive, is the sensual landscape of Egypt, for example, in the hunting scenes, and the atmosphere of the mansions and the suburbs of Alexandria. The prose is a poet's prose. It is the attack, total and deliberate, of a poet against the world of modern novelistic prose.

The flaws that could be raised against it: it slides into the florid and theatrical, falls now and then into literary clowning; they are the products of his exuberance. On the other hand, among his qualities as a writer we can point to energy, compassion, an acute intelligence that catches and dissects ideas, and a strong vocation. From him we can hope for many more works of this audacious kind, which he has dared to construct with great boldness.

March 1960

Context

The following questions were sent to a number of poets, for them to answer individually or to use as a basis for a general statement about the writing of poetry today.

> *(a) Would poetry be more effective, i.e. interest more people more profoundly, if it were concerned with the issues of our time?*
>
> *(b) Do you feel your views on politics or religion influence the kind of poetry you write? Alternatively, do you think poetry has uses as well as pleasure?*
>
> *(c) Do you feel any dissatisfaction with the short lyric as a poetic medium? If so, are there any poems of a longer or a non-lyric kind that you visualise yourself writing?*
>
> *(d) What living poets continue to influence you, English or American?*
>
> *(e) Are you conscious of any current 'poeticisation' of language which requires to be broken up in favour of a more 'natural' diction? Alternatively, do you feel any undue impoverishment in poetic diction at the moment?*
>
> *(f) Do you see this as a good or bad period for writing poetry?*

(a) Yes, it would probably interest more people, but I don't think, in the present state of English society and education, very many more. The dangers would be the over-simplification which we have been familiar with in our own lifetimes, over-simplifications due to the unaccommodating subject-matter and the temptation to try to lush-up a public to whom poetry has always been foreign. If he didn't worry much about that public I don't see why a poet who felt warm enough politically shouldn't cultivate a side-line in political satire on the model of Byron's.

I think the principal issue of our time is the survival of the loving, feeling individual against the political-social spook – so every good poem is eventually taking sides.

(b) Almost not at all. Politics and religion in their present forms do not affect me at the deep level from which poetry starts. On the other hand, I can imagine a poem about the human disaster caused by some doctrinaire political or religious concept.

Apart from its pleasure, poetry must have a score of uses. Perhaps the most important one is that described by Shelley, that it makes the writer or the reader of it go out of himself in that act of sympathy which apparently underlies the main virtues.

(c) The short or medium-short lyric is how poetry happens to me. I have enough trouble with that.

(f) A good period, anyhow in English-speaking countries, first in the sense that there is a good confusion in the world around the poet and in himself to be sorted out. Secondly, the poet now has almost limitless possibilities of form and general treatment, since there is no Dr Johnson to tell him how to write. I welcome this – it makes each poem more of an undertaking, more of a risk. What each poet has got as a guide or control or fertiliser is the nature and history of his language, without there being any widely accepted critical opinion about which aspects of this he ought to be guided by.

Then, although there isn't usually much money from a poem or book published, the poet can get a lot of publicity considering how few people read new poetry. Anthologies keep rolling out, even school anthologies (which is a good reminder to the poet not to be a bore, since some child somewhere who has happened to be preserved from literary fashions may see clearly what he actually wrote). University jobs, contracts for radio programmes or for lectures not infrequently follow publication. The long-term financial rewards for writing a few good poems are probably greater than they have been before in this century, and they may be less embarrassing to collect than in periods of private patronage.

February 1962

University of Madrid Lecture

I feel I should explain why I am not offering you a lecture on some more important subject than my own poems. In fact this is not even a real lecture. It sounds a bit 'pushing', as we say, to come here and talk about my own work. But the fact is that I had been away on sick leave and I hadn't got anything else ready when I was asked to contribute to this English-American week. And I was told that a reading of my own poems with a bit of talk about them was something which you might accept instead of a regular lecture. In fact, I was persuaded into doing this by my great friend Dr Sofia Martín Gemero and Professor Pujals. Now Professor Pujals and I first met by letter. It was at a time when after spending six very happy years in Madrid at the British Institute I had been moved to a job in Athens. (Everyone wants a job in Madrid...) Anyhow, I was in Athens, in about 1956, when I received a letter from Dr Pujals saying things which I thought very flattering about some poems which I had recently published in *The London Magazine*. The poems he liked had Spanish subjects, or backgrounds. Now this was very gratifying, very pleasing to me, especially as coming from someone I didn't know, except that he was a distinguished member of the staff of the Instituto de España in London. And to take the trouble to write to me! When you publish a poem in a magazine you usually get no reaction at all. It is like a sailor shipwrecked on a deserted island who throws a bottle into the sea with a message in it...or like dropping a stone down a well...

And then last year Dr Pujals very kindly wrote an article about my poems in the *Filologia Moderna*.

So by the combined forces Dr Sofia Martín Gemero and Dr Pujals, you can see how I was persuaded to give this talk to you today.

I think there is a certain interest in the biography of any artist. I will give you the relevant facts of mine very briefly. I am told that at the age of two I came back from a childrens' party reciting, although rather indistinctly, some verses from *The Lays of Ancient Rome*, written in the beginning of the nineteenth century, by Macaulay. Some strong visual images and an infectious, swinging metre. I had apparently heard some grown up repeat them. I suppose I had that much of the poet in me that I was already fond of words. Sometime before I was five, because I remember the house where I did it, I ate a whole newspaper. I remember the difficulty I had in finishing it. I suppose I was fond of print. I learned to read rather earlier than most children, mostly through boredom, and read anything I could find, indiscriminately and always enthusiastically. I suppose I was not meant to be a critic. My parents lived abroad and I was brought up by guardians in remote places in the English countryside. I had to find my own entertainment – to amuse myself – most of the time; and I suppose a certain amount of loneliness and boredom nourishes the artistic imagination. What you haven't got you invent. When I was at school I used to tell imaginary adventure stories to the other boys – though some of the others could do that also – and later on I used to make up funny poems to make people laugh. As I grew older, while still a schoolboy, I read a lot of poetry of the nineteenth century – the Romantics, especially Keats, William Morris, Swinburne and Matthew Arnold; and in the twentieth century such Romantics of this period as Masefield and James Elroy Flecker, both of whom wrote poetry which was based on travel abroad. I was lucky enough to travel abroad myself, while still a schoolboy, for holidays to France, Switzerland, Italy and Belgium. I mention this because I used to pray that I should be a traveller abroad when I grew up, just as I used to pray that I should be a poet, and both prayers have been to some extent answered! I think my travels, which have been mostly around the Mediterranean, have had a good deal to do with my poetry, both because of the stimulus of seeing many varied places, and because I have been exposed to some extent to the literature of those countries.

Anyhow, to return to my later schooldays, under the influence of the Romantic poets I have mentioned I began to write poems which curiously enough sounded a bit like bad Keats and Shelley, and from one point of view were not so funny as my earlier ones. But I remember, with the money given me for a school prize, buying not only the earlier works of W.B. Yeats, the great Irish poet who died only a little before the last world war, but also a volume of George Herbert, the seventeenth-century poet. And he has always remained one of my great admirations because of his deep feeling, his essential innocence, and his sparing and curious use of words. His sense of a tight pattern. This was a *new* sort of influence, no longer of the Romantic school, and you will see that it connected with what I was thinking about and reading later.

At Oxford University I continued studying Latin & Greek, which has a healthy influence in the sense of making you careful about how many words you use – not to use too many. The advice that Latin and Greek literature give is: *Think* hard while you *feel* warmly.

There is a story on this topic about a poet who showed a poem of his to Ezra Pound, the American poet and important critic, whose views about poetry made a deep impression on such different poets as W.B. Yeats and T.S. Eliot. Ezra Pound read the poem through and said to the author: 'You could have written the same poem with two syllables less.'

At Oxford I published poetry in the styles that were accepted then: one of the styles owed a good deal to T.S. Eliot, a style which was reserved, ironical and dry. To show you what our admirations in literature were then, I will quote to you a little rhyme written by a university student of that time – even though he was from Cambridge and not from Oxford. There is in English an old prayer which used to be recited by children when they went to bed. It is this, and it calls on the names of the Disciples: 'Matthew, Mark, Luke and John / Bless the bed that I lie on.' In order to show the literary influences of those times, the student wrote: 'Eliot, Rabelais, Dryden, Donne / Bless the bed that I lie on.' T.S. Eliot at that time was writing critical essays which you no doubt have read very much praising the poetry of the seventeenth century, and recommending our return to that tradition. So we might have continued writing this learned sort of poetry, full of references, if it had not been for the International Financial Crisis – the Slump – which prevailed from 1929 on until 1932 and beyond, and, following that, the steady growth of International tensions, the rise of the Nazi State in Germany, with its territorial ambitions, the Italian occupation of Abyssinia, the Civil War in Spain. Millions became unemployed in Europe. Many people in the 1930s were wondering whether they would lose their job in the following month, and they were also wondering how soon their country would be at war.

In this way there arose the so-called Social Poetry of the 1930s, in which the subject of poetry was often Man in his Social Situation, and also the Impending War. Leading figures in this movement were W.H. Auden and Stephen Spender, both of whom had travelled and seen conditions in Europe, not only in England. They used to write for a magazine called *New Verse*, to which I also used to contribute. The general view among these poets, supported by poems and critical articles from the editor, Geoffrey Grigson, was that the poet should not be a withdrawn visionary, but one in the middle of the events of his time, with a view that extended beyond the frontiers of his country. Colloquialism of language, less scholarly than Eliot.

One poem of mine which dates from this time is in the well-known anthology *Contemporary Verse*. It is rather staccato, and awkward, in the manner of the time, but I still think it does what it sets out to do, which is to show how man in a setting of Nature and Spring is at the same time man in a setting of Society, of Politics & Economics.

In 1939, whether we wanted it or not, we in England had to face Man in his Social Setting; a pessimist might say Man in his Preferred Social Setting – the one where he really likes to be: the World War had started.

The Social School of Poetry no longer existed in its earlier sense. And this brings me to the first poem I want to read to you today. At the outbreak of the war between Greece and Italy, the so-called Albanian War, I was in Salonika in Northern Greece, which was the nearest big town to the Front where the fighting was taking place: the date was 1940. Salonika is a very Macedonian sea-town, rather primitive, smelling strongly of fish and fruit and the kind of resinous wood which is burnt everywhere as fuel. There are some splendid Byzantine churches. The town with its bay is set among wild, barren hills, and in winter, when this campaign was mostly fought, it is intensely cold, especially when a North East wind, the 'Varda', sweeps down from Russia. In this poem I am trying to give the impression of what it is like to be near to a war, yet not quite of it. In verse 3, I mention the air-raids which in fact one night entirely gutted or destroyed the inside of the hotel where I was staying. I had spent that particular night in another part of town because I had been celebrating someone's birthday! The air-raids happened at fairly regular times, so we used to arrange to have our meals specially early or specially late so that we didn't have to get up in the middle of them to go to the shelters. I have tried to give the weird, uneasy feeling of not actually seeing the enemy, except his aeroplanes, and yet knowing that anyone you spoke to might be an enemy agent or sympathiser. And indeed you yourself were suspicious in the eyes of other people ['Base Town'].

Turn to 'Olive Trees'. As I have said, I have spent a lot of my life in countries around the Mediterranean, and for me the olive tree is a sort of symbol of this part of the world, and also of the ancient civilisations, especially the Greek civilisation, which flourished there. That is what I am speaking about in the third verse where I am thinking of how these trees which often look so ancient themselves, 'crones' in verse 1, must have been the background to the building of new towns and the destruction or falling to pieces of the same towns. They are like spectators at a play which is human history.

This poem came to me when I was on a long bus journey in Israel, going East from the coast near Haifa and up into the hills. I remember that the bus passed through miles and miles of olive groves as the road climbed. For most of the time I had not got a seat and had to stand; and I was peering out at the olive trees and going over in my mind all the things I had been thinking about olive trees for years – how old they look, and how I like the colour of them, and how I don't like eating 'aceitunas' – how there was something rather grim or dour about them, and yet something beautiful and attractive; in fact I was talking to myself, a little bit to pass the time on the long journey, and I found that what I was saying to myself was beginning to be a poem. And here it is: ['Olive Trees']

You may notice that the hard consonants in the first verse suggest the hard, forbidding quality of the trees; and the soft long sounds in the second verse correspond to the change of thought. And I want the sounds at the end of the fourth verse to give an impression of heaviness and stoniness.

In 1958, shortly before I returned to Spain, I went to Turkey to work at the University of Ankara for six months, and I was taken one holiday time for a journey by car through the plain of Anatolia, where you can drive for two hours without seeing a village or even a house, only sometimes a flock of sheep with their wild-looking shepherd. It was after this journey that I wrote the next poem, 'Feathery Grasses'.

After crossing the plain we drove over the mountains and went to look at the remains of some ancient Greek towns on the South coast of Turkey. These towns, although overgrown with grass and weeds, often still have recognisable remains of temples and theatres standing, with their semi-circular tiers of stone seats. So much loneliness and emptiness and all those ruins put me in a state of melancholy excitement. I was half attracted by it and half afraid. And the impulse to write poetry is partly the impulse to *sort out* and *understand* confused, worrying feelings. So I wrote this poem. What is the trap? What was I afraid of? Later, at his request, I read the poem out to a fellow poet, John Betjeman, and he cried out 'Oh! Eternity'! That is as good an answer as any ['Feathery Grasses'].

In 1956 I left Madrid for some years, and before I left I thought I would like to put down the feelings I had for this city. Look at 'Notes by a Foreigner'. I had for some time been writing a prose journal in order to have some record of what it was like to live here, and so in this poem I am as it were talking to myself, as one does in a journal, and when I say YOU it means ME. I love Madrid, but the way I see it is probably different from the way another person would. And a foreigner sees it differently from a person who belongs to the city. That is the first meaning of the poem, but all poems have different depths of meaning, and the poem is not just about Madrid but about any town, and eventually it is about the strangeness of being in the world at all, the feeling that you may have invented the whole thing. More precious because you have? In the sixth and seventh verses there is a phrase 'dust-doomed' about the famous vivid Madrid sunsets. It is not 'dust' – 'doomed sunsets' etc...I find it hard to make printers and typists use the hyphen and not the dash. I am not quite sure what 'dust-doomed' means, but it sounds good! It is something to do with the dust in the air accounting for the extreme brilliance of the sunset, and the sunset itself having the appearance of doom and flames.

The next two poems were both written in Madrid. Turn to 'From my Window'. The first one is about the essential separation of different groups of people in a large city. The students in the first lines have nothing to do with the rich. And the poet, although he can see the rich behind their windows, is not likely to meet them and he can't even hear their voices, but only sees them waving their hands. And the poor children, who are playing a game of Try to Catch Me, have nothing to do with the other groups. And finally the dog has to find company in the fire until it hears another dog barking a long way off.

The second poem, 'Morning in Madrid', is trying to do one of the things which poetry sometimes can do – to get the inscape or essence of some-thing. It also contains an onomatopoeic tribute to those creatures I admire so much, the Madrid donkeys. I think the poem, being so short, gets a certain lightness from its feminine endings: 'calling', 'falling' – 'drifted', 'lifted'.

The next poem, 'In Athens', has a mood of tenderness and frustration and a certain irony. I was walking one day in Athens near the main square, which is called the Syntagma or Constitution Square, when a girl of about seventeen passed me whom I at first thought I recognised, in fact knew well. Well, I didn't. It must have been that she was like someone whom I knew & loved years and years ago. Yes, but Who? This part of Athens is very near the part where the ancient city stood, near the Acropolis, and I thought of those discussions on love and the emotions in the Dialogues of Plato (Platon) where he speaks of the human soul as being drawn by horses that sometimes pull in different directions – the horses of Impulse and the horses of Reason – in fact how love can play the hell with people – and play silly tricks on them too, as is expressed in one of the same dialogues, I think by Aristophanes, who Plato makes tell the story of how the Gods, to punish humanity, cut everyone in half, just as you cut an apple, and since then everyone has gone around searching for his or her other half. And in the second part of the poem there is a feeling of wonder at how all these things, the girl, the thoughts, the place should have come together – the surprise Twist of Fate – the Twist in the Plotting...

In this poem you will see that I have not used rhyme because the turning, drifting, exploring nature of the thought seemed not to be suitable for rhyme. Too heavy handed.

My poems are often in the technical sense dramatic. That is to say they often present a figure or several figures in a landscape, which may be a city, at a moment of action or strong feeling, and these moments I feel have a bearing on certain truths about life which I am rediscovering. But of course the rediscovery can't happen in the way of being told something, A = B, but only as a total experience of an artistic kind. The last poem I read to you was like that, and so are the two which follow. First 'The Lottery Sellers': a familiar sight not only in Madrid but in other cities where I have lived. One of the sellers is a man, one a woman, and the woman is blind. That is why her gaze is 'lifted over roof tops'. I find, too, that blind people often have strange, remote voices. These then turn into the personifications of Luck & Wealth which they offer their clients.

The next poem presents a very contemporary scene. It is that of a city, and I was living in one like this, where political rioting is taking place, and the satisfactions of a mob, which the army has had to be called in to restrain, have for the moment taken first place. Profounder, more human values such as love and long friendship have been for the time forgotten. As you walk down the empty street at night you see the political slogans on the walls; you see the soldiers, and you reflect that this is the town where two people had a *rendezvous* ['The Rendezvous'].

March 1962

Interview with Peter Orr

ORR: Mr Spencer, can you remember when you first began writing poetry?

SPENCER: I think I should say late in my public school period when I was very much influenced by romantic poetry, by nineteenth-century poetry, by William Morris, by Keats, and made discoveries of people like James Elroy Flecker, and I think I wrote one or two poems then on conventional subjects. I think I wrote one about Venice when I was on a visit, which sounded extraordinarily like other people's and nineteenth-century poets' views about Venice.

ORR: So these influences were very strongly apparent in your poems at an early stage, were they?

SPENCER: Oh yes, I went through an absolutely normal stage of being in love with poetry; reading all I could find, but especially the pulling out from the shelves of romantic poetry. I would say it was mostly of that period, although I do remember when I got a school prize at about seventeen, I was much laughed at for having chosen George Herbert as the book and everyone thought that was extremely stuffy of me. That, I think, is important, because I have a great, great admiration for the Metaphysicals now.

ORR: Apart from the Metaphysicals, what other poets have been an influence on you as a maturer writer?

SPENCER: I think Thomas Hardy, very, very especially. I like the down-to-earthness of his language and his observation. I also liked, at an early stage, Edward Thomas.

ORR: Do you find that it is difficult for you to assimilate these influences and then emerge with a style which is triumphantly and definitely your own?

SPENCER: It was difficult, I am quite sure. Looking back on the things that I used to publish in the early days, I was quite clearly writing under a rather strangling influence of what was considered right in those days and

I am sure that Eliot and Auden were very strong influences. But I think that as one grows older, one just cuts the cackle and I have to turn more and more to my knowledge of myself, what I am really like, and steer away from any accepted style, as far as I know. There is one other point, of course, that I have lived a long while abroad, for about twenty-two years, and I have come a little bit under the influences of what I have read here and there, whether in Greece, with poets such as Elytis or Seferis. Although I don't write like them, it must have given me ideas of different ways of writing from those you would find in England or the States, I suppose.

ORR: It is definitely noticeable, on reading your poems and on hearing your poems, that you don't belong to the English pastoral school.

SPENCER: No, I think I am much more interested, really, in people in a landscape, with some dramatic situation. But very much, of course, in the landscape with them, because I believe the landscape is involved in their feelings. That is what, really, I am looking for all the time, I think, a dramatic situation in some landscape.

ORR: Do you find yourself bound by, or helped by conventional poetic forms, the pure mechanics of poetry, as one might write a sonnet of fourteen lines with a certain rhyme scheme or observe a certain regular metre or stanza form?

SPENCER: I do write sometimes in regular stanza forms, as were customary years ago. But on the whole, I think, I write far more in irregular forms: let us say, not with a regularly recurring pattern, but the pattern growing up more or less like a plant according to the nature of what I am saying. I do think, though, that in each poem I write, I try to set myself a new technical problem. I think I have written very little in the same form from one poem to another, because it is famous that you should keep your mind on some technical thing. It helps the imagination to do its stuff, if you have your mind on a technical problem.

ORR: What about the sound of your poems? Do you think of your poems in musical terms, in terms of their being read aloud?

SPENCER: Yes, in the end I do, although I don't think it is necessary for all poets. But I myself am very attracted by the sound of words. Of course, everyone is really when they write. They hear an imaginary sort of voice, rather monotonous in their ear, chewing over what they are saying. What I hear in my ear is not really the way I would read it out in the end, when I had written it. But I think you hear in your ear a voice which is playing with the contrasting vowels and consonants and textures. That, I think, you hear and definitely I expect to hear it.

ORR: Do you expect your poems to make an impact on a first hearing, as distinct from the impact they may make when studied on the printed page?

SPENCER: Well, I don't think there is very much poetry being written nowadays which can have an impact on first hearing and I, who have to do a certain amount of lecturing and poetry-reading abroad, prefer to help an audience, if it is the first time they are going to be exposed to this poem, by pointing out a few things about the kind of poem it is. Because if you are reading by yourself a poem that is unfamiliar to you, you are in fact, through experience, already looking at the shape of it, and in the first few lines you are observing whether there is a rhyme going on or not. But it is much more elaborate than you can expect an audience of less trained people to be able to get at.

ORR: We hear a great deal today in the form of lament that contemporary poetry appeals to a very tiny audience in this country. Does this mean that the appreciation of poetry is becoming a more exclusive and difficult thing? We have heard it said, and I am sure you have, that poets are now writing poetry for other poets.

SPENCER: I don't think there has really been much change from what there already was. I mean, in Shakespeare's time he and his contemporaries were not writing their lyrics for the general public, were they? In fact, they used to keep them in manuscript and pass them round to other writers and highly educated friends and later on they were published. But they didn't have very grand sales, did they? The plays are a different matter. So I don't think that there is very much change. I think new poetry will always be rather limited in its first audiences until it has been digested through the machinery of criticism and made available to a wider public, usually years afterwards.

ORR: Do you find yourself constantly in the company of other poets, other writers, and perhaps artists and musicians?

SPENCER: Well, I don't very much. Maybe partly by circumstances, because I don't live in an English-speaking community most of the time. But, frankly, I think I rather prefer not to be. I think I like ordinary people, because I am listening, because they are my subject-matter, and I think if I got among a group of poets or writers very often I should be put off. I like listening to the ordinary person talk, not the literary person.

ORR: You think it is better, do you, in your case for the poet to live in a kind of literary isolation?

SPENCER: Yes, because the nature of my life is that I have to keep a lot of company and I don't get enough loneliness, and possibly this is an effort to get a kind of mental loneliness. You must let the pressures build up inside you and not be diluted by literary talk.

ORR: Do you find an interest in or a knowledge of other arts, the visual arts or music, is helpful to you as a poet?

SPENCER: I have, I think, a very strong visual sense and I am practically unmusical (someone said I am tone-deaf), but as for the visual arts, I am very stimulated by them and I am very stimulated by sights and sounds and feelings in the making of a poem.

ORR: Are there any recurrent themes, dominating themes, which you can detect in your own poetry or any constant filter through which all your observation and imagery passes in order to produce your poems?

SPENCER: No, I don't think so: possibly there is one thing. I have been living for a long time near the Mediterranean, that is to say in the scene of various earlier civilisations, and I suppose inevitably there's a sort of excitement and a reference to other civilisations which I find continuously stimulating me to write. I don't mean that is my only way of writing, but I do find that I have written a certain amount about such themes. The fact of being in some sort of continuity with earlier civilisations does have an exciting effect on me. That, I think, I can detect. It is about the only recurrent theme, if there is one, that I can think of.

ORR: Can you say, then, what is the sort of thing that prompts a poem in your mind?

SPENCER: I should say that I suddenly detect myself in a situation, out of which comes a so-far-unformulated excitement, and I suppose all poets must feel or learn to know this. It is like a sort of signal flashing on, or some particular kind of bell going. They know that there is a poem there, if they look attentively. One of the objects of writing is to explore and disentangle and put in some kind of form this nebula of feeling, which troubles and worries until it is listened to and dealt with and turned into a poem. It might happen at any moment and, no doubt, one sometimes does not hear the kind of signal to recognise one is in the presence of a poem. I rather like what a Greek poet said (it was Seferis) that you meet poems like people and certain kinds of poems in different places. A certain kind you may run into in a railway station, you can expect them there, and other kinds in, shall we say, the bathroom.

ORR: And it depends on the sort of poet you are as to whether you produce railway poems or bathroom poems?

SPENCER: Well, yes. What I really wanted to say was that poems are almost hanging about. Perhaps you may call them, if you like, but they only come up at that moment. But a lot of unrecognised poems, I think, are lived through every moment of your life. It depends on how alert or how undisturbed you are, or how excited and attentive you are at that very moment when the opportunity comes.

ORR: In the same way, perhaps, as it has been said of another art, that inside every unhewn block of marble there is a statue?

SPENCER: I suppose so. Something like that, yes. But definitely it is a feeling as if some sort of signal has gone on and the fact that inside you, from that moment, is a so-far-unexplored area of feeling and emotion, which is almost disagreeable to hold on to. And the poet, for all reasons, must then work on this or let it hang about, preferably for some time before he starts working on it, and this will turn into a poem, with luck.

ORR: And it is the exploration of this that makes the whole business of writing poetry worth while?

SPENCER: It isn't the only thing, but I think that is what leads one on at the first moment, if one wants to create something. But the first thing is really working on this: the exploring, trying to find out what it is. I suppose some sense of order is involved in trying to bring out, to give a shape to what is essentially, at the first moment, unshaped.

27th August 1962

Bernard Spencer Writes...

Recently I have been discovering again how limited the poet's control is of what he writes and when. At least it is for me. For instance you have had for some time a poem which you very much want to write, and you even have some 'given' lines or phrases towards it, an idea perhaps from these about the form it is likely to take, and a reasonable confidence that it is a real poem and not a phony one. And in spite of this, what happens? You write instead another poem which swept you off your heels, love at sight, last Tuesday. It amounts to a breach of promise.

The breach of promise may be committed several times again, and at the expense of the same poem. A likely reason is the 'breeding' or 'chain' quality of poems. The excitement of the actual writing of a poem can illuminate for me a different bit of experience, and I am confronted with the compelling demand of another poem which wants to be written, and which would probably not otherwise have 'got through' to me.

I learnt long ago from the Greek poet, George Seferis, to think of poems as sometimes waiting around to be written, perhaps in certain parts of town, until a poet comes along. But then, of course, he must be alert enough to recognise them. And what freaks of accident – or is it more than that – take him to the place where the poem is? And when he has written it, how contrary to what might have been anticipated, and to the writer's current preoccupations or views, the final result may be!

June 1963

NOTES & BIBLIOGRAPHY

NOTES

Archival sources are referred to here with the following short forms: *Reading* is the Bernard Spencer Archive, Special Collections, University of Reading, which has a catalogue by Verity Hunt, published as *Bernard Spencer at Reading* (University of Reading, 2009). *Buffalo* is the Poetry/Rare Books Collection of the University Libraries, State University of New York at Buffalo. *Carbondale* is Special Collections/Morris Library, Southern Illinois University at Carbondale. *Gennadius* is the Seferis Collection, Gennadius Library, American School of Classical Studies, Athens. *Kings* is the Rosamond Lehmann Papers, King's College, Cambridge. *Texas* is the Humanities Research Center, University of Texas at Austin. Other occasional items are sourced in the notes. The enlargement of the Spencer Archive at Reading has made it possible to collate and order a large number of surviving manuscripts for individual poems. I have not attempted here to add substantially to the listed variants that Roger Bowen gave in 1981. The documentation now invites detailed study of the poet's compositional processes for many later poems, such as my essay on 'Boat Poem' cited in the bibliography, and a variorum presentation. What I have done here is to correlate, where possible, the variants Bowen cites with the newly catalogued archive and, on occasion, to amend slightly his transcriptions.

Complete Poetry

AEGEAN ISLANDS AND OTHER POEMS (1946)
Poems before 1940

Allotments: April
The poem was first published in *New Verse* no. 21 (June-July 1936), pp. 4-5. In lines 13-14, Bowen has the barely grammatical 'what I hear / A spade slice', as does *Aegean Islands* (1946 and 1948) and *Collected Poems* (1965). I have preferred 'what I hear / Is spade slice', the *New Verse* reading (p. 4) also in *New Verse An Anthology* (1939), p. 35. Kenneth Allott anthologised the text with this reading in *The Penguin Book of Contemporary Verse* (1950), and Spencer referred to the volume on more than one occasion without pointing out a misprint.

A Hand
The poem was first published in *New Verse* no. 17 (Oct-Nov 1935), p. 4.

Plains as Large as Europe
Bowen corrected the ungrammatical 'certainly' in line 12 of the *Aegean Islands* text to 'certainty', the first publication reading in *New Verse* no. 13 (Feb 1935), p. 4.

There was no Instruction Given
First published in *New Verse* no. 15 (June 1935), p. 2.

Houses are Uniformed
First published, with the title 'Poem', in *New Verse* (Oct-Nov 1935), p. 5.

Evasions
First published in *New Verse* (Oct-Nov 1935), p. 4.

Portrait of a Woman and Others
First published in *New Verse* no. 13 (Feb 1935), pp. 4-5.

A Cold Night
First published in *New Verse* no. 24 (Feb-Mar 1937), pp. 8-9. The Battle for Madrid took place during November 1936, petering out into a siege of the Spanish capital that ended only when it fell to Nationalist forces on 28 March 1939.

Part of Plenty
First published in *New Verse* no. 24 (Feb-Mar 1937), pp. 10-11. Bowen notes that the subject is Nora Gibbs, whom Spencer had married in August 1936. Reading holds a translation of the poem into Spanish by Tomás Ramos Orea dated 1959. This is the one poem of Spencer's that Geoffrey Grigson, the editor of *New Verse*, continued to admire (See 'Bernard Spencer', *The Private Art: A Poetry Note-Book* (London: Allison & Busby, 1982), pp. 62-3), anthologising it in *The Faber Book of Love Poetry* (London: Faber & Faber, 1973), p. 227.

Cage
First published in *Year's Poetry*, ed. D.K. Roberts & Geoffrey Grigson (London: Lane-Bodley Head, 1937), p. 105.

Ill
First published in *New Verse* no. 24 (Feb-Mar 1937), p. 10.

A Thousand Killed
On the basis of lines 2 and 3 ('And am glad because the scrounging impe-rial paw / Was there so bitten'), and the date of first publication in *New Verse* no. 20 (April-May 1936), p. 10, which is before the outbreak of the Spanish Civil War in the summer of that year, it appears the poem was inspired by reading about the First Battle of Tembien (20-24 Jan 1936) in the Second Italo-Ethiopian War of 1935-6, an encounter described as inconclusive. Though the Ethiopians suffered 8,000 casualties, the Italian casualty figures are given as 1,100.

Suburb Factories
Bowen notes that the first published version, in *New Verse* no. 20 (April-May 1936), p. 10, contains an extra verse between stanzas 4 and 5 of the *Aegean Islands* text:

> From the diamonded parks I would wish to delight
> At shapes that attack and are new:
> But it's hard,
> Knowing only for certain; power is here surrendered
> And it changes to the hands of the few.

Waiting
First published in *New Verse* no. 29 (March 1938), p. 12.

How Must We Live?
The earliest of Spencer's post-Oxford poems to see print, this was first pub-lished in a 'Poetry Supplement', *The Listener* (12 July 1933), facing p. 76. In l. 9 I have reverted to 'Blood is quiet', the *Aegean Islands* reading, where Bowen has 'in quiet'.

My Sister
First published as an untitled poem in *New Verse* no. 13 (Feb 1935), p. 5. Bowen notes that Spencer's father, Sir Charles Gordon Spencer, died at Tarwood House, South Leigh, Oxfordshire, in November 1934. Cynthia Peppercorn, bearing a child, was reunited with her brothers, John and Bernard, at the family home.

AEGEAN ISLANDS AND OTHER POEMS (1946)
Poems 1940 to 1942

Aegean Islands 1940-41

There is a typescript in *Gennadius*. First published in *Personal Landscape* no. 1 (Jan 1942), p. 4.

Greek Excavations

There is a signed typescript in *Gennadius*. First published in *Personal Landscape* no. 1 (Jan 1942), p. 5, and in *Citadel* (Feb 1942), p. 7. For the book publication Spencer transposes '– And I suddenly discover this discovered town' from the last line of stanza 1 to the first of stanza 2. *Reading* holds a translation into Spanish by Tomás Ramos Orea dated April 1959.

Salonika June 1940

There is a signed typescript in *Gennadius*. First published in *Aegean Islands*, p. 9.

Delos

There is a typescript in *Gennadius* with the first 9 lines translated into Greek by Seferis. First published in *Personal Landscape* no. 1 (Jan 1942), p. 6. Bowen notes that *Collected Poems* (1965) revises out the repetition of 'violence' in l. 17, and restores the *Aegean Islands* reading published here. See 'The Wind-blown Island of Mykonos' (pp. 258-60 above) for a prose account of the poem's occasion.

Base Town

There is a typescript in *Gennadius*. First published in *Personal Landscape* no. 2 (Mar 1942), p. 15. The town is Salonika (Thessaloniki) in northern Greece.

Death of an Airman

There is a typescript in *Gennadius*. First published in *Citadel* (April 1942), p. 23. The pilot is from the Italian air force, shot down during a raid on Salonika.

Letters

There is a typescript in *Gennadius*. First published in *Personal Landscape* no. 3 (June 1942), p. 11, where l. 9 reads: 'Now public truths are scarce as sovereigns'. Olivia Manning quotes the poem in 'Poets in Exile', *Horizon* no. 10 (Nov 1944), p. 272, introducing it by noting that Nora had returned to London before the Fall of France in June 1940, and was not permitted to rejoin her husband thanks to the worsening war situation. They were reunited in Cairo in January 1945.

Libyan Front
First published in *Aegean Islands* p. 14. This is the first of Spencer's poems set in North Africa. He had arrived in Cairo in early 1941.

Egyptian Delta
There is a typescript in *Gennadius* with l. 5 translated into Greek by Seferis. First published in *Aegean Islands* p. 15.

Acre
First published in *Personal Landscape* vol. 1 no. 4 (1942), p. 5. Spencer went for two weeks of summer leave to Palestine during 1942 and 1943.

Frontier
Gennadius holds a typescript. First published in *Personal Landscape* vol. 1 no. 4 (1942), p. 4.

Cairo Restaurant
Gennadius holds a typescript. First published in *Aegean Islands*, p. 18.

The Ship
First published in *Personal Landscape* vol. 2 no. 2 (1944), p. 7. Bowen notes that the setting is Nahariah, Palestine.

Behaviour of Money
First published in *Personal Landscape* vol. 2 no. 1 (1943), pp. 15-16.

Yachts on the Nile
First published in *Personal Landscape: An Anthology of Exile* (London: Editions Poetry, 1954), p. 64. *Reading* holds a typescript and a carbon of a translation into Spanish by Tomás Ramos Orea, dated April 1959.

Olive Trees
First published in *Aegean Islands*, p. 23. See 'Madrid University Lecture', above p. 295 for an account of this poem's beginnings on a bus in Palestine during the summer of 1942. First published in *Aegean Islands* p. 23. Berthold

Goldschmidt (1903-96) set the poem for tenor and orchestra in *Mediterranean Songs* (1958), a cycle of six texts (Byron's 'Lines Written in an Album, at Malta', Lawrence Durrell's 'Nemea', 'Olive Trees', Flecker's 'The Old Ships', and Shelley's 'Stanzas Written in Dejection near Naples') premièred at the Kaufmann Concert Hall, New York, in 1959.

The Building of the House

First published in *Personal Landscape* vol. 2 no. 2 (1944), p. 8. Variants include ll. 5-6: 'features from it, and eyes to see: such fancies / and all the tumble and ballet of building gear'; l. 9: 'were portrait-maker's touches, cool in feeling'; and 1. 21: 'which never touches us to the bone?'

Peasant Festival

First published in *Aegean Islands*, p. 25. Bowen also suggests 'The Windblown Island of Mykonos' (pp. 258-60 above) as a context for this poem.

Egyptian Dancer at Shubra

First published in *Personal Landscape* vol. 2 no. 3 (1944), p. 6 as 'Dancer at Shubra'. Shubra is a northern district of Cairo on the east bank of the Nile. Compare Ruth Speirs' translation of Rilke's 'Spanish Dancer', which appeared in *Personal Landscape* no. 3 (June 1942), p. 6. She acknowledges Spencer's advice with these translations in her 'Note' to Rainer Maria Rilke, *Selected Poems*, trans. Ruth Speirs (Cairo: The Anglo Egyptian Bookshop, [1944]), n.p.

Passed On

First published in *Personal Landscape*, vol. 2 no 1 (1943), p. 16, as 'Passed Over'. Bowen notes among the variants ll. 4-5: 'in desks and scrapbooks, what he used to call / visitors and uncles'; and l. 13: 'even rough horse-play, crashing a table about.'

In an Auction Room

First published *Personal Landscape*, vol. 2 no. 4 (1945), p. 12.

Sarcophagi

Gennadius holds a typescript. First published in *Personal Landscape*, vol. 1 no. 2 (1942), p. 3. Bowen notes that *Collected Poems* (1965) combines stanzas 3 and 4, and he reverts to the text in *Aegean Islands*, p. 29.

The Beginning
Reading holds a typescript marked up by the printer of *The Twist in the Plotting*. Bowen (1981) has the proof-reading slip 'Constaninople' for 'Constantinople'.

Delicate Grasses
First published in the *New Statesman* (14 May 1960), p. 719, as 'Feathery Grasses'. *Reading* holds a typescript marked up by the printer of *The Twist in the Plotting*, where it was published with the earlier title. The typewritten text for ll. 9-10 reads 'slow as the seconds wear / or dial needles prowl' and is revised to the definitive version in the poet's hand. The uncorrected page proof for *With Luck Lasting* still calls it 'Feathery Grasses', indicating that the title change was made at this late stage. The poem is set among the remains of ancient Greek towns on the south coast of Turkey. Bowen cites the passage from the 'University of Madrid Lecture' introducing this poem: see above pp. 285.

Notes by a Foreigner
First published in *The London Magazine* (Dec 1955), pp. 28-9. *Reading* holds 7 items connected with this poem. These include 3 early notes and drafts, and 1 typed sheet made after the publication of *The Twist in the Plotting*. Bowen cites from a further three-page draft with revisions and the variant title 'The Foreigner', noting the variant ll. 1-2: 'Deep in their kind of eyes / you imagine gleams some truth about this town.' It is set in Madrid. Spencer comments on the poem in 'Poems by Bernard Spencer' and 'University of Madrid Lecture' pp. 285 and 295 above.

From my Window
Reading holds 5 items, including an untitled ink draft much revised in pencil. All begin 'Now that', including the typescript used to set the first published text in *The Twist in the Plotting*, p. 10, which suggests that the revision was made on the lost proof for this publication.

Mediterranean Suburbs
Reading holds 6 items: 2 untitled pencil drafts, 1 draft with variant title 'As It Happens', 1 typescript with earlier title and variant third verse, 1 carbon of typescript with variant title 'Madrid Suburbs' and pencil note (not in Spencer's hand) which reads 'pathos of the lost and the outcast', a

carbon, and the typescript marked up by the printer of *The Twist in the Plotting*, where it was first published, p. 11. Bowen cites the 'As It Happens' draft variants for ll. 12-17: 'a few small boys have left their games to romp / around the scarecrow player. Streets and evening / family, music, beggar; all these are / connected or not, would you say good or not, / are, as it happens, now and in Castilla / under the eternities of that first-starred sky.' In his 5 Nov 1954 letter to Fletcher, held at *Reading*, Spencer writes: 'For British Council reasons I would like the title *Madrid Suburbs* altered to *Mediterranean Suburbs*.'

Fluted Armour

Reading holds 5 items: 1 manuscript draft, 1 crumbled biro fair copy with variants, 1 carbon with biro revision of l. 6 and pencil commentary not in Spencer's hand, 2 copies of uncorrected Galley Twenty-Three, Bernard Spencer 'Three Poems' for *The London Magazine* (August 1955), p. 33, and the typescript marked up by the printer of *The Twist in the Plotting*. Bowen cites 'Reading MS' (BSP 1/15/1 [MS 2413]) l. 1: 'Because of the splintering of every day' (deleted) and notes further autograph revisions. He gives the revision on 'Reading TS' (BSP 1/15/3 [MS 2413]) l. 6 as 'particular things' to 'confusion of particulars'. The pencil commentary on this carbon reads: 'The wine-glass (social life and dissipation) and the storm-cloud (the natural scene and the life of the passions) prevented particular insights or consummations occurring; against those things which he knowingly sought, he, unknowingly, went to the National Gallery and from an apparently disparate set of particular experiences: of suffering and charity in San Sebastian / of sexual love / and of the unflinching quality of art and war – '. Spencer's 5 Nov 1954 letter to Fletcher, held at *Reading*, suggests removing 'Piero di' in the penultimate line if the BBC reader cannot cope with the length of the final two-line phrase.

Out of Sleep

Reading holds 1 item: the typescript marked up by the printer of *The Twist in the Plotting*. Published in *Poetry (London)* no. 11 (Sept-Oct 1947), pp. 12-13.

A Spring Wind

Gennadius holds 1 typescript with 'Seferis' underlined in red, l. 1: 'slam to' and l. 16: 'its tide'. *Reading* holds 1 item: the typescript marked up by the printer of *The Twist in the Plotting*, which has 'slam to' deleted and autograph revision. Published in *The Windmill* vol. 1 no. 1 (1946), p. 55.

This *Gennadius* typescript is most probably the copy sent to the Greek poet by Nanos Valaoritis and described by Spencer in his 1 June 1946 letter to Seferis as 'a great quivering slice of nostalgia of which I've just been delivered!'

On a Carved Axle-Piece from a Sicilian Cart

Reading holds 1 item: the typescript marked up by the printer of *The Twist in the Plotting*. Biro autograph revision to l. 22 with deleted earlier reading: 'the who and what and why of God and us'. Published in *Penguin New Writing* no. 32 (1949), pp. 78-9.

The Boats

Reading holds 3 items: the typescript marked up by the printer of *The Twist in the Plotting*, 1 carbon copy, 1 carbon copy with Spanish-style indented first lines attached to a translation into Spanish by Tomás Ramos Orea, 1959. Published in *Penguin New Writing* no. 37 (1949), p. 82.

At Courmayeur

Reading holds 1 item: the typescript marked up by the printer of *The Twist in the Plotting* with autograph biro revisions for the earlier l. 14: 'to draw more closely' and l. 18: 'is hard and real as rocks.' Published in *Penguin New Writing* no. 37 (1949), p. 81. Bowen notes that the poem is in memory of Nora, and refers readers to G.S. Fraser, 'The Absence of the Dead', *The Traveller has Regrets* (London: Editions Poetry, 1948), pp. 2-3. Courmayeur is an Italian town in the autonomous Valle D'Aosta region at the foot of Mont Blanc.

In a Foreign Hospital

Reading holds 1 item: the typescript marked up by the printer of *The Twist in the Plotting*. *Buffalo* holds 1 typescript and a galley, signed, with l. 16 as 'England is somewhere far enough to my right'. Published in *Poetry Review* vol. 40 no. 3 (June-July 1949), p. 177. Bowen reports that Spencer entered the Beau-Soleil Clinic, Leysin, Switzerland on 2 September 1948 for a thoracotomy. He cites the poet from his 18 November 1948 letter to John Lehmann in *Texas*: 'There is no special connection between Parts I and II of "In a Foreign Hospital". They might easily appear separately. It's just that the title seemed to suit both.' Bowen comments that only one 'part' appears to have been published, and to have survived – making it possible that by 'parts' Spencer might have intended the two verses.

Regent's Park Terrace

Reading holds 1 item: the typescript marked up by the printer of *The Twist in the Plotting*. Published in *Poetry (London)* (Nov-Dec 1947), p. 23. Nora and Bernard Spencer stayed with Tambimuttu at his flat in Regent's Park Terrace, London NW1, during the autumn of 1945.

Letter Home

Reading holds 6 items: 1 untitled biro draft, 1 crumpled biro draft, 1 carbon with biro revision for 1. 9, 1 fair copy including vision to 1. 9, 1 carbon, and the typescript marked up by the printer of *The Twist in the Plotting*, where it was first published, p. 20. Bowen reports the 1. 9 revision from the deleted 'names of cargoes and iron harbours', and cites the poet's 5 November 1954 letter to Fletcher held at *Reading*: 'a little reminder of Cairo (Zamalek).' The paper on which the first draft is written suggests composition in Madrid during the early 1950s and is the same brand used for 'In Memoriam'.

Morning in Madrid

Reading holds 5 items: 1 near complete pencil draft with final title and variants, 1 draft with variant title 'Early Morning Madrid', 1 carbon with the variant title, 1 carbon of final version, and the typescript marked up by the printer of *The Twist in the Plotting*, where it was first published, p. 21.

The Café with the Blue Shrine

Reading holds 5 items: 1 untitled pencil draft, 1 manuscript with variant title 'Flamenco', 1 carbon, 2 copies of uncorrected Galley Twenty-Three, Bernard Spencer 'Three Poems' for *The London Magazine* (August 1955), p. 32, and the typescript marked up by the printer of *The Twist in the Plotting*. Bowen cites this variant from the revisions on the second item above, ll. 18-20: 'doubtless approved a different harmony / of world and when and home we never came / within years or vineyards of; who watched the swaggerers stand.' He also notes on the last of these items, the deleted variant in l. 18: 'heard in his bones that song', with autograph revision.

Castanets

Reading holds 6 items: 3 early pencil drafts, 1 revised biro draft, 1 biro fair copy, and the typescript marked up by the printer of *The Twist in the Plotting*. Bowen notes among variants in the second of these ll. 9-12: 'I watch her body kindle and glow / and a knife in her glance / and wonder at the icy / shiver of pleasure now'. Published in *The London Magazine* (Dec 1955), p. 29.

In Athens

Reading holds 12 items: 1 early pencil draft, 1 draft in biro, 1 biro draft with variant ending, 1 typescript, 1 near complete draft with a single revision, 1 biro draft marked '(New version)', 1 carbon copy, 1 carbon copy with Spanish-style indented first lines attached to a translation into Spanish by Tomás Ramos Orea, 1959, the typescript marked up by the printer of *The Twist in the Plotting*, a copy of the poem in the *New Statesman and Nation* (6 April 1957), p. 446, and 2 double-sided typed sheets of 'Poems from *The Twist in the Plotting*', one of which contains Spencer's note: 'a girl who passed me on a corner near the Royal Palace, Syntagma Square'. Bowen cites the earlier ending from 'Reading MS' (BSP1/27/3 [MS 5370]) which I have amended as follows, the last 3 lines being lightly deleted and line 9 interpolated:

> An alteration of pulse,
> and a word your body is trying to make you hear
> is all you are left with on a city corner,
> as she goes past, hair flapped across her cheek,
> so near where they talked well on love
> two civilisations ago, and found
> splendid and jeering images: 'the Blind',
> 'the Wonder', 'the Unknowable'
> A word your body is trying to make you...?
> and then–because we love and still look onwards
> – the last wry joke: the split
> apple that famishes for its perfect half.

Spencer expresses versions of such ideas about love in the last of 3 letters to Rosamond Lehmann from the summer of 1932, held in *Kings*. He comments on the context of the poem in 'Poems by Bernard Spencer' and 'University of Madrid Lecture', see above pp. 285 and 296-7.

The Rendezvous

Reading holds 8 items: 1 untitled pencil draft on two sheets, 1 almost complete biro draft, 2 incomplete biro drafts, 1 biro fair copy, 1 uncorrected Galley Four of Bernard Spencer 'Three Poems' for *The London Magazine* (April 1957), p. 45, the typescript marked up by the printer of *The Twist in the Plotting*, and a double-sided typed sheet of 'Poems from *The Twist in the Plotting*.' Bowen cites the BSP 1/28/5 [MS 2413] l. 11 variant: 'since smashed windows, cars on fire'. In an 8 April 1956 note to Fletcher, Spencer notes that the poem is 'unpublished and hot off the pen. No typewriter available', and he indicates the imagined sensitivity of the poem's relation to the current Cyprus crisis between Britain and Greece: 'If you think it's any good, the subject etc might have a special interest for the reading. But politic <u>not to specify too much</u>.' In a second note, two days later, he writes: 'If you use the poem, "The Rendezvous", at the I.C.A., please read "glass crashing" for "smashed windows" in l. 10. This avoids repetition of the word "window" in two different contexts.'

The Lottery Sellers
Reading holds 7 items: early pencil draft, 1 typescript with variant l. 1: 'pewter sky', 1 carbon of previous item, 1 carbon with variant l. 1: 'gun-grey', 1 carbon of the above, 1 uncorrected Galley Four, for Bernard Spencer 'Three Poems' in *The London Magazine* (April 1957), p. 46, and the typescript marked up by the printer of *The Twist in the Plotting*. Bowen cites '[Melanie] Isaacs MS' variant for the opening: 'Under a pewter sky / – passers are muffled and the snow-wind races', and a 'Reading TS' (BSP 1/29/7 [MS 2413]) with the deleted l. 15 variant: 'on a hell-cold corner' and autograph revision.

Train to Work
Reading holds 3 items: 1 almost complete biro draft, with one deletion, written on the back of a biro draft of 'The Rendezvous', 1 carbon copy, and the typescript marked up by the printer of *The Twist in the Plotting*, where the poem was first published, p. 27.

At 'The Angler'
Reading holds 11 items: 1 notes for poem including pub name, 'The Angler', 1 manuscript draft of ll. 12-20, three ink drafts with the variant stanza 4 given below, 1 biro fair copy with the variant stanza, 1 typescript with the revised stanza 4 in autograph ink, 2 carbons, the typescript marked up by the printer of *The Twist in the Plotting*, and a copy of the printed poem in *The New Statesman and Nation* (16 Feb 1957), p. 208. Here is the earlier stanza that Bowen cites:

> A little of the ideal suffices lovers:
> for instance, with the end of storm
> how swans curved near as if to bring good omen
> to us – whom love's worst love had wrung
> too frequently – and in their trance of calm
> possessed like many lamps the water where they hung.

He describes this as derived from a 'Bowen MS', now in *Reading* (BSP 1/31/5 [MS 5370]) though this has a different variant final stanza. He also lists further revisions to the stanza, including l. 24: 'blinded the water where they hung', appearing on (BSP 1/31/3 [MS 2413]).

The Administrator

Reading holds 7 items: 2 manuscripts, 1 typescript, 3 carbons, and the type-script marked up by the printer of *The Twist in the Plotting*. Bowen notes the autograph revision of l. 10 from 'impulsive' to 'passionate', and the adding of the l. 18 repetition of 'but cold' on the typescript used to set *The Twist in the Plotting*. First published in *The London Magazine* (July 1960), p. 67, without the second 'But cold'.

Night-time: Starting to Write

First published in *The Twist in the Plotting* p. 30. *Reading* holds 3 manu-scripts, 1 with the title 'Writing at Night', 2 typescripts, 1 marked up by the printer for *The Twist in the Plotting*, and 2 carbons. Bowen cites a couple of variants from the typescripts: 'Idly I note these sounds' in l. 7 and '– must play a loved-loathed role' in l. 11. His 1981 text contains 'be dammed the call to sleep' for 'be damned' – as it is in the three previous printings. I have restored the swear word.

Sud-Express

First published in *The Twist in the Plotting*, p. 31. *Reading* holds 7 items: 1 early manuscript draft, 1 typescript, 4 carbon copies, and the typescript marked up by the printer of *The Twist in the Plotting*. The poet comments on it in 'Poems by Bernard Spencer' p. 285 above.

Boat Poem

Reading holds 6 items: 4 pages of earliest draft notes, 3 pages of handwritten drafts in blue spiral 'Victoria' notepad, 1 complete draft on 2 pages torn out and reinserted in 'Victoria', 1 typescript of 2 pages, 1 carbon, and the typescript submitted to Hodder and Stoughton with the poem dated 'July 1962', corrected to '61'. *Texas* holds a carbon. Published in *The London Magazine* (Feb 1962), pp. 17-19 with l. 28 omitted. Bowen notes that the setting is Ibiza. For a full transcription of the materials for this poem and a discussion of its occasion, context, the poet's work on it, and their sig-nificances, see Peter Robinson, 'Bernard Spencer's "Boat Poem"', *English* vol. 58 no. 229 (Winter 2009), pp. 318-39.

Table Tennis

Reading holds 6 items: 1 page of biro notes, 3 biro drafts, 1 carbon with biro corrections, and the typescript submitted to Hodder and Stoughton with the poem dated '1960'. *Texas* holds a carbon. Published in *The London Magazine* (June 1962), p. 5.

The Leopards

Reading holds 7 items: 2 early biro drafts, 4 biro drafts, and the typescript submitted to Hodder and Stoughton with the poem dated '1960'. *Texas* holds a carbon. Published in *The London Magazine* (June 1962), pp. 5-6.

A Sunday

Reading holds 3 items: 1 manuscript draft with deleted earlier title 'Plaza de Toros' and l. 9 as 'laughter like gravel falling', a carbon copy, and the typescript submitted to Hodder and Stoughton with the poem dated '1960'. *Texas* holds a carbon. First published in *The London Magazine* (June 1962), p. 6. Bowen notes the setting as Chinchon, near Madrid.

Cripples

Reading holds 6 items: 1 sheet of notes, 1 rough draft, 1 manuscript with deleted title 'Crutches', a further manuscript, a carbon, and the typescript submitted to Hodder and Stoughton, where the poem is dated 'July Sept 61'. *Texas* holds a carbon. First published *The London Magazine* (June 1962), pp. 6-7. Bowen cites a variant reading for l. 9: 'heave acres of vineyards towards months of sun'. I have adjusted the spelling to 'wantonness' from 'wantoness' in l. 11, which is how the word appears on the first 5 items.

Watchers

Reading holds 6 items: 2 early drafts of first stanza, 1 manuscript with variant title 'High Trapeze', 1 manuscript with deleted variant title 'The Sleepers' and 'The Watchers' with article deleted, 1 typescript with a single word deleted, and the typescript submitted to Hodder and Stoughton, with the poem dated 'July 1961'. Bowen notes a cancelled variant in the third item above: 'These are like faces drained in sleep. There stays / no thought in them for field or hearth or children'. *Texas* holds a carbon as 'Watchers'. Published in *The London Magazine* (Jan 1963), pp. 7-8.

The Wedding Pictures

Reading holds 4 items: 1 early draft, 1 manuscript, 1 typescript, and the typescript submitted to Hodder and Stoughton, with the poem dated '1962'. First published in *The London Magazine* (Jan 1963), pp. 8-9.

By a Breakwater

Reading holds 4 items: 2 manuscript pages with deleted variant title 'At Dover', 1 manuscript on 2 sheets with deleted variant title 'By The Breakwater', 1 manuscript page, and the typescript submitted to Hodder and Stoughton, with the poem dated 'Jan 1962'. Bowen notes the deletion of the original last line in item 2 above: 'After ten years I feel myself walking and turning to look again down the wind.' First published in *The London Magazine* (Jan 1963), pp. 7-8.

Lop-sided

Reading holds 6 items: 1 sheet of biro notes and phrases, 1 early draft called 'Meteorology', 1 complete draft with this title cancelled and replaced with the definitive one, 1 typescript, 1 carbon (from a different typewriter), and the typescript submitted to Hodder and Stoughton, with the poem dated '1960'. Bowen cites the following variant from the second item above: l. 9: 'We had noticed no adequate preliminaries.'

Donkey

Reading holds 4 items: 1 early biro draft, 1 manuscript draft in back of the pink Ankara notebook, with variant ending, 1 biro fair copy with variants in stanza 3, and the typescript submitted to Hodder and Stoughton, the poem dated '1959'. First published in *The London Magazine* (Nov 1960), p. 30. In l. 15 I have reverted to the *With Luck Lasting* reading of 'kindling wood' where Bowen has 'kindly'.

Full Moon

Reading holds 4 items: 1 early pencil draft, 1 typescript, the typescript submitted to Hodder and Stoughton with the poem dated '1956', and 1 uncorrected Galley Four, for Bernard Spencer 'Three Poems' in *The London Magazine* (April 1957), p. 46. Bowen cites from Spencer's 12 Aug 1963 letter to Clover Pertiñez: 'The poem about the moon was written in Athens during my time there (1955-56)... The full moon – and the cry of the mating cats – play a great part in my memories of the town'.

The Agents

Reading holds 5 items: 1 untitled unfinished manuscript page, 1 manuscript draft with considered alternative title 'Her Agents', 1 biro fair copy, 1 photograph of a manuscript not in Spencer's hand with 4 passages underlined, and the typescript submitted to Hodder and Stoughton, the poem dated '1957'. Bowen cites the following Petrarchan variant from the second of these, l. 18: 'such long years of frost-fire'. Published in *The London Magazine* (Nov 1960), p. 3. The l. 14 phrase 'like glass jags that top a wall' is a memory of ll. 16-17 in Montale's 'Merrigiare pallido e assorto', which Spencer had translated about a decade before as 'a wall / crowned with sharp splinters of bottle.' See above, p. 247. Ruth Speirs' 11 Sept and 8 Oct 1963 letters to Lawrence Durrell held at *Carbondale* suggests that her complex relationship with Spencer may be contributing to the poem's theme.

Chestnuts

Reading holds 1 item: the typescript submitted to Hodder and Stoughton, on which the poem is dated '1959'. Bowen cites Spencer's 2 Feb 1960 letter to Fletcher, held at *Reading*: 'I got the idea when I was staying in Buckinghamshire last September-October.' Bowen notes that Spencer's brother, John Spencer-Bernard, was bequeathed Nether Wynchendon House and estate near Aylesbury in 1954.

Blue Arm

Reading holds 7 items: 2 sheets of notes and phrases, 1 manuscript draft, 1 almost complete biro fair copy with a revision, 1 photocopy of a manuscript, 1 carbon typescript, and the typescript sent to Hodder and Stoughton, with the poem dated '1960'. Bowen also lists a Pertiñez MS, initialled, and with variants including: l. 6: 'sunhaze'; l. 7: 'Perhaps it is all an answer'; l. 12: 'the blue arm fumbles a window'. Published in *The London Magazine* (Nov 1960), p. 32. Bowen restores, from the magazine publication and Pertiñez MS, the evidently correct reading of 'peeling' for 'peelings' as the rhyme-word at the end of l. 1 (it being a participle and not a plural noun). He also cites Spencer's 31 May 1960 letter to Fletcher (held at *Reading*) about the contents and title of *The Twist in the Plotting*: 'If you would consider putting in the poem 'Blue Arm' of which I enclose a copy (it is new) and calling the collection by that title. It would mean knocking out the poem 'Night Time; Starting to Write', which is on rather the same theme.' It wasn't substituted, and had to wait for *With Luck Lasting* to be collected.

Near Aranjuez

Reading holds 4 items: an MS draft, a typescript with l. 13 as 'the Romans found' deleted and replaced with autograph revision, two uncorrected proofs of 'Three Poems' for *The London Magazine* (August 1955), p. 33, and the Hodder and Stoughton typescript where it is dated 1955. In the uncorrected page proof of *With Luck Lasting*, 'On the Road' is the penultimate poem, and the book concludes with 'Near Aranjuez'. The two must have been reversed on the lost corrected proof returned to Hodder and Stoughton.

On the Road

Reading holds three typescripts and a translation into Spanish by Tomás Ramos Orea, dated May 1959. The typescript submitted to Hodder and

Stoughton has it as the penultimate poem in the collection, dated (erroneously) 1948. First published in *Penguin New Writing* no. 32 (1947), p. 79. The poem appears to have been selected out of *The Twist in the Plotting* by Ian Fletcher on the grounds that its anthologising in Kenneth Allott's *The Penguin Book of Contemporary Verse* (1950), p. 231-2, had made it too familiar with readers. See Spencer's 31 May 1960 letter to Fletcher in *Reading*. Bowen cites from 'Poems by Bernard Spencer': '[it] has a setting in France, at a place along the River Loire. The theme is the possibility of entirely perfect and happy episodes in life, although the title implies that they do not usually last very long.' See above, p. 284.

COLLECTED POEMS (1965)
Poems from Vienna

The Empire Clock
Reading holds 4 items: 2 sheets of notes, a one-page draft, and a typescript with biro corrections from which Bowen cites variants in l. 2: 'muffled gnashing' and l. 5: 'long voiceless'. First published *The London Magazine* (Sept 1963), p. 4. The Spencers lived at Reischachstraße 3/9, Wien 1, from October 1962 to September 1963.

On the 'Sievering' Tram
Reading holds 4 manuscript drafts. Bowen lists an initialled MS in the possession of Clover Pertiñez. First published in *The London Magazine* (Sept 1963), pp. 4-5. Sievering is a suburb in Vienna, part of Döbling, the 19th district. Piers Spencer was born on 7 February 1963.

The Invaders
Reading holds 3 items: some draft notes on a programme for a guest performance of *The Beggars' Opera* by The Royal College of Music at the Konservatorium Der Stadt Wein on 2 and 3 April [1963], and 2 other draft sheets. First published in *The London Magazine* (Sept 1963), pp. 5-6. Austria and Vienna were divided into sectors and occupied by the WWII Allies between 1945 and 12 May 1955, some seven years before Spencer was transferred to the British Council in the Austrian capital.

A Number
Reading holds 2 items: a sheet of notes for the poem, and two drafts on 1 sheet of British Council headed paper. Bowen cites a variant l. 17: 'I thought

you were counting out the stitches that you were always counting.' He notes that the last line was added after the birth of Piers Spencer. First published in *The London Magazine* (Sept 1963), p. 6.

Properties of Snow

Reading holds 3 manuscript drafts. First published in *The London Magazine* (Sept 1963), pp. 6-7. The phrase in l. 5 'the killed from a battle whispering by' recalls Thomas Hardy's 'In Time of "The Breaking of Nations"' ll. 9-10: 'Yonder a maid and her wight / Come whispering by'.

Clemente

Reading holds 14 items: first notes for the poem on front and back of an envelope containing travel ticket and receipt for Salzburg–Innsbruck, 22 Feb 1963, 12 manuscript drafts, and 1 incomplete typescript. Bowen cites a variant from 'Bowen MS' (BSP 1/56/12 [MS 5370]): 'Addressed by a girl in Madrid to winter-haunted Vienna: / 'item...item...item...Clemente died...item.' // With what was his smile, once, / with what he would boast of, / Clemente who wangled you the cruel drinks.' *Texas* holds a magazine galley proof. First published in *The London Magazine* (Dec 1963), p. 13.

You

Reading holds 3 items: a page of early notes, and 2 drafts of the poem. First published in *The London Magazine* (Jan 1964), p. 47. The notes are on the back of a timetable for trains from and to Vienna via Leoben and Klagenfurt, dated 21 May 1963, helping date work on the poem and perhaps suggesting its occasion.

Dr Karl Lueger

Reading holds 1 manuscript. First published in *The London Magazine* (Jan 1964), p. 48. Karl Lueger (1844–1910) was the founder of the Christian-Social Party and mayor of Vienna from 1897 to 1910. The degree and character of Lueger's anti-Semitism is contested, something the poem is likely aware of. His monument, a statue with allegorically sculptured plinth by Josef Mullner completed in 1926, is in Dr-Karl-Lueger-Platz.

To Piers Spencer, five months old

Reading holds 4 items: 1 sheet of notes, 2 biro drafts with variants, and 1 completed manuscript. First published in *The London Magazine* (Jan 1964), pp. 48-9. The poet's son, born on 7 February, was five months old in June 1963, making this most likely the last poem Spencer completed before his death.

Traffic in April

Reading holds 4 items: notes towards the final stanza on the back of a British Council envelope, 1 sheet of notes for the poem, 1 draft with variant title 'Traffic in Spring', and a further draft with both variant title and final one. First published in *The London Magazine* (Jan 1964), p. 49.

UNCOLLECTED AND UNPUBLISHED POEMS
Early Poems 1929-1932

'The lights with big elegant fingers'
Published *Sir Galahad* vol. 1 no. 1 (29 Feb 1929), p. 31.

Schedules
Published *Sir Galahad* vol. 1 no. 2 (14 May 1929), p. 19.

Collection
Published in *Oxford Outlook*, vol. x no. 50 (Nov 1929), p. 362.

Festa
Published in *Oxford Poetry* (1929), pp. 46-7.

'Above, the fingers of the tree'
First published in *Oxford Poetry* (1930), p. 36.

Departure
Published in *Oxford Poetry* (1930), p. 37.

'Those near and dead who think there is another'
Published in *Oxford Poetry* (1930), p. 38.

After Love
Published in *Oxford Poetry* (1931), pp. 34-5.

Poem ('After the wheels and wings of this intense day')
Published in *Oxford Poetry* (1931), pp. 36.

Clouded, Still, Evening
Published in *Oxford Poetry* (1931), pp. 37.

Poem ('White factories lancing sky')
Published in *Oxford Poetry* (1931), pp. 38.

Two Poems ('My pulling on my shoes') ('Her hands waking on her lap')
Published in *Oxford Outlook* vol. xii no. 57 (Feb 1932), pp. 42-3. The second also published in *Oxford Poetry* (1932), p. 45.

'Who sees the rain fall into the spring land'
Published in *Oxford Outlook* vol. xii no. 58 (May 1932), p. 132.

'For seeing whole I had been too near my friends'
Published in *Oxford Poetry* (1932), pp. 46.

'Such height of corn'
There is a typescript contained with the three letters of probably summer 1932 from Spencer to Rosamond Lehmann in *Kings*. Published in *Oxford Poetry* (1932), p. 47.

UNCOLLECTED AND UNPUBLISHED POEMS
Uncollected Poems 1935-1946

'Most things having a market price'
Published in *New Verse* (June 1935), p. 2.

'I, Jack, walking on the hill's shoulder'
Published in *New Verse* (June 1935), pp. 2-3.

The Runner
Published in *New Verse* (June 1935), p. 3.

Winter Landscape
Published in the *Spectator* (24 April 1936), p. 751. Bowen notes that the occasion and place of this poem, Port Meadow, a stretch of common land to the north and west of Oxford, are suggested by Spencer's brief memoir, 'Talking of Barry', *Esfam* (May 1944), pp. 2-4.

The House
Published in *New Verse* (April-May 1936), p. 11.

Going to the Country
Published in *New Verse* (Feb-Mar 1937), pp. 9-10.

Picked Clean from the World
Published in *New Verse* (Jan 1938), p. 4.

They Tell a Lie
Gennadius holds a typescript attached to 'Death of an Airman'. Bowen notes that the first two stanzas, dated 'Groppi's, Cairo, June 1941', have been inscribed inside the cover of Seferis's copy of *Aegean Islands*, sent to him in 1946. The poem is also cited in Seferis's diary, *Days: 1st January 1941 to 31st December 1944* (Athens: Icarus, 1977), pp. 106-7, where he recalls meeting Spencer at Groppi's on 27 June 1941 and being shown this recently completed poem. It is also cited in Seferis's essay, 'The Greek Poems of Lawrence Durrell', *Labrys* (July 1979), pp. 91-2, trans. Anthony Tyrrell.

In Memoriam
Reading holds 4 items: an untitled pencil draft with many revisions, an ink manuscript of the last four lines on airmail paper used by Spencer when in Madrid, a typescript with question marks beside the last four lines and the author's name, and another typescript made by Bowen from the previous item. Bowen also notes that it appears in a list of 22 poems (held in *Reading*) some untraced, others existing at that date in manuscript, and some published between 1946 and 1955, providing a putative period for the composition of this work.

The Top-Storey Room
Published in *The Windmill* vol. 2 no. 1 (1946), p. 54.

UNCOLLECTED AND UNPUBLISHED POEMS
Uncollected Poems 1947-1963

Pino
Reading holds three items: a sheet with travel details for 'Alb[ergo] Nazionale, Pino Torinese', a one-page typescript containing the inserted un-cancelled autograph penultimate line 'the road of foreboding and of dreadful hope', and a typescript made by Bowen from the poem's publication in *Poetry (London)* no. 15 (May 1949), p. 5. Spencer writes to Fletcher in a 6 Feb

1961 letter held at *Reading* asking him if he has a copy of this poem, unused in *The Twist in the Plotting*, which he describes as 'about an Italian village'. Bowen also notes the revision, but publishes the magazine version. I have opted to include the line in the poem here.

The Clock
Reading holds 3 items: a pencil draft, a 2-page manuscript, and a typescript. Bowen notes that it is in the list with 'In Memoriam' and has a Madrid setting.

For Signorina Brunella Mori
Reading holds 3 items: a typescript, a carbon, and a photocopy. Bowen notes that it is listed with 'In Memoriam' and 'The Clock'.

A Ward
Reading holds 4 items: 2 manuscript drafts with variant title 'The Grapes', 1 biro draft with this title struck through and replaced by 'A Departure', and 1 typescript. Bowen notes of the third item above that it has substantial differences from the typescript, including this stanza 3:

> She might have found one, she did as much, that nurse
> who ran back, while we stared, and fetched from the curtains
> (or from remotest hills) a swinging cluster of
> foggy-blue grapes, and carried them through a silence;

Bowen also notes that Spencer was admitted to St George's Hospital, Brompton Road, London, SW1, in August 1959.

Black Cat
Reading holds 2 items: an initialled manuscript, and a typescript made by Bowen. He notes a deletion following l. 16: 'kicking up gravel, in a remembering mood (vein).' The whole manuscript is also cancelled in pencil. Bowen had it published in *The London Magazine* (Dec 1979-Jan 1980), p. 102.

Castille
Reading holds 5 items: 2 untitled pencil drafts, 1 ink draft with pencil revisions, 1 ink draft, and a typescript in which the first word of stanza 4 is 'How' rather than Bowen's reading of 'Now'. Since this forms a parallel construction with the 'how' at the beginning of l. 10, I have preferred it for the text published here. Bowen cites the following variant final stanza from 'Reading MS' (BSP 1/69/1 [MS 2413]:

If I am gentle I shall come to know
Contradiction bitterer than ours
The gilded Christs and a landscape shaped like pain
The dust and the oxen's feet and the bones and crowns and flowers.

In the last line Bowen has the ungrammatical 'fast' for 'feet', and Spencer has added 'pace' below it, indicating that he meant a noun.

This Day

Reading holds 1 two-page notebook draft, which Bowen described as 'heavily deleted' and suggesting 'a poem of greater length'. He cites a first stanza as one of many variants: '"I love you" her first words were / "I love you" first; and then the rendezvous, / the silly phone, her diffident low voice / goodbyes, endearments, were the ones I knew.' *Reading* also holds 1 manuscript of the 8-line poem, in which l. 4 reads: 'her looks, her voice, were only those I knew' and not the less apposite 'her books' as Bowen has it in his transcription.

Witness

Reading holds 5 items: 1 early biro notes, 1 early sketch of the second 2 stanzas, and 3 manuscript drafts. Bowen notes the existence of a 'Reading TS' dated Dec 1962 not in the archive and a 'Reading MS', one of the above, described as 'with minor variants'. 'Lais' refers to either Lais of Corinth or Lais of Hyccara, ancient Greek courtesans both.

Written on a Cigarette Packet

Reading holds 5 items: 2 parts of a 'Senior Service' cigarette packet with first drafts on the back, 2 manuscript drafts on writing paper attached to each other, and a biro draft with revisions. Though published in *The London Magazine* (Jan 1963), p. 7, and thus a 'Poem from Vienna', Ross did not include this in his *Collected Poems* (1965). The bar 'El Tenis' also figures in a passage from 'Madrid Notebook', see above p. 270.

From the Military Academy

Reading holds three items: 2 manuscript drafts on British Council paper, and 1 biro draft. Bowen notes the existence of a 'Reading TS' not in the archive, and a 'Reading MS with autograph revisions'. Bowen cites a Jan 1963 letter of Spencer's to Pertiñez: 'The "bugles" poem in the new lot is another one with reference to Breton de los Herreros' and adds that Spencer lived on this street for a time during his second posting to Madrid, Sept 1958 to July 1962.

The Train Window

Reading holds 3 items: 1 manuscript draft with variant titles 'From a Train Window' and 'A Train Window', 1 manuscript draft with variant title 'A Train Window', and a typescript made by Bowen from the above. His typescript reads 'foam-bursts' in the final line, but the manuscript revision of 'wavelets' reads 'foam-breaks'. He again notes the existence of a 'Reading TS' that is not in the archive. Bowen had this poem published in *The London Magazine* (Dec 1979-Jan 1980), pp. 101-2.

UNCOLLECTED AND UNPUBLISHED POEMS
Occasional and Unfinished Poems

from Conducted Tour after Edward Lear

Reading holds 4 items: 1 handwritten ink variant text, not in Spencer's hand, with alternative readings added in biro, probably by Bowen, 1 original typescript of text from *Gennadius*, and 2 photocopies of this typescript. The three limericks, from the Salonika and Athens period, are dated 1940. Identified as Spencer's by Robert Liddell in correspondence with Bowen, though the latter did not note their existence in 1981.   ἀπό πίσω (pronounced 'apo peeso') means 'from behind'. I am grateful to Roderick Beaton for his help with the Greek.

'From Cairo this: scorn upon verse from Alex...'

Reading holds a copy contained in a 30 March 1979 letter from Gwyn Williams in Aberystwyth to Bowen. The text, signed 'B.S.', is from Gwyn Williams, *Flyting in Egypt: The Story of a Verse War 1943-45* (Port Talbot: Alun Books, 1991), p. 14. This booklet tells the story of an exchange of satirical verses between expatriate writers in Alexandria and Cairo. A 'flyting' is a slanging match in verse. It began in Nov 1943 with verses called 'Challenge to the Cairo Poets' by Williams that include 'Spencer's the chill embodiment / of neo-classic sermons on the mount.' Part of his note to Spencer's reply reads: 'Bernard Spencer answers on behalf of Cairo. I have only recently noticed that this piece is fourteen lines and may be considered a sonnet, though in an unusual rhyme scheme. And what ingenious rhymes. So far as I remember, this was Bernard's only contribution to the flyting. How many devils could dance on a pin is said to have been a favourite set subject for argument by mediaeval philosophers. Where Bernard accuses Robert Liddell of fouling "an English nurse's idyll" I take it that he refers to an epigram by Robert called *Dead Sea Plage* which ends: "...Today the

Sodom sunshine blisters / Queen Alexandra's Nursing Sisters." Robert, Bernard and I went down to the Dead Sea together by bus from Jerusalem. I think Bernard swam but I don't think Robert did.' This will have been in the summer of 1942 or 1943. The volume also contains 'Against Cairo: An Ode' (p. 19) by Lawrence Durrell with a verse on Spencer:

No dunciad could omit thee Spencer
Who to the great Leviathan Story,
Became a blubber hacker here – or flenser
Paring like brutish dory,
Till when you've done
In place of skin and bone
Is gristle left alone.

Gwyn Williams's epigram entitled 'B.S.' reads: 'Cold imagist / couldst limn more just / and warm a vision / thy metres / might win a brief evasion / from Lethe's waters' (p. 16).

'For madmen, darkness whip and chain...'
Reading holds 1 completed pencil, almost fair-copy, draft. It appears to be a poem from, or remembering Spencer's time, in Cairo. There are a few added possible or variant readings, some of which I have been able to incorporate into the text, others not.

'I met you, George, upon a refuse dump...'
Published in *Epithalamia by Various Hands for the Nuptials of George Sutherland Fraser and Eileen Lucy Andrew* (London, printed by Wyndham Printers Ltd., for Tambimuttu, 1946), n.p. [5]. The other hands are Helen Scott, John Waller, Erik de Mauny, Iain Fletcher, Tambimuttu, Gavin Ewart, David Gascoyne, Anthony Schooling, Hamish Henderson, Nicholas Moore, and the *Reading* copy presented by Fletcher includes an unbound 'Appendix' by Laurence Clark.

Casa di P——
Reading holds 3 items: a biro manuscript not in Spencer's hand, a photocopy of an undated letter from Clover de Pertiñez to Ed[ward Burra], the painter, which contains the handwritten text, and an untitled probably authorial typescript-carbon given by J.P. Fitzgibbon to Bowen in a 19 April 1980 letter. In a 27 March 1980 letter he notes: 'Bernard wrote it after that memorable evening and the next day he gave me what I consider the original with all his typing mistakes.' I have moved 'Casa di P——' to this new section of occasional poems, from its place in Bowen's general sequence of

uncollected work. My reasons are that this *'poesie à clef'* circulated privately among friends in Madrid in the early 1950s. Though retaining the title, I have preferred the Fitzgibbon text over the one Bowen derives from Pertiñez, because in places its substantive variants, to my mind, improve the poem – and it is, in any case, from a carbon given by Spencer to Fitzgibbon. Pertiñez, for example, has 'he was the avenging nightmare', meaning 'my headmaster', while Fitzgibbon has 'She was', namely 'the enormous Bawd'. Pertiñez has 'Fitz' for 'John' at the beginning of line 14 (different ways of referring to the same person). Her manuscript also has no punctuation at the end of that line, and then 'and invented', where Fitzgibbon has 'And I invented', allowing Spencer to collaborate in the evening's nightmarish figures. Where Bowen's l. 19 reads: 'my art mistress? Who robbed', Fitzgibbon has 'my art-mistress', who robbed'. All three texts have 'shifting' in line 2, rather than the 'shrinking' in Bowen's text. *La Mujer Vencida* (The Conquered Woman) is a 1951 novel by Ramos Lía, which helps date the piece. The 'rich invalid from Worthing' may refer to Nora's father, who visited Spencer in Madrid about this time.

'The girl in the black mantilla with the ink splash eyes...'
Reading holds 2 items: 1 pencil draft, and Bowen's typescript from the draft not included in his edition. Bowen's first verse reads: 'The girl in the black mantilla with the ink splash eyes / stands leaning there singing (slant of the guitars) / some warm and throaty thing about two lovers / and "the rays of the moon."' The autograph manuscript has a revision of these lines vertically up the left margin, and I have preferred what appears a later draft. In the second verse he transcribes an extra line in parenthesis: 'Dusty from the same door extends the plain / (and one is aware outside of the huge plain) / centuries of poverty and war have torn', but there is a pencil question mark beside his parenthetical line. In the manuscript there is no parenthesis, and Bowen's second line probably represents an earlier reading, with the preferred line substituted above. I have followed this interpretation, and have preferred 'hacked clear' for 'cut clear', where 'hacked' is an alternative pencilled above, 'and the Spanish stars' for 'with Spanish stars', and 'knives or distant' for 'knives in distant' – where Bowen appears to misread the tiny handwriting.

'Look at my suit...'
Reading holds 2 items: 1 ink draft, and Bowen's typescript from the draft not included in his edition. Bowen's transcription leaves out 'new pen' and introduces capital letters for the two questions at the beginnings of lines 8

and 9. The fountain pen used to write these lines is the same as for early drafts of 'From my Window' and 'Mediterranean Suburbs'.

'Rocks like a Dürer landscape, torn and hacked...'

Reading holds 1 draft of 2 manuscript pages. It is very difficult to read, and to produce a continuous text I have had to decide between overwritten variants, and undeleted first readings, and to leave aside marginal attempts at revisions of passages that are not firmly located in the text. Although various variant readings have had to be left aside, I have not interpolated or corrected or revised for consistency, as shown by the erratic capitalisation at the beginnings of lines and the punctuation throughout. I am grateful to Roderick Beaton for his help with the Greek word 'vouni', which is a colloquial variant of βουνό.

The story is of battles and of conquest all the way...

Reading holds 1 tiny manuscript of this draft poem with variants, on the back of an invitation to cocktails on Thursday March first at seven, the Randels, Kilkis 4, Philothei [Athens], probably dating it to Spencer's brief posting there between Sept 1955 and summer 1956. The pencil manuscript is difficult to decipher, and to produce a continuous text I have had to choose where there are variants without deletions. So, for example, line 4 first had 'quite horrid children' with 'delinquent' written underneath 'quite horrid', suggesting a revision but with no cancelling. Though a few variant readings have had to be left out, I have interpolated nothing, as is evident in the inconsistencies of punctuation.

Translations

GEORGE SEFERIS: The King of Asine and Other Poems

John Lehmann published this first book of poems by Seferis in English in 1948. Despite the high quality of these versions, the volume has not been reprinted until now. The title page describes the poems as 'Translated from the Greek by Bernard Spencer, Nanos Valaoritis, Lawrence Durrell'. The volume had a frontispiece portrait of Seferis 'from a drawing by Ghika', and an introduction by Rex Warner. Bowen did not include these translations on the grounds of 'their collaborative nature' and reports Durrell's account of the work in a letter to him of 16 June 1979 [actually 1978. See BSP 4/3/29] that 'apart from "Asine" which is almost entirely Durrell's version, no single poem can be identified as the work of any one translator. The volume was the result of "committee" sessions, with Valaoritis bolstering the "kitchen Greek" of the two English poets' (p. x). However, Roderick Beaton concluded in *George Seferis: Waiting for the Angel* (2003) that the 'contribution of George Katsimbalis to this volume, though not credited, was considerable' (p. 494). He observed at the centenary conference in 2009 that Seferis also contributed suggestions. Further, Valaoritis reported to me by e-mail in 2009 that poems 4, 7, 10, 15, and 24 from 'Myth of Our History' are by Durrell and Katsimbalis; 'Santorin' and 'Mycenae' are by Valaoritis alone; and he implied thus that the rest are by Spencer and Valaoritis. Parts 3 and 16, as 'Remember the baths in which you plunged' and 'And the Name is Orestes', attributed to Spencer and Valaoritis, appeared in *New Writing and Daylight* no. 7 (1946), p. 47. 'The King of Asine' is probably by Spencer and Valaoritis, though with corrections by Seferis from the Durrell version. There is, in *Personal Landscape* vol. 2 no. 3 (1944), pp. 9-10, a translation, no translators acknowledged, called 'The King of Asini' [sic]. This is similar enough to the 1948 text for the later to appear a revision. Beaton refers to correspondence and drafts exchanged between Durrell and Seferis from the early months of 1944, which include Durrell's 'We are having trouble translating you so that you don't sound like Eliot' (p. 229). Thus his description in 1978 of working with Spencer and Valaoritis will refer to 1944, while the division of labour that Valaoritis reports includes collaboration with Spencer in London during 1946, when Durrell appears to have been in Patmos. I have included the entire contents of the volume here because Spencer's name appears first, non-alphabetically, in the list of translators, suggesting that the order was to indicate levels of input, while the value of the translations themselves surely overrides the question of who wrote exactly which words.

The epigraph to 'Myth of our History' is made up of lines 2 and 3 of 'Fêtes de la Faim'. Seferis's Note on his title is given as follows: 'I have chosen the word MYTH for the title of this work, because I have clearly used a certain mythology in the poem; and the word HISTORY because I tried to convey, in a certain sequence, a state of mind as independent from mine as that of characters in a novel.' The poet referred to in part 2 is Dionysios Solomos, citing the first chapter of his *The Woman of Zakynthos*. The title-phrase in part 3 is Orestes speaking at Agamemnon's tomb in Aeschylus, *The Libation Bearers*. The quotation at the start of part 4 is spoken by Socrates in Plato's *Alcibiades*. The 'M.R.' of part 6 is the composer Maurice Ravel. The Simplegades in part 10 are the clashing rocks in the story of Jason and the Argonauts. 'Hydra' in the title to part 13 is an island off the north east of the Peloponnese. In part 15 *Quid πλατανων Opacissimus?* [What dark thickest plane-tree wood?] is from the younger Pliny's *Letters*, referring to the resources of a villa. 'Astyanax' in part 17 is the son of Hector and Andromache. The final word in the epigraph to 'Ancient Dances' is Seferis' original title 'Gymnopaidia', in its plural form, made familiar by Erik Satie with his piano pieces, 'Gymnopédies'. In 'The King of Asine' the castle in line 1 is the ruined acropolis of Asine near the village of Tolos in Argolida. Seferis' epigraph is from Homer's catalogue of ships (*Iliad*, II, 560).

ODYSSEUS ELYTIS: 'The Mad Pomegranate Tree'

Described as 'Translated from the Greek by Nanos Valaoritis and Bernard Spencer' when first published in *New Writing and Daylight* no. 7 (1946), pp. 48-9. Bowen notes the existence of another translation from Elytis in *Penguin New Writing* no. 35 (1948), pp. 43-4. However, this is a re-publication of the same poem.

EUGENIO MONTALE: Four poems

Bowen notes of these four translations, which he published for the first time in 1981, that the *Reading* pencil drafts on sheets torn from a notebook, with revisions, were inserted in Spencer's copy of *Ossi di seppia* (Turin: Einaudi, 1942). When I first examined the archive in 2007, there was no sign of Spencer's copy, and the original manuscript for 'Don't ask us for the word which cuts and shapes' was missing. *Reading* currently holds for 'The Lemon Trees', a version of 'I limoni', 3 pencil-draft pages and a photocopy made by Bowen of the above with the original Italian attached. For 'Don't ask us for the word which cuts and shapes', a version of 'Non chiederci la parola', there is only the Bowen photocopy and attached original. For 'Bring me the sunflower so that I can transplant it', a version of 'Portarmi il girasole', a 1-page pencil draft and Bowen's photocopy with the original. For 'To shelter, pale and preoccupied', a version of 'Merrigiare pallido e assorto', there is again a 1-page draft and Bowen's photocopy with the original. Bowen speculates that these translations were made probably in Palermo or Turin between September 1946 and August 1948, but the fact that travel arrangements for 'Alb[ergo] Nazionale, Pino Torinese' (see note to 'Pino' above, pp. 327-8) are on the same lined paper torn from an exercise book suggests the later place and date as more likely.

GEORGE SEFERIS: Two poems

Reading holds three items: 2 copies of a BBC rehearsal script, and a type-script made by Bowen of the two translations, not included in 1981. 'The Mourning Girl' and 'Denial', attributed to Spencer alone, appear in 'Poems by Seferis', Selected by Ian Scott-Kilvert, Producer D.S. Carne-Ross, broadcast on The BBC Third Programme, Sunday 8th December 1957, 9.55-10.15 p.m. They are versions of ᾽Η ΛΥΠΗΜΕΝΗ᾽ and ᾽ΑΡΝΗΣΗ᾽ from *Rhymed Poems* in the bilingual *Collected Poems 1924-1955* translated by Edmund Keeley and Philip Sherrard (London: Jonathan Cape, 1969), pp. 400-1 and 404-5. In 'The Mourning Girl' I have corrected 'hearts' to 'heart's', and in 'Denial' changed 'Full' to 'full'. 'Denial' was published in *The London Magazine* (Dec 2008-Jan 2009), p. 72.

Selected Prose

The Exhibition of Dutch Art at Burlington House
Published in *Sir Galahad*, vol. 1 no. 1 (21 February 1929), p. 16. *Reading* holds a photocopy of the page from the magazine.

Note on Auden
Published in the Auden Double Number of *New Verse* (November 1937), p. 27. It appears between similarly brief statements by Allen Tate and Charles Madge.

Ideas about Poems
Published as 'Ideas about Poems III', one of a series that included statements by Lawrence Durrell, Gwyn Williams, and George Seferis, in *Personal Landscape* vol. 1 no. 4 (1942), p. 2. Bowen notes the echoes here of the 1937 note on Auden. 'Johnny, I hardly knew ye' is an anonymous Irish ballad, published by Padraic Colum in his *Anthology of Irish Verse* (1922). 'A handsome young airman lay dying' is one of many wartime flyer parodies of a folk song called 'The Dying Hobo'. Yeats wrote that 'passive suffering is not a theme for poetry' in his Introduction to *The Oxford Book of Modern Verse 1892-1935* (Oxford: Oxford University Press, 1936), p. xxxiv. He wrote that 'the Muses were women who liked the embrace of gay warty lads' on 22 May 1936. See *Letters on Poetry from W.B. Yeats to Dorothy Wellesley* (Oxford: Oxford University Press, 1940), p. 63.

Keith Douglas: An Obituary Note

The magazine *Personal Landscape* concluded publication with this note, signed 'B.S.', in the final issue vol. 2 no. 4 (1945), p. 20.

The Wind-Blown Island of Mykonos

Published in *The Listener*, vol. 36 (5 September 1946), pp. 307-8. It had been broadcast on the BBC Home Service. At the end of the piece, Spencer cites a slightly variant translation of the last 4 lines to part 8 in Seferis' 'Myth of our History' and see above, p. 213.

Dialogue on Poetry

Reading holds a copy of the newspaper *Insula* no. 64 (15 Abril 1951) with on p. 8 this as 'Dialogo sobre la Poesia' por María Alfaro y Bernard Spencer. Published here is a translation of that text made by myself with the help of Ornella Trevisan. María Alfaro was the author of a recently issued volume of translations: Lord Byron, *Poemas líricos* (Madrid: Adonais, 1950). She cites Stéphane Mallarmé in 'Le mystère dans les lettres' from *Divagations* (1897): 'tendre le nuage, précieux, flottant sur l'intime gouffre de chaque pensée.'

Madrid Journal

At the time of Bowen's edition, the notebook containing this journal was thought to have been lost. *Reading* holds a letter from Julia Dohnal in London, dated 9 September 1992, returning the notebook to Anne Humphreys, and explaining 'Enclosed is an exercise book which Margaret Bennet gave to me the other evening. She told me some time ago that she was leaving them in her Will to you (and some others to Piers) and wanted me to be the "messenger". Quite rightly she realised it was important that you had them now – no point in hanging on to them.' The green-covered notebook, containing 17 pages of handwritten text, is now in the *Reading* archive. To this I have added the last page from a 'Madrid Notebook', which consists of 3 pages of fragmentary notes in a Basildon Bond letter pad, the first 3 short paragraphs being *aide memoire* of incidents which appear to have taken place in London. The page I have included is clearer, and fits the mood and context of the 'Madrid Journal'. In the second sentence of his journal, Spencer writes 'traperos' or 'vasuleros'. I have corrected the non-existent second word to 'basureros'. The date of the journal appears to be from the earlier 1950s, coextensive with the composition of 'Notes by a Foreigner' first published in Dec 1955. The notebook paragraphs may have a later date.

New Poetry

The source is a *Reading* archive radio script. The producer was D.S. Carne-Ross. Anthony Jacobs and Derek Hart read poems, and passages from the original Gascoyne recording were replayed. The programme was pre-recorded on Wednesday 27 February 1957 and transmitted on Monday, 4 March 1957, from 9.45 to 10.15 on the BBC Third Programme. Spencer introduces John Holloway, 'Warning to a Guest' and 'In the Dark', *The Minute and Longer Poems* (Hessle: Marvell Press, 1956), pp. 46 and p. 65, J.C. Hall, 'The Island' in *Mavericks: An Anthology* ed. Howard Sergeant and Dannie Abse (London: Editions Poetry and Poverty, 1957), pp. 18-19, two passages from David Gascoyne, *Night Thoughts* (London: André Deutsch, 1956), and C.A. Trypanis, 'Miss Fitzsimon', 'Winter's Afternoon Walk' and 'Picture of the Nativity in the Church of Krena in Chios', *The Stones of Troy* (London: Faber & Faber, 1957), pp. 45, 42 and 37.

I Will Abroad

Reading holds two carbon typescripts of this book review. I have not been able to discover if it was ever published or broadcast. The title is, of course, an allusion to 'The Collar' ('I struck the board, and cried, "No more." / I will abroad') by George Herbert, one of Spencer's favourite poets, as he acknowledged on at least three occasions. The three volumes reviewed are Gerald Brenan, *South from Granada* (London: Hamish Hamilton, 1958), Peter Mayne, *Saints of Sind* (London: John Murray, 1956), and Christopher Kininmonth, *The Brass Dolphins: A Description of the Maltese Archipelago* (London: Secker and Warburg, 1957). 'Malagueñas' are a type of Andalusian flamenco, deriving from Malaga.

Ankara Notebook

Reading holds the pink Turkish notebook containing 7 manuscript pages. This notebook also contains a draft of the poem 'Donkey'. Spencer held a posting at the University of Ankara between January and July of 1958. The first paragraph of the '*Ankara, March*' section concludes with the following, heavily deleted phrase: 'A ghostly love-pain twining the imagined naked bodies and writhing on the springs.'

Anatolia Notebook

Reading holds the orange unlined notebook containing the 11 pages of manuscript with three illustrative drawings: of the well bucket apparatus, a shepherd with a black sheep, and woman in peasant costume. These notes provide a context for the poem 'Delicate Grasses', p. 94 above, which was inspired by the same journey. The brief passage about the Dürer mountain background may also help date 'Rocks like a Dürer landscape torn and hacked...', p. 203 above, though, equally possibly, the prose may be a later recollection of the same idea.

Poems by Bernard Spencer

Reading holds a 6-page handwritten draft of Spencer's comments on the poems. The source for the text published here is the *Reading* archive radio script, a copy of which also exists in the BBC archive. Rehearsal and pre-recording: Thursday, 30 July 1959, transmission Third programme, week 37. The script includes biro-ed cuts of commentary and two poems ('Fluted Armour' and 'Full Moon') made during the recording. I have transcribed the uncut recording script in its entirety, excluding the poems, which were recorded by an unidentified reader, with the exception of the last, 'Feathery Grasses', read by Spencer himself.

Lawrence Durrell

Published in *Insula* no. 160 (March 1960), p. 6. *Reading* holds a copy of the newspaper. Though there are papers on Durrell's writings among Spencer's lecture notes, held at *Reading*, these do not include an English draft of this article. The text published here is a translation made by myself with Ornella Trevisan. The quotation about the poet Ivan Zarian is from *Prospero's Cell* (London: Faber & Faber, 1945), p. 14, about Theodore Stephanides, p. 15, and the fortune-teller, p. 13. *Clea*, the last of the *Alexandria Quartet*, was first published in the December following this article's appearance.

Context

Reading holds 4 items: 3 pages of notes, and a 3-page manuscript. Spencer attempted an answer to question (d) in the first of these items, but passed entirely on (e). For (d) he wrote: 'None consciously. Graves, Frost, Cummings? T. Hardy: the dramatic situation. Figures in a landscape.' Published in *The London Magazine* (February 1962), pp. 41-2, alongside responses to the same questions from Robert Graves, George Seferis, Stephen Spender, C. Day-Lewis, Philip Larkin, Lawrence Durrell, Roy Fuller, Robert Conquest, Laurie Lee, Thomas Blackburn, Derek Walcott, Judith Wright, D.J. Enright, Thom Gunn, Charles Causley, Vernon Watkins, Ted Hughes, Sylvia Plath, Edwin Brock, Hugo Williams, John Fuller, Julian Mitchell, Elizabeth Jennings, Anthony Thwaite, and Norman Nicholson.

University of Madrid Lecture

Reading holds the manuscript. The lecture exists as 11 numbered, hand-written pages, in blue biro on lined paper, to which is attached a cyclostyled handout entitled 'Poems by Bernard Spencer' containing 9 works. The text published here has been lightly edited for consistency of accidentals and capitalisations. I have also indicated, when necessary, where the poems were to be read. The article mentioned near the beginning is Esteban Pujals, 'Poemas de Bernard Spencer', *Filologia Moderna* no. 3, Madrid, April 1961, pp. 19-27. Spencer adds the marginal comment: 'I ought really to read that. So much better!' In a marginal note beside the sentence 'I think there is a certain interest in the biography of any artist', Spencer wrote '*What kind of a poet / What is involved* in writing poetry / What poets are trying *to do.*' Beside the phrase 'I used to tell imaginary adventure stories to the other boys' is the marginal remark: 'Once told a story which went on for two years. Tolstoy put to shame.' Spencer cites the first couplet of a quatrain by John Davenport in *Cambridge Poetry* (London: Hogarth Press, 1929): 'Eliot, Rabelais, Dryden, Donne / Bless the bed that I lie on, / Blake and Rimbaud, Marvell, Voltaire, / Swift, Joyce, Proust and Baudelaire.' By *Contemporary Verse* Spencer has written 'BOOK', which may mean that he showed the audience or read from a copy of *The Penguin Book of Contemporary Verse*, ed. Kenneth Allott (1950), which contains 'Allotments: April' (1936) and 'On the Road' (1947). His subsequent remarks make it clear that he has the first of these poems in mind. The word 'aceitunas' is the Spanish for 'green olives'.

Interview with Peter Orr

Reading holds a carbon transcript of 'The Poet Speaks (XV): Bernard Spencer Talks to Peter Orr'. Published in *The Poet Speaks: Interviews with Contemporary Poets Conducted by Hilary Morrish, Peter Orr, John Press and Ian Scott-Kilvert*, ed. Peter Orr, Preface by Frank Kermode (London: Routledge & Kegan Paul, 1966), pp. 233-7 and dated 27th August, 1962.

Bernard Spencer Writes...

Reading holds 5 fragmentary sets of notes towards the composition of this statement. It was published in *Poetry Book Society Bulletin* no. 37 (June 1963). Spencer recalls the last paragraph from George Seferis' 'Mathaios Pascalis his Ideas about Poems', *Personal Landscape* vol. 2 no. 3 (1944), p. 2, where he writes: 'Poems of the same kind meet usually in special places; they have their clubs. On this point I rely on my own experience which informs me that heroic poems meet in ships on a calm sea; poems about slumber in battle fields; poems about rapes in waterless islands; poems about death, in green meadows at noon; poems about happiness on peaks of mountains; poems about self-indulgence on staircases (think of *Ash Wednesday*); and limericks in the bathroom.'

BIBLIOGRAPHY

Primary

POETRY

Aegean Islands and Other Poems (London: Editions Poetry London, 1946)

Aegean Islands and Other Poems (Garden City, NY: Doubleday, 1948)

The Twist in the Plotting (Reading: University of Reading School of Art, 1960)

With Luck Lasting (London: Hodder & Stoughton, 1963)

With Luck Lasting (Chester Springs, PA: Dufour Editions, 1965)

Collected Poems (London: Alan Ross, 1965)

Collected Poems ed. Roger Bowen (Oxford: Oxford University Press, 1981)

Poems by Bernard Spencer Selected with a Note by John Press (Warwick: Greville Press, 2003)

TRANSLATIONS

Odysseus Elytis, 'The Mad Pomegranate Tree' translated by Nanos Valoritis and Bernard Spencer, *New Writing and Daylight* 7 (1946) and *Penguin New Writing* 35 (1948)

George Seferis, *The King of Asine and Other Poems*, translated from the Greek by Bernard Spencer, Nanos Valoritis, Lawrence Durrell (London: John Lehmann, 1948)

George Seferis, 'The Mourning Girl' and 'Denial', translated by Bernard Spencer, from the script for 'Poems by Seferis', selected by Ian Scott-Kilvert, produced by D.S. Carne-Ross, broadcast on the BBC Third Programme, Sunday 8th December 1957, 9.55-10.15 p.m.

Eugenio Montale, 'The Lemon Trees', 'Don't ask us for the word', 'Bring me the sunflower', 'To shelter pale and preoccupied', *Collected Poems* ed. Roger Bowen (Oxford: Oxford University Press, 1981), pp. 103-7.

PROSE

'The Exhibition of Dutch Art at Burlington House', *Sir Galahad*, vol. 1 no. 1 (21 February 1929), p. 16.

Review of John Lehmann, *A Garden Revisited*, *Oxford Outlook* no. 12 (February 1932), pp. 71-2.

Note on Auden, Auden Double Number of *New Verse* (November 1937), p. 27.

'Ideas about Poems III', *Personal Landscape* vol. 1 no. 4 (1942), p. 2.

'Talking of Barry', *Esfam*, Cairo, (May 1944), pp. 2-4.

'Keith Douglas: An Obituary Note', *Personal Landscape* vol. 2 no. 4 (1945), p. 20.

'The Wind-blown Island of Mykonos', *The Listener*, vol. 36 (5 September 1946), pp. 307-8.

Article about Hospital Life, *Envoy* (the India Club), c. 1949.

María Alfaro and Bernard Spencer, 'Dialogo sobre la Poesia', *Insula* no. 64 (15 April 1951), p. 8.

'New Poetry', broadcast BBC Third Programme, Monday, 4 March 1957.

'Poems by Bernard Spencer,' recorded for BBC Third Programme on 30 July 1959, broadcast week 37.

'Lawrence Durrell', *Insula* no. 160 (March 1960), p. 6.

'Context', *The London Magazine* (February 1962), pp. 41-2.

'Bernard Spencer', *The Poet Speaks: Interviews with Contemporary Poets Conducted by Hilary Morrish, Peter Orr, John Press and Ian Scott-Kilvert* ed. Peter Orr, Preface by Frank Kermode (London: Routledge & Kegan Paul, 1966), pp. 233-7.

'Bernard Spencer Writes...', *Poetry Book Society Bulletin* no. 37 (June 1963).

'University of Madrid Lecture' in 'Bernard Spencer (1909-1963) Centenary Supplement', *Agenda*, Fiftieth Anniversary Issue, vol. 44 no. 4–vol. 45 no.1 (Winter 2009), pp. 248-54.

ARCHIVES

Bernard Spencer at Reading: Catalogue of the Bernard Spencer Collection at the University of Reading, compiled by Verity Hunt with an Introduction by Peter Robinson (Reading: University of Reading, 2009).

Selected Secondary Reading

Dannie Abse, 'Without Self-Importance', *The Two Roads Taken: A Prose Miscellany* (London: Enitharmon, 2003), pp. 142-52.

Bergonzi, Bernard, 'Out of the Shadows', *PN Review* 27, vol. 7 no. 1 (1982), pp. 55-7.

Betjeman, John, 'Louis MacNeice and Bernard Spencer', *The London Magazine* vol. 3 no. 9 (Dec 1963), pp. 62-4.

Bolton, Jonathan, '"The Historian with His Spade": Landscape and Historical Continuity in the Poetry of Bernard Spencer', *Personal Landscapes: British Poets in Egypt during the Second World War* (Basingstoke: Macmillan, 1997), pp. 69-84.

Bowen, Roger, 'Native and Exile: The Poetry of Bernard Spencer, *The Mal-ahat Review* no. 49 (1979), pp. 5-27.

——— 'The Edge of a Journey: Notes on Bernard Spencer', *The London Magazine* (Dec 1979-Jan 1980), pp. 88-102.

——— 'Introduction', Bernard Spencer, *Collected Poems* (Oxford: Oxford University Press, 1981), pp. xiii-xxxxiii.

——— 'Bernard Spencer: The Quiet Exile', *'Many Histories Deep': The Personal Landscape Poets in Egypt, 1940-45* (Madison: Fairleigh Dickinson University Press, 1995), pp. 114-39.

Caesar, Adrian, 'Bernard Spencer and his Manuscripts', *White Light and Sand: An Exhibition of Poetry in the Middle East between 1939 and 1945*, University of Reading Library, Dec 1st 1981 to Jan 1st 1982. Copy in Ruth Speirs archive, Special Collections, University of Reading. MS 2492.

——— *Dividing Lines: Poetry, Class and Ideology in the 1930s* (Manchester: Manchester University Press, 1991), pp. 123-8.

Connolly, Cyril, 'Poets in a Predicament', *The Sunday Times* (14 July 1963), p. 24.

Durrell, Lawrence, 'Bernard Spencer', *The London Magazine* vol. 3 no. 10 (Jan 1964), pp. 42-7.

Dodsworth, Martin, 'Bernard Spencer: The Poet of Addition', *The Review* no. 11-12 (1964), pp. 71-80; reprinted as 'Bernard Spencer', *The Modern Poet: Essays from The Review* (London: Macdonald, 1968), pp. 90-100.

Ewart, Gavin, *'Personal Landscape'*, *The London Magazine* (Nov 1981), pp. 80-3.

Fraser, G.S., 'Review of *Collected Poems*', *The London Magazine* no. 5 (Nov 1965), pp. 81-2.

Fuller, Roy, 'Review of *With Luck Lasting*', *The London Magazine* vol. 3 no. 4 (July 1963), p. 91.

Grigson, Geoffrey, 'Bernard Spencer', *The Private Art: A Poetry Note-Book* (London: Allison & Busby, 1982), pp. 62-3.

Hitchens, Christopher, 'A Thousand Killed: What a Little-Known British Poet Named Bernard Spencer Knew', *Slate*, 9 Sept 2004, www.slate.com /id/2106466/.

Hugo, Richard, 'Some Kind of Perfection', *The Real West Marginal Way: A Poet's Autobiography*, ed. Ripley S. Hugo et al. (New York: Norton, 1986), pp. 154-8.

MacCaig, Norman, 'Hearthrug Head', *New Statesman* (30 August 1963), p. 263.

Manning, Olivia, 'Poets in Exile', *Horizon* no. 10 (October 1944), pp. 117-9.

Morrison, Blake, 'Beach Poets', *London Review of Books* (16 Sept–6 Oct 1982), p. 16-18.

Piette, Adam, 'Pronouns and Place in Bernard Spencer's "In Athens"', *The Reader* no. 13 (Autumn 2003), pp. 49-52.

Porter, Peter, 'Home Thoughts from Abroad', *The Observer* (7 Feb 1982), p. 29.

Pujals, Estéban, 'Poemas de Bernard Spencer', *Filologia Moderna* no. 3 (April 1961), pp. 19-27.

———— 'En Memoria de Bernard Spencer', *Filologia Moderna* no. 13 (October 1963), pp. 19-27.

———— 'La Inspiracion Mediterranea de Bernard Spencer', *Drama, Pensiamento y Poesia en la Literatura Inglesa* (Madrid: Ediciones Rialp, 1965), pp. 433-47.

Robinson, Peter, 'Fatal Twists', *Essays in Criticism* vol. 32 no. 4 (October 1982), pp. 389-97.

———— 'Twists in the Plotting: Bernard Spencer's Second Book of Poems', *Publishing History* no. 62 (2007), pp. 81-102.

———— 'Bernard Spencer in *The London Magazine*', *The London Magazine* (Dec 2008–Jan 2009), pp. 66-72.

———— 'Introduction', *Bernard Spencer at Reading: Catalogue of the Bernard Spencer Collection at the University of Reading*, compiled by Verity Hunt (Reading: University of Reading, 2009), pp. 11-19.

———— '*The Twist in the Plotting*: Special Collections Featured Item for November 2009', http://www.reading.ac.uk/special-collections/featured-items/sc-featured-items.aspx

———— 'Bernard Spencer's "Boat Poem"', *English* vol. 58 no. 224 (Winter 2009), pp. 318-39.

———— (ed.), 'Bernard Spencer (1909-1963): Centenary Supplement', *Agenda*, Fiftieth Anniversary Issue, vol. 44 no. 4–vol. 45 no. 1 (Winter 2009), pp. 234-62.

Skelton, Robin, 'Britannia's Muse Awaking', *The Massachusetts Review* vol. 8 no. 2, Spring 1967, pp. 353-4.

Thwaite, Anthony, 'Fine Particular Moments', *Times Literary Supplement* (1 Jan 1982), p. 7.

Index of titles and first lines

(Titles and sub-titles are shown in italics, first lines and first-line titles in roman type.)

A black Cordoba hat tilted, 124
A Bottle in The Sea, 214
A Cold Night, 56
A Hand, 49
A high pink wall, 134
A little further, 220
A lukewarm, trouser-treasured, sixpence for God, 153
A Number, 142
A pressure on the ears, 129
A Spring Wind, 101
A Sunday, 124
A Thousand Killed, 60
A turn in the road, 78
A ward dim like a wagon-lit; quick footsteps, 185
A Ward, 185
Above London sailed my room, 180
Above, the fingers of the tree, 156
Acre, 77
Aegean Islands 1940-41, 67
After Love, 159
After the wheels and wings of this intense day, 161
All day they had worshipped at the Virgin's picture, 86
All morning round and round the castle we were searching, 233
Allotments: April, 45
And if the wind blows it does not cool us, 218
And the Name is Orestes, 217
And yet we must reckon how we advance, 237
Anywhere your agents search me, 132
Argonauts, 208
As a trained racket hand's sweep, 172
Astyanax, 217
At Courmayeur, 105
At Dover the wind came spotting rain and whirled, 128
At evening from the Military Academy, 191

At first we heard the jingling of her ornaments, 87
At 'The Angler', 116

Back will go the head with the dark curls, 111
Base Town, 71
Because it was the Queen's birthday, 154
Because the heavy lids will not drag up, 122
Behaviour of Money, 81
Beneath a gun grey sky, 114
Black Cat, 186
Bloody lonely without you, 190
Blue Arm, 134
Boat Poem, 120
Bored and humbled by every disintegrating day, 99
Breathing in leaf only, 162
Bring me the sunflower, 246
Bulky with mackintosh and scarf, 127
By a Breakwater, 128

Cage, 58
Cairo Restaurant, 79
Calligraphy, 236
Casa di P——, 199
Castanets, 111
Castille, 187
Chestnuts, 133
Clemente, 144
Clouded, Still, Evening, 162
Cobbled with rough stone which rings my tread, 47
Collection, 153
Conducted Tour after Edward Lear, from, 195
Cratered the land, unploughed, 75
Cripples, 125

Dancer's naked foot so earthly planted, 73

Death of an Airman, 73
Delicate grasses blowing in the wind, 94
Delicate Grasses, 94
Delos, 70
Denial, 249
Departure, 157
Dolphins banners and the sound of cannon, 215
Donkey, 130
Don't ask us for the word which cuts and shapes, 245
Doubtful-edged and almost daylight, 131
Dr Karl Lueger, 146

Egyptian Dancer at Shubra, 87
Egyptian Delta, 76
Empty chairs, 224
Epiphany, 1937, 225
Epitaph, 225
Evasions, 54
Excellent ritual of oils, of anointing, 90
Expectant at the country gate the lantern, 59

Festa, 154
First the demure green handkerchiefs let droop, 133
Five boats beside the lake, 104
Five Japanese Poems, 224
Fluted Armour, 99
For madmen, darkness whip and chain, 197
For seeing whole I had been too near my friends, 167
For Signorina Brunella Mori, 184
Frock-coated Dr Karl Lueger, 146
From Cairo this: scorn upon verse from Alex, 196
From my Window, 97
From the Military Academy, 191
Frontier, 78
Full Moon, 131
Give me your hands, 222
Going to the Country, 175

Greek Excavations, 68

He belongs under a blow-torch sky, 130
Her hands waking on her lap, 164
Her hank and swing of hair, 112
Here terminate the works of the sea, the works of love, 220
His absentness, his evading, 159
Houses are Uniformed, 52
How many deaths and partings spilled, 89
How many times have you smiled a reckoning smile, 54
How Must we Live? 63
However far I go voyaging, still Greece wounds me, 226
Hydra, 215

I am sad because I let a broad river flow between my fingers, 218
I, Jack, walking on the hill's shoulder, 171
I met you, George, upon a refuse dump, 198
I read of a thousand killed, 60
I take the twist-about, empty street, 113
I wish there was a touch of these boats about my life, 120
I woke with this marble head in my hands, 208
Ill, 59
In a Foreign Hospital, 106
In Acre it wasn't simply the peeping alleys, 77
In an Auction Room, 89
In Athens, 112
In Memoriam, 178
In my breast the wound opens again, 219
In the Manner of G.S., 226
In these whitewashed courtyards where the South Wind blows, 241
Into the track, into the track again, into the track, 217
It was yours and mine, this sun, 230

Its pale walls partly clambered on by
creeper, 93
I've been smoking since morning
without a break, 229

Jerusalem derelict city, 238

Let me out of my life, 55
Letter Home, 108
Letters, 74
Letters, like blood along a weakening
body, 74
Libyan Front, 75
Light thrown, 79
Like air on skin, coolness of yachts at
mooring, 83
Listen, the poet laureates, 243
Look at my suit, 202
Looking up from her knitting, 142
Lop-sided, 129

M.R., 210
Mathias Pascalis among the Roses,
229
Mediterranean Suburbs, 98
Money was once well known, like a
townhall or the sky, 81
Morning, 231
Morning in Madrid, 109
Most things having a market price,
170
Muted wood-wind is one noise of the
traffic, 139
My end of Europe is at war, 69
My old friend what are you looking
for? 231
My pulling on my shoes, 164
My Sister, 64
Mycenae, 222

Near Aranjuez, 135
Night-time: Starting to Write, 118
9.20; the Underground groans him to
his work, 115
Notes by a Foreigner, 95
Now ranging cracker-brilliant areas,
175

Now that you are going, take with you
the child, 217
Now when so much has passed before
our eyes, 219
Now when the University students
have abandoned, 97

Old Man on the River Bank, 237
Olive Trees, 84
*On a Carved Axle-Piece from a Sicilian
Cart*, 103
On that kind island the brick-coloured
earth, 125
On the Road, 136
On the 'Sievering' Tram, 140
One of them was licking the bars of its
circus-cage, 123
Open your eyes and unfold, 231
Our native place is enclosed, all
mountains, 213
Our roof was grapes and the broad
hands of the vine, 136
Our speed's perpetual howling like a
strong wind, 119
Our Sun, 230
Out of Sleep, 100
Over the long-shut house, 68
Over the mountains a plane bumbles
in, 118

Part of Plenty, 57
Parted, the young and amorous touch
tragic hands by letter, 177
Passed On, 88
Peasant Festival, 86
Picked Clean from the World, 176
Pino, 182
Pino, a hill-top village, slanting street,
182
Plains as Large as Europe, 50
Poem (After the wheels and wings), 161
Poem (White factories lancing sky), 163
Poem (Who sees the rain fall), 166
Portrait of a Woman and Others, 55
Properties of Snow, 143

Quid πλατανων Opacissimus? 216

Regent's Park Terrace, 107

Remember the Baths by Which You Were Slain, 208

Returning West from our visit to the Embassy, 148

Rhyme for the runnels feeling among the crops, 76

Rocks like a Dürer landscape, torn and hacked, 203

Said the larger and fatter of two police, 195

Sails on the Nile, 236

Salonika June 1940, 69

Santorin, 221

Sarcophagi, 90

Schedules, 152

Skirmish of wheels and bells and someone calling, 109

Sleep, like the green leaves of a tree, wrapped you round, 216

Smouldering moon and stars like flaming crosses, 187

Snow on pine gorges can burn blue, 143

Some of his messages were personal, 88

Some student I look after from this desk, 117

South Wind, 211

Spring shakes the windows, 101

Square figures climb off and on, 140

Still another well within a cave, 207

Stoop if you can to the dark sea forgetting, 221

Stratis the Mariner among the Agapanthus Flowers, 235

Stratis the Mariner on the Dead Sea, 238

Stroked like a reflection high up on the train window, 192

Suburb Factories, 61

Subways have similar gunbarrel perspectives, 145

Such height of corn, so many miles, 168

Sud-Express, 119

Sunset; the streets of flats, new and forbidding, 98

Surfacing out of sleep she feared, 100

Table Tennis, 122

Tell me, you Romans, who but the dark Brunella, 184

That canary measures out its prison, 58

The Administrator, 117

The Agents, 132

The apple trees were all 'salaams' of clusters, 116

The Beginning, 93

The bell and the parade of winking girls, 199

The Boats, 104

The Building of the House, 85

The Café with the Blue Shrine, 110

The Clock, 183

The dour thing in olive trees, 84

The earth slumped in, 178

The Empire Clock, 139

The flowering sea and the mountains towards the waning moon, 225

The garden with its fountains in the rain, 210

The girl in the black mantilla with the ink splash eyes, 201

The harbour is old, I cannot await any longer, 213

The hills begin their march again, 157

The House, 174

The human hand lying on my hand, 49

The Invaders, 141

The King of Asine, 233

The Lemon Trees, 243

The Leopards, 123

The lights with big elegant fingers, 151

The Lottery Sellers, 114

The lumps of coal in the mist, 225

The Mad Pomegranate Tree, 241

The messenger, 207

The Mourning Girl, 248

The noises round my house, 107

The old man bearded with illness weakens upstairs, 64

The pride of Clemente was that the drinks he brought were fiercer, 144

The Rendezvous, 113

The Return of the Exile, 231

The Runner, 172

The Ship, 80

The simple beach and the sea, 80

The Soul too, 208

The spiky distance was the town, 173

The story is of battles and of conquest all the way, 204

The Top-Storey Room, 180

The Train Window, 192

The urgent ringing of the electric alarum, 152

The village craftsman stirred his bravest yellow, 103

The Wedding Pictures, 127

Their faces are untenanted, 126

Their opaque, restless eyes, 95

There are no asphodels, no violets, no hyacinths, 235

There that terrible house, those corridors, 174

There was no Instruction Given, 51

They Tell a Lie, 177

They would bar your way in the street, 141

Thick wool is muslin tonight, and the wire, 56

This climbers' valley with its wayside shrines, 105

This Day, 188

Those near and dead who think there is another, 158

Though passion for her is my life's mere commons, 188

Three red pigeons in the sun, 216

Three rocks, some burnt pines, and a deserted chapel, 214

To Piers Spencer, five months old, 147

To shelter, pale and preoccupied, 247

To sit in the heavily curtained, old ladyish, waiting-room, 62

Traffic in April, 148

Train to Work, 115

Two Poems, 164

Ungated fields of yellowish earth, 135

Upon the hidden beach, 249

Valleys away in the August dark the thunder, 106

Waiting, 62

Walk on a fallen sky, 108

Watchers, 126

We never knew them, 211

We that set out on this pilgrimage, 219

Wealth came by water to this farmless island, 70

Westward the ocean melts in the range of mountains, 211

What do they seek our souls as they travel, 212

When she carries food to the table and stoops down, 57

When the great convent clock strikes, 183

Where white stares, smokes or breaks, 67

White as a drawing on white paper, 61

White factories lancing sky, 163

Who sees the rain fall into the Spring land, 166

Winter Landscape, 173

Winter's white guard continual on the hills, 71

Witness, 189

Written on a Cigarette Packet, 190

Yachts on the Nile, 83

You form and feel words over on your lips, 147

You play the tape-recorder back, 189

You push the soiled door-curtain back, 112

You sat on the rock waiting, 248

You, 145

Your blood sometimes froze like the moon, 214